Columbia University

Contributions to Education

Teachers College Series

No. 295

AMS PRESS
NEW YORK

THE JUDICIAL POWER OF THE NEW YORK STATE COMMISSIONER OF EDUCATION

ITS GROWTH AND PRESENT STATUS WITH A DIGEST OF DECISIONS

BY

JOHN SEILER BRUBACHER, LL.B., Ph.D.

Teachers College, Columbia University
Contributions to Education, No. 295

Bureau of Publications
Teachers College, Columbia University
NEW YORK CITY
1927

Library of Congress Cataloging in Publication Data

Brubacher, John Seiler, 1898-
The judicial power of the New York State Commissioner of Education.

Reprint of the 1927 ed., issued in series: Teachers College, Columbia University. Contributions to education, no. 295.
Originally presented as the author's thesis, Columbia.
Bibliography: p.
1. New York (State). University. Office of the President of the University and Commissioner of Education. 2. Educational law and legislation--New York (State) I. Title. II. Series: Columbia University. Teachers College. Contributions to education, no. 295.
KFN5648.Z9B7 1972 344'.747'07 78-176602
ISBN 0-404-55295-1

Reprinted by Special Arrangement with Teachers College Press, New York, New York

From the edition of 1927, New York
First AMS edition published in 1972
Manufactured in the United States

AMS PRESS, INC.
NEW YORK, N. Y. 10003

ACKNOWLEDGMENT

The writer desires to acknowledge his indebtedness to those who have aided in the inception and completion of this study. To his father, Dr. A. R. Brubacher, President of the New York State College for Teachers, he is under obligation for suggesting the study and for encouraging and criticizing it in its progress to completion. To Mr. Irwin Esmond, Chief of the Law Division of the New York State Education Department, he is thankful for sources of information and constructive criticism. To Professors George D. Strayer and N. L. Engelhardt but especially Professor Edward H. Reisner, all of Teachers College, he is indebted for sound advice and inspiring guidance. To his wife, Winifred Wemple Brubacher, he is grateful, for having been, throughout the preparation of this study, the best of companions at work and play.

J. S. B.

CONTENTS

THE JUDICIAL POWER OF THE NEW YORK STATE COMMISSIONER OF EDUCATION

CHAPTER I

INTRODUCTION

On April 17, 1822, the legislature of the state of New York invested the Secretary of State, the then *ex officio* Superintendent of Common Schools, with appellate jurisdiction to make a final determination of certain specified controversies arising under the state laws pertaining to common schools.[1] With one minor exception [2] the chief school executive of the state has now been in possession of this judicial power for just about a century. The present, therefore, seems a fitting time to take inventory of the growth and significance of this aspect of state educational administration. The investigation, too, is timely from a legal point of view and should be conducted in conjunction with it. Since the latter part of the nineteenth century, there has been a strong trend toward relieving the courts and vesting administrative officers and departments with the decisions of a growing number of social controversies.[3] Although much has been written in this regard on such bodies as the Interstate Commerce Commission, the Federal Railroad Labor Board, state public service commissions, state tax commissions, state workman's compensation commissions, and the like, there is as yet no treatment in either educational or legal literature of the state department of education as an actual or even possible administrative judicial tribunal. To cast further light on this part of our educational and judicial machinery will therefore be the object of the following pages.

[1] Laws of N. Y., 1822, ch. 256.

[2] *Post*, p. 64.

[3] Pound, Roscoe, The Present Crisis in American Law, Harper's Magazine, Jan. 1926; *Ibid.*, Justice According to Law, Columbia Law Review, vol. xiii, pp. 696-713, and vol. xiv, pp. 1-26, 103-21; Freund, E., Growth of American Administrative Law.

Before dealing directly with the judicial power of the New York State Commissioner of Education, it may be well to put the power in its proper perspective by: (1) a somewhat more complete account of the growth of executive or administrative justice as contrasted with judicial justice; (2) a brief survey of the extended fields in which the state of New York has come to exercise its police power; and (3) a discussion of the way in which, concomitantly with the expansion of social welfare legislation, a progressive development of centralized state administrative organization has come.

1. Administrative justice is the result of both old and new forces. A complaint of long standing against the dispensation of justice by the courts has been their delay. The delay is the more objected to when it is on account of what the layman calls mere technicalities. In the end not only is much time consumed, but the costliness of litigation is greatly increased. Methods designed to overcome these difficulties have always been popular. Since executive and administrative officers are charged with getting results quickly and efficiently, they naturally are inclined to cut through delays and technicalities where the determination of disputes is entrusted to them. Their decisions of controversies have been popular on another score too. The courts are interested in a rule of law which will effect justice in the great majority of cases. On this account, they will adhere to the rule even though it may occasionally work injustice in individual cases. The administrative officer, on the other hand, is not so much concerned with rules and justice in the abstract; his interest centers rather on specific cases and justice in the concrete. Since he attempts to dispose of each case on its individual merits, the layman extols the justice of his tribunal.[4]

A force of more recent origin in promoting the development of executive officers' exercise of what the courts call *quasi-*judicial power is the state's ever-widening activity in the field of police regulation.[5] As the state enters more and more into the supervision of public health, banking, insurance, agriculture, relations of employer and employee, and public utilities such as transportation, light, heat, and power, it is unavoidably getting deeper and deeper into matters involving highly developed tech-

[4] For a more complete discussion, see Pound, Roscoe, *op. cit.*, vol. xiv, pp. 12-26.

[5] Pound, Roscoe, *op. cit.*, vol. xiv, p. 20; Freund, *op. cit.*, p. 112; Albertsworth, Judicial Review of Administrative Action, Harvard Law Review, vol. xxxv, p. 127.

nical knowledge and skill. It should quickly become evident that the controversies which arise under this new form of legislation are so intricate that technically rather than judicially trained men are needed to settle them.

2. New York State was early in the field of state regulation of hitherto private and local activities. Almost first in its public welfare legislation after its induction into statehood was education. The supervision of secondary and higher education brought about by the act of 1784 [6] and the provisions for a common school fund shortly after the commencement of the nineteenth century [7] were bits of legislation that were among the first of their kind. The state's interest in public utilities commenced as early as 1811 when it established a canal commission.[8] A state policy for the relief of the poor was undertaken not quite a decade later.[9] After a number of minor regulatory acts, the first real state banking law was passed in 1838.[10] Responsibility for the insane was first assumed by the state when it established insane asylums toward the middle of the century.[11] But in the general problem of health New York lagged behind, having no permanent law till 1850.[12] The antecedents of the present Labor Law are to be noted first in 1853 when a statute was enacted regulating the hours of labor.[13] Not long thereafter, the state took up the defense of the public from impure foods and thus laid the basis of what is contained in the present Agricultural Law.[14] The first state aid for the maintenance of public highways came rather late, not till the end of the century.[15] More instances of this sort of legislative activity on the part of the state might be noted and especially the subsequent extensive growth of the humble beginnings already mentioned. To do so, however, would be to go too far afield of the present purpose.

3. These great extensions of the police power of the state did not evolve without one other development which forms a very significant part of the background of the judicial power of the Commissioner of Education in New York State. As the state

[6] Laws of N. Y., 1784, ch. 51, Session 7.

[7] Laws of N. Y., 1805, ch. 66; *Ibid.*, 1812, ch. 242.

[8] Laws of N. Y., 1811, ch. 288.

[9] Fairlie, J. A., Centralization of Administration in New York State, p. 82; Columbia University Press, New York City, 1898, 210 pp.

[10] Laws of N. Y., 1838, chs. 51, 260.

[11] Fairlie, *op. cit.*, p. 83.

[12] Fairlie, *op. cit.*, pp. 126-27.

[13] Laws of N. Y., 1853, ch. 641.

[14] Laws of N. Y., 1862, ch. 467; *Ibid.* 1877, ch. 415.

[15] Laws of N. Y., 1898, ch. 115.

legislates on the kind of activities described, it has felt more and more the need of reaching out its own administrative arm to see to the accomplishment of its purposes. A very few instances will illustrate this. The state's charitable enterprises, commencing with its interest in the poor in 1819, became so great in the course of time that a central state board of charities was inaugurated in 1867 to supervise and coördinate public charities.[16] In the matter of health the local units provided for by the temporary act of 1836 and the later permanent act of 1850 were found wanting. Their coördination under state authority three decades later finally led at the end of the century to the creation of a state board of health.[17] Again, while the state had earlier regulated the hours of labor, required seats for women in mercantile establishments, and the like, it was not till 1883 that it established administrative machinery in the field of employer-employee relations. At this time it created a bureau of labor statistics.[18] Three years later the governor was given power to appoint a factory inspector.[19] In the same year a state board of arbitration was erected,[20] and finally in 1901 a commissioner of labor was created.[21] As the state has come to be the unit of administration it has progressively had to increase its own effectiveness. Not least in its armory of weapons for guaranteeing its own interests has been the vesting of *quasi*-judicial power in some of the central agencies described.

The field of education, "in which central control first appeared and in which it has been farthest developed," [22] may well receive separate and more extended consideration at this point. The state supervision of secondary and higher education, provided for in the act of 1784, was put in the hands of a state board of regents, and there it remained till the beginning of the twentieth century. Unfortunately, it was as late as 1890 before an inspector of secondary schools, subordinate to the regents, was appointed.[23] The beginnings of a permanent state body of officials in connection with elementary schools came in 1812.[24] In that year the income of the common school fund, established in 1805,[25] became great enough to distribute to the various common schools of the state.

[16] Fairlie, *op. cit.*, p. 84.
[17] *Ibid.* pp. 130-32.
[18] Laws of N. Y., 1883, ch. 356.
[19] Laws of N. Y., 1886, ch. 409.
[20] Laws of N. Y., 1886, ch. 410.
[21] Laws of N. Y., 1901, ch. 9.
[22] Fairlie, *op. cit.*, p. 20.
[23] *Ibid.* 67.
[24] Laws of N. Y., 1812, ch. 242.
[25] Laws of N. Y., 1805, ch. 66.

To manage this enterprise, invest the capital and distribute the income, the first state superintendent of common schools in the United States was established. This office was abolished after the distinguished career of its first incumbent, Gideon Hawley, by the transfer of the duties of the superintendent of common schools to the secretary of state in 1819. This temporary setback to so auspicious a start toward a strong state policy in education was characteristic of the provincialism of the times. By 1841, however, the pressure of school affairs had come to take so large a portion of the time of the secretary of state that a deputy superintendent of common schools was instituted whose whole time could be devoted to school affairs.[26] The creation of this office showed recognition for the necessity and return to importance of a separate and independent administrative organization for common schools. In 1854 this became a fact in the erection of a separate State Department of Public Instruction with a superintendent in charge.[27] The cause of centralization was further improved in 1856 when the office of school commissioner was established.[28] By giving the commissioner limited authority over the school activities of an assembly district and by making him subordinate to the superintendent of public instruction, the extreme localism of the district system was on the way to considerable curtailment. A similar office, a county superintendency, had been tried out in the previous decade,[29] but, while a success educationally, it failed of popular support. For the next fifty years the department of public instruction, organized basically on the above lines, remained the state's administrative machinery in relation to elementary education.

From the foregoing it will be clear that throughout the nineteenth century New York State had a dual system of state control for education—the regents for secondary and higher education and the department of public instruction for elementary education. The next direction of growth in state administrative control was the Unification Act of 1904. Dissatisfaction with the dual system was heard as early as 1836 from the chairman of the "literature fund" in the legislature and from Governor Marcy's message to the legislature of the next year,[30] but nothing ever

[26] Laws of N. Y., 1841, ch. 260.

[27] Laws of N. Y., 1854, ch. 97.

[28] Laws of N. Y., 1856, ch. 179.

[29] Laws of N. Y., 1843, ch. 260.

[30] Fitch, C. E., The Department of Public Instruction, A Review of Its Administration, Ann. Rept. Dept. of Pub. Instn. 1904, pp. 27-28.

eventuated from either of these. A little coördination was obtained when the office of superintendent of public instruction was created. It was provided, then, that the incumbent of that office be *ex officio* a member of the board of regents.[31] A ferment in the legislature in 1869 to abolish the regents and substitute a state board of education was never pressed to a vote. The next year a bill drawn according to the suggestions of the superintendent of public instruction, making the regents subordinate to the superintendent and vesting the election of the latter in the legislature, was passed in both assembly and senate but failed to escape the governor's veto.[32] Success finally crowned these abortive efforts for greater centralization of control when the act of 1904 provided for a State Education Department consisting of a Board of Regents with legislative functions and a Commissioner of Education, selected by them to serve during good behavior, who was to be the executive head.[33] This organization continues at the present time, and has proved most efficient for state educational administration.

The tendency toward centralization among local authorities continues. In 1910 the school commissioner areas were divided into supervisory districts with a district superintendent in charge.[34] This has produced closer supervision of the district system and minimized its evils. Unfortunately, the township law of 1917, a long step in the direction away from localism, was repealed on account of popular opposition before it had had a fair chance to prove itself in operation.

Not only has the administrative organization been thus highly centralized, but appropriate powers have been conferred to guarantee the authority of the state in its educational policies. Fairlie thinks that state financial aid is the key to these powers, for he remarks:

> This development of central control has, moreover, been closely connected with the increase of State grants. For although State aid does not seem to have been given for the purpose of establishing control, the State appropriations have rendered necessary State supervision, and, as these

[31] Laws of N. Y., 1854, ch. 97.

[32] Fitch, *op. cit.*, pp. 62-64.

[33] Laws of N. Y., 1904, ch. 40.

The title, Superintendent of Common Schools, Superintendent of Public Instruction, and Commissioner of Education will be used interchangeably in the following pages, the reference in any particular place always being to the state's chief educational executive of that date.

[34] Laws of N. Y., 1910, ch. 607.

State grants have increased, the control over the local authorities has been made more and more complete and effective.[35]

The very creation of the office of superintendent of common schools in 1812 bears this out, for supervision of the state school funds was to be its main function. The uniform state Regents Examinations were brought into existence in 1865 in order to make a fairer distribution of the state "literature fund." [36] In more recent times consolidation of districts has been promoted by offering additional state grants to those consolidating.[37] The commissioner's judicial power itself might be taken as a final instance. Since the chief function of the superintendent of common schools was financial and continued so at the time of the enactment of the law of 1822, it may well be inferred that the new judicial power was at first largely ancillary to it. From these roots the power has grown to a position where it is second to no other as an instrumentality for making the arm of the state effective in matters of education.

It was remarked on an earlier page that the strongest present factor pushing the state in the direction of administrative judicial tribunals was the need for technically rather than judicially trained minds to apply the intricate kind of social welfare legislation which is issuing from the legislative press in such abundance to-day. It may be well to clinch this point for education at this juncture by sketching only briefly the extent of the present education law. The Education Law, as amended July 1, 1925, is a volume of no less than 408 pages! Between the covers of this volume are provisions regulating more or less minutely the formation, alteration, dissolution, and consolidation of school districts; the proceedings of district meetings; the powers and duties of school officers, as, trustees, district superintendents, school commissioners, etc.; the assessment and collection of school taxes; issuance and validation of school bonds; school buildings and school sites; the apportionment of state subsidies; transportation of pupils; powers and duties of city boards of education; certification of teachers, their tenure, and their contracts; medical inspection; compulsory education; colleges for teachers, normal schools, training classes, and teacher institutes; retirement and pension of teachers; teacher salaries; libraries and museums;

[35] Fairlie, *op. cit.*, p. 33.

[36] *Ibid.* p. 67.

[37] Laws of N. Y., 1913, ch. 129; *Ibid.* 1914, ch. 101.

courses for retarded children, courses in physiology and hygiene, physical education, citizenship, agriculture, etc.; schools for the deaf, dumb, and blind, for Indians, for colored children; industrial schools; state scholarships; incorporation and supervision of universities, colleges, academies, libraries, museums, etc. The recent State Departments Law,[38] reorganizing and consolidating the state administrative machinery, has even further widened the sphere of activity of the Education Department by giving it control over the state colleges of agriculture, home economics, and forestry, and the state veterinary college; the agriculture experiment station; the state school for clay working and ceramics; and the former motion pictures commission.

[38] Laws of N. Y., 1926, ch. 544, enacted as art. 11 of ch. 78 of the Consol. Laws.

CHAPTER II

THE NATURE AND OPERATION OF THE JUDICIAL POWER OF THE NEW YORK STATE COMMISSIONER OF EDUCATION

1. The Purpose and Constitutionality of the Commissioner's Judicial Power

The state superintendency of common schools had been in existence for ten years before judicial power was incorporated into the functions of the office. During this time, however, so many controversies arose over the proper administration of the school law that Superintendent Hawley was frequently called upon to make expositions of it.[1] That this duty of the superintendent rapidly became formidable can readily be seen from the first annual report to the legislature of Superintendent Hawley's successor, Secretary of State Yates, the state's first ex officio superintendent of common schools. After remarking about the number of opinions he was called upon to render on the school law, Superintendent Yates called the legislature's attention to the fact that,

> . . . still there exists no legal authority to enforce any of his decisions, nor to put an end to the vexatious controversies submitted to his decision. The school act is already too complicated, in many of its provisions, to increase the difficulty, by driving the parties into an expensive litigation, to settle probably a point of no great importance in itself but which derives all its interest from the passions and prejudices of the parties concerned. It were better, perhaps, in such cases, to have a speedy decision, at the risk of being wrong, than to injure, if not derange, the whole system, by a long, oppressive, and procrastinated legal controversy.[2]

For the remedy of this situation, Superintendent Yates proposed the following amendment to the school law:

[1] Decisions of the Superintendent of Common Schools, Preface, p. iv, Croswell, Van Benthuysen & Burt, Albany, N. Y., 1837, 479 pp.

[2] Annual Report Superintendent of Common Schools, in Assembly Journal, 1822, pp. 621-22.

> And be it further enacted, That it shall be lawful for any person conceiving himself aggrieved by the decision of any district meeting, or of the commissioners of schools, in the forming or altering, or in refusing to form or alter any school district, or of the commissioners, in refusing to pay any school monies to any district, to appeal therefrom, to the acting superintendent of common schools, whose decision thereon shall be final.[3]

The legislature proved sympathetic. In fact, so appreciative of the situation did it prove that it granted an even wider jurisdiction than the superintendent asked for. The final mind of the legislature read as follows:

> And be it further enacted, That it shall be lawful for any person, conceiving himself aggrieved by any decision which has been, or hereafter may be made by any district meeting; or by the commissioners of schools in the forming or altering, or in refusing to form or alter any school district, or in refusing to pay any school monies to any district; or by the trustees in paying any teacher, or in refusing to admit any scholar, gratuitously, into any school; or concerning any other matter under this act, or the act hereby amended, to appeal therefrom to the acting superintendent of common schools, whose decision thereupon shall be final.[4]

The original purpose of this legislation is already sufficiently clear except to say that it was hardly a year old before Superintendent Yates offered the further contemporary justification for it that it prevented many applications to the state legislature for relief.[5] At a number of other points in the nineteenth century, occasions arose necessitating an interpretation of the purpose of the judicial power, but explanations pretty generally took their color from pronouncements of Superintendent Yates.[6] Later interpreters of the legislation have supported it for still other reasons. Fitch, in his review of the administration of the old Department of Public Instruction, found the design of the legislation very acceptable because it relieved the courts of much litigation that would have been annoying and burdensome.[7] Within limits to be noted later,[8] the courts have aligned themselves with this view. Perhaps this was implied in Superin-

[3] *Ibid.* p. 674.

[4] Laws of N. Y., 1822, ch. 256, sec. 7.

[5] Ann. Rept. Supt. Com. Schs. 1823, Appendix A, p. 2.

[6] Easton *v.* Callendar, 11 Wend. 91, 95 (1833); 3 Denio 175, 176 (1846); Anonymous, Jud. Decs. 10, 11 (1887); Appeal of Cunliff *et al. v.* Wood *et al., Ibid.* 771, 774 (1888); Ann. Rept. Supt. Com. Schs. 1830, p. 30; Ann. Rept. Dept. Pub. Instn. 1875, p. 53. See also: Safford *et al. v.* Commissioners etc., Decs. Supt. Com. Schs., 44 (1829); Trustees etc. *ex parte, Ibid.* 241, 243 (1835).

[7] Fitch, in Ann. Rept., Dept. Pub. Instn. 1904, p. 24.

[8] Sections 3 and 7 of this chapter.

tendent Yates' argument to the legislature, but certainly not in the explicit language employed by courts of a later day. Without mentioning their own convenience they have now asserted a more direct and affirmative justification of the act of 1822 in that it keeps school litigation "within the compass of the department of public instruction as best fitted to mete out justice between the parties." [9] The "finality" of the commissioner's judicial power has commended itself to one court in recent times on the ground that it enabled the commissioner to devote his attention primarily to the schools and not the courts.[10] This certainly reads more into the original purpose of the power than was actually meant, for the early superintendent of common schools had no professional duties as they are conceived to-day, such as supervision of instruction, determination of minimum curriculum requirements, certification of teachers and the like. While the statute has become overlaid with these new interpretations, one must not think that the former purposes do not still hold, for they do. These later tendencies merely show that, happily, the law does change and attempt to reflect changing educational values through the flexibility of judicial interpretation.

In short, the commissioner's judicial power may now be justified on the ground that the state's interest in education has become so extensive and so technical that if the state's policies are to be carried out effectively, a method of settling controversies that is cheaper, more expeditious, and more cognizant of professional intricacies, than either the courts or the legislature can afford, must be found. No one is more competent to fill this rôle than the commissioner of education.

The constitutionality of this legislation has never been seriously in question. In 1880 the point was pressed that in as much as appeals before the commissioner of education did not provide for trial by jury, the legislation permitting them was unconstitutional. The merits of this objection, however, were not examined at length, since the party raising it had voluntarily submitted himself to the commissioner's jurisdiction and was thereby held

[9] People *ex rel.* Bowers *v.* Allen, 19 Misc. 464, 466 (1897). Acc.: Bullock *v.* Cooley, 225 N. Y. 566, 576-77 (1919); Superintendent Skinner took the same view in his annual report of 1900, p. 30, where he said, "These decisions often involve questions of school polity as well as of the construction of statutes, and are largely questions with which the courts are not familiar and of which they have no special knowledge. . . ."

[10] People *ex rel.* O'Reilly *v.* Finley, 175 App. Div. 204, 206 (1916).

to have waived his constitutional right.[11] Some twenty years later the complaint was that the "finality" of the commissioner's decisions was ousting the courts of their jurisdiction and that therefore the act of 1822 was unconstitutional. Unfortunately, again the court did not go into the merits of the objection, since it held that the relator in the suit had not made out a case which would rightly put him in a position to raise the constitutional question. The court, nevertheless, strongly intimated that it thought there was no merit to the contention. In the first place, the court pointed out that the school district involved in the case was a creature of the state and, therefore, the legislature could suit itself as to the terms under which it might take appeals. A second ground suggested by the court was similar to that in the case of jury trial, namely, that if one voluntarily submits to the jurisdiction of the commissioner, he must accept his decision on the terms specified in the statute.[12]

2. The Nature of the Controversies Which May Be Appealed to the Commissioner of Education

While the superintendent of common schools originally asked only to have a final decision in matters concerning the formation and alteration of school districts and in the distribution of state funds to them, it has already been seen how the legislature in addition accorded him similar power in the payment of teachers' salaries, the gratuitous admission of pupils to common schools, and "concerning any other matter under this act."[13] In spite of the alteration of the act of 1822 in 1827[14] and again in 1830,[15] there was no notable change in the matters subject to appeal for the next twenty-five years. By that time, however, school libraries had become so important that the decisions of district trustees, librarians, and meetings in relation to their school district libraries became reviewable by the superintendent of common schools.[16] As new subordinate officers were created to facilitate the administration of the common school system, their acts and decisions were usually made subject to the superintendent's appellate

[11] People *ex rel.* Yale *v.* Eckler, 19 Hun 609.
[12] People *ex rel.* Underhill *v.* Skinner, 74 App. Div. 58, 61 (1902).
[13] *Ante,* p. 10.
[14] *Post,* p. 65.
[15] Laws of N. Y., 1830, ch. 320, sec 7; see also *post* 65 f.
[16] Laws of N. Y., 1847, ch. 480.

jurisdiction as in other cases already provided for by law.[17] The long-awaited consolidation and revision of the school laws which came in 1864 produced a few changes by way of addition, though none by way of subtraction. Specific new matters of appeal became the following: refusal to apportion "a part of a school district" its share of the state moneys; refusal of a supervisor to pay school moneys to a school district; and, finally, any grievance under any act other than the school act, but nevertheless pertaining to common schools.[18] So far as the enumeration of the kinds of controversy which the commissioner of education may take cognizance of is concerned, this statement of the law in 1864 is practically its status at the present time.[19]

As a matter of fact, the variety of appeals which are brought before the commissioner of education is far greater than the specific ones enumerated. The expansion of his jurisdiction is brought about in the general provision of the education law which gives the commissioner power to adjudicate controversies "concerning any other matter under this act." [20] A good many years elapsed before doubts were raised about the limits of this clause. The first time it was contested in court was in People *ex rel.* Owen v. Masters.[21] In that case the respondent, a town superintendent, who at that time was the teacher licensing officer in the state, refused to examine the relator for a teacher's certificate on the ground that the relator's moral character was unsatisfac-

[17] E.g., Laws of N. Y., 1856, ch. 179, creating the office of school commissioner; *Ibid.* 1910, ch. 607, sec. 398, relating to the district superintendency of schools.

[18] Laws of N. Y., 1864, ch. 555, title 12, sec. 1.

[19] Section 890 of ch. 140 of the laws of 1910, as amended to 1925, reads in part as follows:

"Such appeal or petition may be made in consequence of any action:

"1. By any school district meeting;

"2. By any school commissioner and other officers, in forming or altering, or refusing to form or alter, any school district, or in refusing to apportion any school moneys to any such district or part of a district;

"3. By a supervisor in refusing to pay any such moneys to any such district;

"4. By the trustees of any district in paying or refusing to pay any teacher, or in refusing to admit any scholar gratuitously into any school or on any other matter upon which they may, or do, officially act;

"5. By any trustees of any school library concerning such library, or the books therein, or the use of such books;

"6. By any district meeting in relation to the library or any other matter pertaining to the affairs of the district;

"7. By any other official act or decision of any officer, school authorities, or meetings concerning any other matter under this chapter, or any other act pertaining to common schools."

[20] Wording of an act of 1822, *ante* p. 10.

[21] 21 Barb. 252 (1855).

tory. The relator appealed to the state superintendent who, finding his moral character satisfactory, ordered the town superintendent to give him an examination on the educational subjects. This the respondent town superintendent did and found the candidate competent therein. But, in subsequently issuing the teacher's certificate, the town superintendent omitted all mention of the former's moral character. The teacher then went to court and asked for a writ of mandamus to compel the town superintendent to issue him a perfect certificate. When the licensing officer set up the relator's moral character as a bar to relief in this tribunal, the latter introduced the superintendent's decision as conclusive on the question of his moral character. The town superintendent contested this decision on the ground that the superintendent had had no jurisdiction to hear the appeal in the first place. As the certification of teachers was not specifically one of the matters subject to appeal, he seemed to have excellent reason for making this contention. On the other hand, the validity of the superintendent's jurisdiction was advocated because of his authority to hear appeals "concerning any other matter under this act." The court sided with the town superintendent and denied the mandamus, holding that this clause could not be given "a full literal interpretation and operation." To confer such broad jurisdiction on the state superintendent would lead to what the court thought the absurdity of requiring the town superintendent to certify the truth of something which he thought false. Such a centralization of power also seemed inconsistent with what the court pointed out as the evident localism of the school law, for that placed the selection of teachers in an officer whom the people themselves elected. This view was further reinforced by the fact that town superintendents were not compelled by law to recognize the certificates issued by other town superintendents. The court concluded with the statement, "This whole policy would be frustrated by allowing the discretion of the town superintendent to be controlled or interfered with in this respect by the state superintendent."

Judging from the localism of the first half of the nineteenth century, it hardly seems questionable but that this restriction on the extent of the operation of the judicial power was in keeping with the times. There was, however, a broader precedent which the court might have followed in People *ex rel.* Owen v. Masters had it been cited in the argument of the case and had the court been favorably inclined to it. In 1841 certain school commissioners refused to sanction an appropriation for a new schoolhouse on the ground that it was too large. When their refusal was appealed they contested the superintendent's jurisdiction to review the discretionary act of a local school officer. The superintendent answered, "The discretion exercised in this case, like that of granting or refusing a certificate to a teacher, is the subject of appeal. The authority of the superintendent upon appeal extends to all matters arising under the school laws." [22] It is this conception of the clause under consideration that has obtained since the latter part of the nineteenth century, at least in the decisions of the Commissioner of Education.

The leading modern case is one of Andrew S. Draper's. In the Matter of the Appeal of Edson v. The Board of Education of Binghamton,[23] the board's acts with reference to textbooks were involved. The board's contention was that the general clause conferring power on the superintendent of public instruction to hear appeals from "any other official act or decision concerning any other matter under this act or any other act pertaining to common schools" [24] should be given no broader connotation than the specific clauses preceding it and of which it was a part. Textbooks, as will be remembered, were not among the specified acts subject to appeal. In replying to this, Draper made a very strong claim for the superintendent's judicial power:

> The contention of the respondent's counsel that the phrase "any other official act" refers only to acts by the same body or of the same nature as those specified in the first six subdivisions of the section, can not be adopted. . . . Enacted in the early days of the school system, it (the judicial power) has from time to time been added to with the evident purpose of making it clear that the jurisdiction of the superintendent is intended to be statewide and is to cover all controversies touching any official act of local school officials.[25]

This certainly does not seem wholly consistent with the customary rule of statutory construction contended for by the

[22] Anonymous, Jud. Dec. 7 (1841); University of State of N. Y., Albany, N. Y., 1914, 1508 pp.

[23] Jud. Decs., 1222 (1887). See also: Matter of Appeal of Cunliff *et al. v.* Wood *et al.; Ibid.* 771 (1888).

[24] Wording of act of 1864, ch. 555.

[25] Matter of Appeal of Edson *v.* Board of Education of Binghamton, Jud. Decs., 1222, 1224.

respondent board of education,[26] but, nevertheless, the conclusion seems such sound public policy that the courts of the state should and would uphold it. Although the decision in People *ex rel.* Owen v. Masters has never been expressly overruled, and although no similar case has since been presented to the courts, the general tenor of the opinions of the courts and the long acquiescence in the more liberal policy enunciated by Andrew S. Draper lead to the conclusion that the courts, too, would to-day uphold the Matter of Appeal of Edson v. Board of Education of Binghamton.[27]

It will be remembered that the statute provides that those aggrieved by "any act or decision" may appeal. It probably needs no special proof that this phrase is broad enough to include a failure to act or decide as well as affirmative conduct, but, nevertheless, the point is brought out since the court has been called upon to sustain the superintendent of public instruction on this matter.[28]

So far the discussion has concerned *what* acts the commissioner of education has jurisdiction to hear on appeal. Some different principles apply to a consideration of *whose* acts may be appealed. The leading case on this point is People *ex rel.* Hylan v. Finegan.[29] There there was a dispute between the board of education and the municipal authorities of New York City as to the disposition of certain state school funds which had been paid to the city. Without entering into the facts of this controversy it suffices for our purpose to note that when the acting commissioner of education, Dr. Finegan, was apprised of the situation, he himself instituted a proceeding to settle the dispute and cited both of the contestants to appear before him. The municipal authorities then brought action in the courts to restrain the commissioner from hearing the appeal, on the ground that he had no jurisdiction to do so. The commissioner rested his case on the general power

[26] See Matter of Appeal of Sweeney, 35 State Department Report, 573, 578 (1926) and court cases cited.

[27] It should not be thought that the Matter of the Appeal of Edson *v.* Board of Education of Binghamton overrules People *ex rel.* Owen *v.* Masters. The courts may review the decision of the commissioner of education but there is only the faintest dictum of the converse proposition and that weakened by the fact that it is the commissioner's. See Davidson *et al.,* 17 State Dept. Repts. 448, 452 (1918).

[28] People *ex rel.* Yale *v.* Eckler, 19 Hun 609 (1880). Hutchinson *v.* Skinner, 21 Misc. 729 (1897). See also Matter of Appeal of Crandall, 22 State Dept. Repts. 303 (1922), where a board of education failed to defeat a teacher's right to appeal for salary due by protracted delay in its consideration of the claim.

[29] 227 N. Y. 219 (1919). In accord, see People *ex rel.* Trustees *v.* Town Auditors, 126 N. Y., 578 (1890).

to hear any party aggrieved by "any other official act or decision of any officer, school authorities, or meetings concerning any other matter under this chapter, or any other act pertaining to common schools." [30] The court of appeals, however, took the position that this general section was to be interpreted in the light of the preceding sections; that these sections all applied to acts of "bodies or individuals generally, or, for the time being, made agencies of the education department and which are subject to the undisputed authority of the Education Law and bound to obey its commands"; [31] that "the city of New York does not admit in this matter that it stands in the position of an agency of the education department. . . . On the contrary, it denies and repudiates these propositions and insists that it stands as a municipality under the statutes which constitute its charter." [32] In a nutshell, Chief Judge Hiscock points out:

> If the proposition of the commissioner of education is correct, then he would have power to settle controversies between bodies within the department of education and third parties outside of its jurisdiction involving large property rights which, because of the finality of his decision, would be more far reaching than that possessed by the Supreme Court of the state.[33]

Legal students would doubtless support this decision as sound doctrine. It raises, however, several interesting questions. Suppose the appellant before the commissioner is an agency outside of the Education Department and the respondent an agency of the department, or, in other words, suppose the parties in the case just discussed were reversed, would the decision have been different? So far as this investigation has been carried no adjudication on this exact point has been found, but it is here submitted that if the outside agency voluntarily submits its grievance to the jurisdiction of the commissioner, it would be bound by the latter's decision. A second moot question growing out of the New York City case might be to inquire what attitude one should now assume toward the broad position taken by the superintendent of public instruction in the Matter of the Appeal of Edson v. the Board of Education of Binghamton.[34]

If there is to be a restricted view of *whose* acts are subject to

[30] See note 19, p. 13.
[31] People *ex. rel.* Hylan *v.* Finegan, 227 N. Y., 219, 224-25.
[32] *Ibid.* pp. 225-26.
[33] *Ibid.* p. 226.
[34] *Ante,* p. 15 f.

the commissioner's jurisdiction, would not the court of appeals, had the Binghamton case been carried to it, have overruled the position taken by Draper on *what* acts are appealable? It is here claimed that the two cases are not inconsistent with each other. The inference is strong in reading Chief Judge Hiscock's opinion as a whole that he recognizes the *broad* jurisdiction of the commissioner in his own bailiwick, and it is equally as plain that Draper's claim for his jurisdiction extended no further than to official acts of school officials.[35]

Some matters, even though they concern official acts of agencies subordinate to the Education Department, are expressly exempted from his jurisdiction. Suits for the collection of fines and penalties where imposed by the Education Law are, and have been, exclusively brought in the courts.[36] The same procedure has been followed in the case of condemnation proceedings for procuring property for a school site.[37] Again a city's charter might have the effect of exempting the city from the commissioner's jurisdiction.[38]

In addition to *what* acts and *whose* acts may be the subject of appeal, there is a further question of who may properly "conceive himself aggrieved" by such acts within the meaning of the statute.[39] This must be done because the commissioner has power, conferred as far back as 1864,

> To decline to entertain, or to dismiss, an appeal, when it shall appear that the appellant has no interest in the matter appealed from and that the matter is not a matter of public concern, and that the person injuriously affected by the act or decision appealed from is incompetent to appeal. . . .[40]

[35] In fact, prior to 1919 there were two decisions in the department expressly refusing relief on the ground that the superintendent of public instruction in the one case and the commissioner of education in the other had no jurisdiction over persons then or no longer recognizing the superior authority of the chief state educational officer: Matter of Appeal of Bonnefond, Jud. Decs. 17 (1886); Matter of Rau, 1 State Dept. Repts. (unofficial) 420 (1912). Since 1919 see Matter of Appeal of Eaton, 26 State Dept. Repts. 84 (1921).

[36] Anonymous (1866). p. 293, Laws of N. Y. etc. and a Digest of Decisions, Weed-Parsons & Co., Albany, N. Y., 1868, 720 pp.; Matter of Appeal of Kennedy, 2 State Dept. Repts. (official) 625 (1914).

[37] Matter of Hemenway, 134 App. Div. 86 (1909); Matter of Appeal of Balcom *v.* Trustees of Sch. Dist. No. 11, etc., Jud. Decs. 967 (1891); Laws of N. Y. 1910, ch. 140, sec. 463, subdiv. 2, as amended to 1925.

[38] Steinson *v.* Board of Education, 27 Misc. 687 (1899), reversed in 49 App. Div. 143 and reversal affirmed in 165 N. Y., 431, but on other grounds.

[39] *Ante,* p. 10.

[40] Laws of N. Y., 1864, ch. 555, title 12, secs. 2, subdiv. 3; continued in laws of 1910, as amended to 1925, ch. 140, sec. 891, subdiv. 3.

An outstanding case under this part of the school law is that of People *ex rel.* Board of Education v. Finley. In that decision the board of education of the city of New York wanted the superintendent, against his personal judgment, to issue a list of teachers eligible for certain teaching positions. The board went as high as the court of appeals in an effort to gain a writ of prohibition to prevent the superintendent from appealing the case to the commissioner of education at Albany. Counsel for the board, among other arguments, tried to belittle the superintendent's proposed appeal on the ground that he only "conceived" himself aggrieved and that it was not the purpose of the law for the commissioner to entertain such trivial grievances. The court, however, turned this point to good advantage, holding that the purpose of the statute was

> . . . to be a broad one, leaving it to the commissioner to decline to entertain or dismiss appeals which seem to him to involve visionary or remote grievances and interests. Of course we agree with counsel for the appellant that the mere fact a person "conceives" himself to be aggrieved would not furnish the basis for an appeal; that the right to such appeal must rest on real reasons and not on mere mental attitude of the person who desires to take an appeal. But we do think the word "conceives" is of some importance in connection with the other language which we have quoted as indicating that the statute is to be liberally construed in permitting appeals to the commissioner in disputes arising in the administration of our school system.[41]

But even granting the liberal spirit underlying the statute, it has been a settled policy of long standing in the department that, "There should be some real grievance, some positive and serious injury sustained" to justify an appeal.[42] Yet the question still rises, What is a "real grievance, some positive and serious injury sustained"? A few concrete illustrations may make this clearer. Where a controversy happened to be merely a personal one, and where the educational welfare of the district was really not involved, the commissioner summarily disposed of the case with the remark that,

> The remedy of appeal in school controversies, provided by statute, was not designated to permit the exploitation of personal enmity or the indulgence by the parties of immaterial and groundless recrimination and abuse.[43]

[41] 211 N. Y., 51, 58 (1914).

[42] Matter of the Appeal of Bishop, Jud. Decs. 15 (1893).

[43] Matter of Appeal of Barry. 8 State Dept. Repts. 607 (1916). Acc.: Anonymous, Code of Pub. Instn. 1856, p. 293 (1859).

In a similar spite litigation the appellant was dismissed because he was as guilty of wrongdoing as the respondent.[44] An appellant who wished to have the proceedings of the district meeting set aside merely because he had not received notice of the meeting was bowed out for failure to show that any one had been prejudiced by the fact.[45] And certainly one who was not a qualified voter of a district had no standing to complain of the irregularity of the district trustee's election.[46] In another case it was held, that while a resident parent might be aggrieved because his son was not admitted gratuitously to the schools, an employer of the child would not have a similar standing.[47] A similar result was reached where an agency of the Christian Science Church appealed because the board of education refused to accept the excuse of a teacher belonging to its membership who had been absent and treated by one of their practitioners. The commissioner said here that the appellant's injury "must be personal in its nature, and the mere fact that members of the appellant's church or denomination or persons of the same religious belief are injured does not constitute the appellant an aggrieved person within the meaning of the statute." [48] So, too, where a teacher has been wrongfully dismissed from her employment, she is the one to appeal, and not a taxpayer, even though the latter be a parent.[49] On the other hand, when People *ex rel.* Board of Education v. Finley [50] was in the courts below,[51] it was decided that the city superintendent of schools might well be aggrieved both as superintendent and private citizen at the action of his board in directing him to do an act against his better judgment. The commissioner has taken the same view because, when the controversy at the bottom of Board of Education *v.* Finley ultimately reached his tribunal, he decided that the superintendent was properly aggrieved both as city official and as lay citizen.[52].

[44] Matter of Petition of Cunningham. Ann. Rept. State Dept. of Ed. 1913, p. 437 (1912).

[45] Matter of Appeal of Bishop *et al.* Jud. Decs. 15 (1893); Matter of Appeal of the Hartford Club *v.* Muller, *Ibid.* 19, 21 (1902).

[46] Matter of Appeal of Chase, Ann. Rept. Dept. Pub. Instn. 1892, p. 149 (1891).

[47] Matter of Appeal of Tiernan *v.* Board of Education, Jud. Decs. 1320 (1897).

[48] Matter of Appeal of Gilmore, 24 State Dept. Repts. 716, 718 (1921).

[49] Matter of Appeal of Catel, 6 State Dept. Repts. 513 (1915); Anonymous (1868), p. 496, Code of Pub. Instn. Containing the Laws and Decisions Relating to Common Schools, Weed, Parsons & Co., Albany, N. Y. 1887, 1070 pp.

[50] *Ante,* p. 19.

[51] People *ex rel.* Board of Education *v.* Draper, 78 Misc. 329 (1912).

[52] Matter of Appeal of Maxwell, 3 State Dept. Repts. (official) 539 (1914).

3. ARTICULATION OF THE COÖRDINATE AND EXCLUSIVE ORIGINAL JURISDICTIONS OF THE COMMISSIONER AND THE COURTS

The statute of 1822 merely made an appeal to the superintendent of common schools for the redress of grievances under the school act optional with the party aggrieved. In 1841, however, the legislature considered it good public policy to encourage litigants to carry their complaints to the superintendent rather than the courts. Consequently, it provided in the enactments of that year that no costs should be allowed a successful plaintiff in the courts where the court would certify that the defendant school officer acted in good faith and where the plaintiff might in the first instance have carried his case to the superintendent.[53] The statute included an important exception in favor of suits for penalties under the school law and in suits to enforce the decisions of the superintendent.

In as much as the law of 1841 is continued in the present Education Law,[54] and in as much as appeal to the commissioner is still permissive and not mandatory within certain limits, it becomes pertinent to inquire into the way in which this option has come to be exercised. Much seems to depend on the nature of the aggrieved party's cause of action. The earliest statement of the present practice is found in People *ex rel.* Light v. Skinner:

> The party who feels himself aggrieved, if he has a clear legal right, may, no doubt, enforce it in the courts, while in a matter in which he merely has a grievance the statute provides that he may appeal to the superintendent, and if he does so, he must accept the terms under which it is granted.[55]

This statement of a complainant's alternatives, however, is confusing, since the distinction between legal rights and mere grievances may not always be clear. The principle of this decision has been strengthened and made more explicit in subsequent determinations. The class of cases formerly referred to as "grievances" is now identified with disputes arising within the educational system which are of a distinctly technical or profes-

[53] Laws of N. Y. 1841, ch. 260, sec. 33. Applying the statute see: *Ex parte* Bennett, 3 Denio 175 (1846); Whitbeck *v.* Billings, 1 Hun 494 (1874). In Matter of Humphrey, 94 Misc. 377 (1916), the plaintiff brought suit to recover expenses incurred on behalf of local educational authorities in court litigation. The judge criticized the expense account presented because it might have been smaller had the case been heard before the commissioner of education.

[54] Laws of N. Y., 1910, as amended to 1925, ch. 140, art. 33, sec. 857.

[55] 74 App. Div. 58, 61 (1902).

sional nature. In this sphere the power of the commissioner of education has been dignified with exclusive jurisdiction. Thus, the Appellate Division of the Supreme Court has recently declared,

> The authority and jurisdiction of the Commissioner of Education are exclusive in all matters relating to the supervision and control of the public school system, the discipline of the schools and the management of the school property, and the authority and discretionary acts on the part of officers or agencies of education.[56]

Perhaps it is better to say that the commissioner's jurisdiction in this sphere is exclusive at least for hearing in the first instance.[57] This exclusive jurisdiction, however, does not extend to the second class of cases mentioned in People *ex rel.* Light v. Skinner above, and described as involving a "legal right." In such an instance, an appellant may seek relief from either the courts or the commissioner at his pleasure. But what is the nature of a dispute arising under the educational law which infringes legal rights and yet is not to be classed as of a professional nature and thus within the exclusive jurisdiction of the commissioner? It is not easy to describe. Such a controversy involves "rights which had become vested";[58] it may arise "where the right of a party depends upon the interpretation of a statute and it is claimed that a school board or official has proceeded to act in violation of an express statute and thereby the party complaining is being deprived of valuable rights";[59] or it may involve "a cause of action on the part of a taxpayer for an improper use of the funds and property of the board of education or the determination of constitutional questions or illegal acts on the part of officials."[60] It is not always easy to determine which sort of case confronts one.[61] This jurisdictional problem is well summed up in the following dictum,

[56] Matter of O'Connor *v.* Emerson, 196 App. Div. 807, 310 (1921), affd. 232 N. Y., 561.

[57] Lewis *v.* Smith *et al.*, 109 Misc. 694, 696 (1919), affd. without opinion in 190 App. Div. 884; People *ex rel.* Merral *v.* Cooley *et al.*, 75 Misc. 188, 191 (1912); Matter of McCarthy, 106 Misc. 193, 196 (1919), reversed in 188 App. Div. 930 but on other grounds.

[58] Matter of McCarthy, *supra.*

[59] Matter of O'Connor *v.* Emerson, 196 App. Div. 807, 810 (1921). But the fact that the question may involve the construction or application of a statute does not deprive the commissioner of jurisdiction: Matter of Levitch *v.* Board of Education, 243 N. Y., 373, 375 (1926).

[60] Stein *v.* Brown, 125 Misc. 692, 694 (1925).

[61] *Instances of the first group:* Welker *v.* Lathrop, 210 N. Y. 434 (1914); People *ex rel.* Keyser *v.* Board of Education, 32 Misc. 63 (1900); People *ex rel.* Walrath *v.* O'Brien, 112 App. Div. 97 (1906); Lewis *v.* Smith, *supra. Instances of the second*

In this state it is a settled policy that all questions of school administration and methods shall be determined by the commissioner of education and that his decision is not subject to review by the courts so far as it pertains to such administration and but incidentally, if at all, affects property rights. . . . This delegated power in the commissioner is not, however, general and unlimited. In order to oust the courts of their normal jurisdiction, it is not enough that the schools or the school system are more or less involved; in all matters outside its general policy, administration and control, where the educational system conflicts or interferes with the rights and interests of the people, in the absence of express statute to the contrary, the courts retain and will exercise full jurisdiction.[62]

But even after this pronouncement, a peculiar advantage still clings to seeking justice from an administrative tribunal such as the commissioner of education rather than the law courts. Superintendent Skinner has described this best in one of his decisions:

There is a further reason for preferring the remedy by appeal to a common-law action. . . . In an appeal the Superintendent can dispose of all questions connected with and arising therein in a single decision: where the action of a decision of a school officer or the proceeding of a school meeting is wrong he can not only reverse it, but direct the appropriate remedy so as to afford redress to all persons who have been injuriously affected; while an action at law inures only to the benefit of the person who brings it, and only gives pecuniary damages, without substituting a correct proceeding in the place of an erroneous one.[63]

Once the courts have assumed jurisdiction, the commissioner will in no way interfere. Such a policy is almost as old as the commissioner's judicial power itself.[64] Not even would the superintendent of public instruction be enticed into issuing an order to enforce the collection of a judgment by the supreme court against school trustees.[65] And much less would he give an opinion on a case pending in court with the purpose of having it in any way influence the judgment to be handed down there.[66] An in-

group: Matter of O'Connor *v.* Emerson, *supra;* Stein *v.* Brown, *supra;* Matter of McCarthy, *supra;* Anonymous, Jud. Decs. 1450 (1883); Matter of the appointment and qualification of Members of the Board of Education in the city of Plattsburgh, 3 State Dept. Repts. (official) 557 (1914).

[62] Matter of Miller v. Gould, 121 Misc. 270, 272 (1923). But see also Matter of Levitch *v.* Board of Education, 243 N. Y., 373 (1926).

[63] Matter of Appeal of Barnett *v.* Stanton, Ann. Rept. Dept. Pub. Instn. 1895, p. 184 (1894); Ann. Rept. Dept. Pub. Instn. 1896, pp. xxxii-xxxiii.

[64] Whittier *v.* Inhabitants of School Dist. No. 11, etc., Jud. Decs. 13 (1826); Anonymous, Laws of N. Y., etc. and Digest of Decs. 1868, p. 294 (1863); Anonymous, Code of Pub. Instn. 1887, p. 503 (1875); Alverson *v.* Joy, jr., Jud. Decs. 14 (1890); Matter of Appeal of Town, 1 State Dept. Repts. (unofficial) 385 (1912).

[65] Anonymous, Code of Pub. Instn. 1887, p. 504 (1873).

[66] Anonymous, Decs. Supt. Com. Schs., p. 285 (1836).

teresting variation from this discreet policy occurred in 1917. A district decided to purchase a new school site and erect a new school building thereon. A minority group brought action in the courts to restrain the board of education from carrying out the will of the district. The board of education sought to have the commissioner made party to the suit. The judge of the court where the petition was presented put in a long distance telephone call to the Education Department at Albany for its opinion. The deputy commissioner was of the mind that the case should first be disposed of through the department and telegraphed the contending parties to that effect. As a result, this was finally stipulated between the parties. A public meeting of the district was called and an agreed statement of facts and questions was drawn up to be presented to the commissioner.[67] The case was clearly one of the first group mentioned above where the commissioner was more technically competent to decide the issues presented than was the court. It is consequently satisfying to see this instance of coöperation between the courts and an administrative tribunal rather than a spirit of jurisdictional jealousy.

4. Procedure in Appeals Before the Commissioner of Education

The original act of 1822 [68] made no mention of the procedure to be followed in the bringing, hearing, and disposition of appeals authorized by the act. Not till the important consolidation and revision of the education law in 1864 did the legislature speak on this important phase of judicial proceedings before the then superintendent of public instruction. The legislature of that year enacted, and it has remained the enactment to date, that, "The superintendent, in reference to such appeals, shall have power: (1) To regulate the practice therein. . . ." [69]

The fact that the legislature was tardy in this regard does not mean that the matter had not become acute earlier. Apparently from the very start the number of appeals pressed upon the attention of the superintendent of common schools was so great that the superintendent had to act somehow or other to extricate himself. Superintendent Azariah C. Flagg was the first to try

[67] Matter of Erecting a New School Building, etc., 12 State Dept. Repts. 412 (1917).
[68] *Ante*, p. 10.
[69] Laws of N. Y., 1864, ch. 555, title 12; continued in Laws of 1910, as amended to 1925, ch. 140, sec. 891.

to expedite matters. Addressing himself to the legislature in his annual report for 1825 he said that he considered it "advisable that a system of rules should be published, prescribing the necessary prerequisites in bringing an appeal before the superintendent. It is believed that the number of decisions might be greatly diminished and many unprofitable controversies avoided, by a few judicious regulations in regard to appeals."[70] Proceeding, presumably, on the theory that no mode of inquiry being prescribed by statute, he had authority to make such reasonable rules therefore as would enable him to exercise the judicial power conferred upon him, the superintendent the next year promulgated the first set of rules regulating the procedure in appeals before him.[71]

Only a summary of the rules will be attempted here. The first requirement was that appeals be brought within thirty days after the commission of the act complained of unless a good excuse were offered. A statute of limitations such as this would naturally at once work toward expedition of appeals. Second, contending parties were recommended to submit their grievances on an agreed statement of facts. In the third place, if they could not agree, each was required to submit his case on affidavits. In this event the appellant was required to serve a copy of his complaint upon the respondent at least ten days before presentation of the appeal and then at that latter time produce proof of the service. As a fourth consideration neither party was required to appear in person before the superintendent. Instead, however, he might include in the letter forwarding his case any arguments which he thought logically grew out of the affidavits presented. It will be seen at once how economical in time and money this manner of disposing appeals is. Fifth, if the appeal concerned the formation or alteration of a district, a number of details was demanded, chiefly a map. This had to show the district or districts concerned; the old, new, or proposed lines of districts; the schoolhouse or schoolhouses; relative distances therefrom of the parties aggrieved, and the roads. In addition to the map the superintendent required a list of all the taxable inhabitants in the territory involved with their assessed valuations, together with the number of children 5 to 15 years of age belonging to each person. The final regulation, rather weakly stated, was that, where the

[70] Ann. Rept. Supt. Com. Schs. in Assem. J. 1826, Appendix G, p. 4.
[71] Ann. Rept. Supt. Com. Schs., in Assem. J. 1827, document No. 43, exhibit L, p. 36.

controversy happened to be over state aid, the commissioner of common schools "ought to retain the money . . . until the appeal is decided."

These rules of procedure remained in force for the next quarter of a century with little change. In the copy of the rules appended to Superintendent Dix's Decisions of the Superintendent of Common Schools, published in 1837,[72] additions appear. After service of the copy of the appeal on the respondent, all proceedings from which relief was sought were to be suspended. In addition, if errors were detected in the annual reports of trustees, they were to be given time to amend them.

By the time of their next appearance, in the publication of the Code of Public Instruction in 1856,[73] the rules of procedure regulating appeals had materially changed. The first of the new regulations required the appeal to be in writing and signed by the appellant. The second required service on the respondent to include a copy of all matters subsequently to be relied upon by the appellant. It also made it necessary to transmit another copy of the same to the superintendent of public instruction. The third requirement was a carry-over from the former rules, namely, that appeals must be brought within thirty days of the origin of the grievance or a good excuse offered for the contrary. Fourth, the respondent was given ten days within which to put in a defense. Fifth, the respective parties were only required to put in their cases on affidavits in so far as the facts between them were in dispute. The sixth regulation described the type of oath that would be recognized. In the seventh place the respondent was required, as previously, to serve upon the appellant a copy of all the matters he would rely on in answering the appeal of the appellant. No replication by the appellant to the respondent's answer nor rejoinder by the respondent to the appellant's replication were to be permitted except with express permission of the superintendent of public instruction. This provision was distinctly different from the procedure in a regular court where these extended pleadings are not so restricted, but then it had the virtue of expediting procedure which is of prime importance in the administration of educational concerns. Naturally, proof of service was another of the regulations. The ninth regulation gave an interested inhabitant of a district the privilege of answer-

[72] P. 444.

[73] P. 322.

ing an appeal with or without the trustees. The tenth provision was exactly similar to the fifth of the former regulations concerning the formation and alteration of districts.[74] The new regulations next made a great improvement on the former ones in mandatorily suspending for the time being the proceedings whose operation was the subject of appeal. This change is but one of several that already might be pointed to indicating the gradual growth of strong centralized power in the chief state school officer as a result of his judicial activities. The last provision concerned the recording and filing of the superintendent's decision.

The volume containing these rules contained also, for the first time, some practical suggestions on the bringing of appeals.[75] Outstanding among these was the request that what the department wanted was,

> . . . facts, and not arguments, far less, injurious imputations upon the motives of parties. The facts should be distinctly averred, so that an indictment for perjury would lie if they are wilfully misstated. Therefore, they should not be stated by way of recital under a "whereas," or in any similar way. Every material fact should be stated with all practicable particularity as to time, quantities, numbers, etc. Where a statement is ambiguous or doubtful in meaning, that construction is adopted which is most unfavorable to the party making it. The appellant should make out his own case; so that if no answer is put in, the superintendent will have, in the appeal itself, all the facts to inform him what order ought to be made.

After this followed suggestions that the appeals be drawn on foolscap paper with an inch margin in the fashion of other legal proceedings, that the pages be fastened at the top and not at the side so that when written on both sides the bottom of one side would be the top of the other, and that they be indorsed with the title of the case so as to indicate the kind of grievance and the district, town, or county to be affected. A last important request was for the post-office address of the party whose papers were concerned.

So satisfactory did the foregoing rules and suggestions prove that in spite of some minor alterations only a few notable changes have been made to the present time. In the publication of school laws, decisions, and rules of procedure in 1866,[76] the formula of 1856 was carried over verbatim with the one important exception that the bringing of an appeal itself no longer stayed proceedings

[74] *Ante,* p. 25.
[75] Code of Pub. Instn. 1856, pp. 320-22.
[76] Laws of New York, etc. and Digest of Dec., pp. 232-33.

unless the same was specifically requested. In a similar volume in 1887,[77] the only outstanding change to be mentioned here was the provision of serving appeals other than by personal service. By requiring for the first time in this publication the post-office address of attorneys, when employed, it may be properly inferred that by this period appeals had grown to involve matters of grave enough concern to make it worth while to engage professional talent, a very noteworthy milestone in the growth of the importance of the commissioner's judicial functions. In the 1926 Handbook on the Law and Rules of Practice Relating to Appeals to the Commissioner of Education, whether appeals shall be submitted on the papers filed, with or without oral argument, or the filing of briefs is left for the commissioner to determine. If hearings are had, however, it is provided that they may take place before the deputy commissioner if the commissioner so authorizes it. Whereas formerly the number of children between the ages of 5 and 15 was required in proceedings relating to the formation, alteration, or consolidation of districts, the number between the ages of 5 and 21 is now required. This evidently reflects the growth of the state's interest in secondary education. The sum of these changes in the handbook so far shows the constantly expanding burden and importance of work that is flowing through the judicial processes of the commissioner. Finally, a very important addition to the rules of practice is the twentieth one, permitting the commissioner in his discretion, in his determination of an appeal, to consider any official reports on file in the education department pertaining to the case before him. This not only quickens procedure, but it also gives the commissioner an excellent background of the controversy which the papers, briefs, and oral arguments might never afford.

Some rules of practice, or procedure, have grown up and are stated apart from those already mentioned. The set of longest standing is that relating to the removal from office of a school officer guilty of malfeasance in office. The first statement of these is found in the code of 1856[78] as an annotation to the section of the law giving the superintendent power to remove such an officer. Since the procedure is not materially different from the other rules of procedure and since the present statement is not

[77] Code of Pub. Instn., 1887, pp. 123-24.

[78] Code of Pub. Instn. 1856, p. 112, Weed, Parsons & Co., Albany, N. Y., 1856, 492 pp.

essentially different from the early one, no further mention need be made of it now. A more recent evolution in procedure is that in connection with the provision of the school law relating to the validation of school bonds before the commissioner.[79] In such a case a petition stating all the material facts relating to the appropriation and sale of the bonds must be served on the purchaser of the bonds and filed with the district clerk. Together with proof of service, the same must then be filed with the commissioner of education. Any person interested in the proceeding may file an answer within ten days after the service and filing of the petition. The commissioner's decision is filed with the district clerk and a copy delivered to the petitioner and the purchaser of the bonds.

In the following consideration of the application of the foregoing rules, the most important thing to point out first is the spirit in which those rules are administered. No hard and fast interpretation is given them, for the department realizes they are a means to, and not an end in justice. Superintendent Dix disregarded the form of the appeal papers if they were correct in substance.[80] The department's primary aim is to gain the educational interests of the state through a maximum allowance for the merits of each individual case. Because of this elastic and individualized application of the rules, the lay reader is cautioned not to think too quickly that the commissioner's action is either arbitrary or capricious. One of the clearest illustrations of this spirit is the administration of the rule requiring appeals to be brought within 30 days of the commission of the act complained of. If the appellant has no excuse for his remissness, the commissioner will rigorously apply the rule.[81] But if the appeal concerns some controversy which ought to be put at rest, or the appellant was unavoidably delayed, or some similar good reason exists, and the rights of none of the parties will be prejudiced by dispensing with the rule, the commissioner will act liberally.[82]

[79] Laws of N. Y., 1917, ch. 413. For procedure, see Handbook, pp. 25-26.

[80] Ann. Rept. Supt. Com. Schs. 1836, p. 30.

[81] E.g. Matter of Appeal of Babcock *et al.* *v.* Henderson, Ann. Rept. Dept. Pub. Instn. 1888, p. 849 (1887); Matter of Appeal of Schoonmaker, 30 State Dept. Repts. 219 (1923). The commissioner dismissed the appeal in the latter case without prejudice to bringing an action in the courts.

[82] Trustees Joint School District No. 6 Town of Tyrone *v.* Commissioners, etc., Decs. Supt. Com. Schs., p. 172 (1834); Anonymous, Code of Pub. Instn. 1887, p. 550 (1869); Appeal of Fulton *et al.,* Jud. Decs., 126, 132 (1896); Matter of Appeal of Bigler, 1 State Dept. Repts. (unofficial) 415 (1912); Matter of Appeal of Stevens, 2 State Dept. Repts. (unofficial) 416 (1913); Matter of Appeal of School District No. 4 of Mount Pleasant, etc. 2 *Ibid.* (official) 599 (1914).

The flexibility of procedure before the commissioner may further be illustrated by comparing it in one or two aspects with the corresponding procedure in the courts. In the Appeal of the Board of Education of Union Free School District No. 15, Town of Hempstead, etc., the village of Lawrence voted to set itself off from the union free school district of which it was a part. When this action was appealed to the commissioner, the village contested the right of the commissioner to hear the appeal on the technical ground that no final action in the separation had been taken since the school commissioner had not issued his certificate and no appeal lay, according to court rules, from any except final acts. The commissioner quickly answered this by stating that, "The remedy by appeal to the Commissioner of Education is specially provided by statute and ordinary rules of procedure in appeals from judicial decisions, and decrees do not necessarily apply except so far as they have been included in the rules of practice adopted by the Commissioner." [83] An *obiter dictum* in the matter of charges against Weick makes an even wider claim,

> It is probably true that the jurisdiction of the Commissioner of Education to review on appeal the dismissal or removal of teachers by local school authorities is broader and more extensive than that prescribed by statute where it is attempted to review by *certiorari* in the Supreme Court the judicial acts of a municipal board in respect to dismissals or removals of officers. The Commissioner of Education exercises a close and effective supervision over the administration of school affairs, and he may under certain special conditions direct the performance of acts by local authorities without the same regard for judicial procedure as would be required where a remedy is sought in the courts. . . .[84]

Turning now to more particular applications of the rules of practice, an appellant finds on the very threshold of his appeal that pains must be taken with his moving papers. At the outset they must be "legible and intelligible" to catch the ear of the commissioner.[85] Short shrift was the order where the object of an appeal was the removal of a school commissioner, but the appellant failed even to allege an offense for which the respondent was remov-

[83] Ann. Rept., State Ed. Dept., 1913, p. 475 (1912).

[84] 10 State Dept. Rept. 459, 462 (1917); Acc.: Appeal of Mufson *et al.*, 18 *Ibid.* 393 (1918).

[85] Anonymous, Laws of N. Y. etc. and A Digest of Dec. 1866, p. 294 (1864). Acc.: Matter of Appeal of Holcomb *v.* School District No. 17, Jud. Decs. 15 (1889); Matter of Appeal of Frisbie, Ann. Rept. Dept. Pub. Instn. 1891, p. 84 (1890); Matter of Appeal of Thompson, Jud. Decs. 197 (1909).

able.[86] If the education law requires certain things to be stated in the appeal, nothing less will do. The condemnation of a schoolhouse demands that the order of condemnation set forth that the building is "wholly unfit for use and not worth repairing." Merely to state that the building is "wholly inadequate to accommodate the pupils attending said school" will obviously fall short of both the letter and the spirit of the statute.[87] When the appellant fails to serve notice of the appeal on the respondent, he can hardly expect to be heard by the commissioner in so one-sided a proceeding.[88] The commissioner is likely to be quite rigid in the application of his own rule of practice which requires the filing of a map with the moving papers.[89] It will readily be seen that it would be next to impossible to dispense with this in determining the problems arising in the formation, alteration, and consolidation of school districts.

If the appellant's papers in themselves are sufficient to make out a case, and the respondent fails to oppose them in any way when he might do so, the appellant's case will stand admitted and a decision rendered accordingly.[90] Sometimes the moving papers contain more than the appeal and answer, including also a replication by the appellant to the answer of the respondent and in some instances a rejoinder by the latter to the replication. In one case where the appellant filed a replication he did not counter the allegations of the respondent's answer, but set forth an entirely new complaint which, not being in the original appeal, was held a surprise on the respondent to which he did not have to pay attention.[91] Apparently the commissioner is not much inclined to favor defenses of the respondent which are in the nature of a counterclaim or an offset against the appellant. So, where a teacher was seeking payment of the balance of her salary the trustee was not allowed to reduce her claim by setting up the fact that the appellant had several unexcused absences from school and had kept the register irregularly.[92] Perhaps the commissioner thinks his judi-

[86] Application of Pendleton *et al.*, Jud. Decs. 440 (1907).

[87] Appeal of Barney *v.* Burdick, Jud. Decs. 850 (1902).

[88] Application for Annulment of Teacher's Certificate, etc., 13 State Dept. Repts. 15 (1917).

[89] Anonymous, Code of Pub. Instn. 1887, p. 497 (1868).

[90] Matter of Appeal of Choate *et al. v.* Thayer., Jud. Decs. 975 (1888); Matter of Appeal of Griffin *v.* Lounsbury *et al.*, *Ibid.* 376 (1896).

[91] Matter of Appeal of Frasier *v.* Houghton, Jud. Decs. 1270 (1891).

[92] Matter of Appeal of Bradley, 5 State Dept. Repts. 599 (1915). The offset of one trustee against a teacher's claim for salary was her destruction of the school organ

cial machinery is not well designed to handle such cases of controverted or unliquidated money damages. Neither does the commissioner favor an original action by way of a collateral attack, e.g., contesting a trustee's right to office by an appeal resisting a tax list issued by him. Such a grievance should be appealed earlier and directly.[93] But he has entertained an appeal based on the assignment of a claim for reimbursement for repairs to a school building.[94]

When the moving papers are completed, the case is ready for the commissioner's examination and final adjudication. As noted in the rules of practice, the commissioner may listen to oral argument on the appeal. If he does, the hearing generally takes place in some one of the offices in the State Education Building at Albany. The deputy-commissioner sometimes presides. In one case, at least, the deputy and two assistant commissioners were present with the commissioner.[95] The formalities ordinarily attending on a court proceeding are dispensed with. Usually there is not even any examination of witnesses—their contributions being presented in affidavits—just argument on the briefs and appeal papers.

Whether the commissioner determines the appeal with or without oral argument, the appellant must not only allege a cause of action but he must also present *evidence* that his allegations are true.[96] If he fails to do this, the department will not feel itself obligated to conduct its own investigation to ascertain just what the facts are.[97] On the other hand, if the truth of the facts, as alleged and denied, is too difficult to unravel from the appeal papers alone, the statute does give the commissioner a discretionary power to direct certain local school officers to take evidence and forward it to him.[98] In other instances the commissioner may

and part of the school library. When the teacher countered with the fact that the organ was her only source of kindling wood and that the library books destroyed were so dirty as to be a menace to health, the commissioner remitted the trustee to the courts to settle the claim. Matter of Appeal of Kimm *v.* Board of Education, Jud. Decs. 594 (1889).

[93] Anonymous, Laws of N. Y., etc. and Digest of Decs. 1868, p. 298 (1860).

[94] Matter of Appeal of Hill *et al.* *v.* Doan, Jud. Decs. 1261 (1885).

[95] Matter of Appeal of Certain Members of Board of Examiners, etc., 34 State Dept. Repts. 183 (1926).

[96] Matter of Appeal of Seery, Jud. Decs. 406 (1894).

[97] Anonymous, Laws of N. Y., etc. and Digest of Decs. 1868, p. 299 (1859); Anonymous, Code of Pub. Instn. 1887, p. 502 (1884).

[98] Laws of N. Y., 1883, ch. 413; *Ibid.* 1910, ch. 607, sec. 595, subdiv. 12. For an example of a case where this was done, see Matter of Appeal of McDonough *v.* Smith, Jud. Decs. 515 (1890).

send out a deputy from the State Department at Albany to ascertain just what the situation is.[99] In at least two cases where the choice of school site was a very close one, the superintendent of public instruction himself visited the scene of controversy before making his determination of the appeals.[100]

In any event, of course, the burden of proof is on the appellant.[101] This burden is pretty firmly fixed on him since the commissioner frequently resorts to the presumption that the acts and decisions of his subordinates were the proper ones under the circumstances. The appellant must, therefore, bring forward evidence to rebutt this prima facie case. There are many illustrations, a few of which are cited.[102] This presumption not only aids in the disposition of appeals, but it is, of course, also good administrative policy for the commissioner to stand back of his lieutenants in the field. While the appellant's evidence must outweigh this presumption, yet,

> . . . a preponderance of proof does not necessarily mean the greater number of witnesses. In the consideration of the weight of the evidence produced, due regard should be given to the kind and quality of the evidence, the degree of credibility to which the testimony of the witness is entitled, the apparent probability or improbability of its truthfulness, and the interest of the witness in the matter at issue.[103]

[99] Matter of Appeal of Hall *et al.*, Jud. Decs. 911 (1905). Matter of Appeal of Decker *et al.*, *Ibid.* 798 (1907).

[100] Matter of Appeal of Abbott *et al.* *v.* Jones, Jud. Decs. 935 (1888); Matter of Certain Taxpayers, etc., Ann. Rept. Supt. of Pub. Instn. 1893, p. 143 (1892).

[101] Matter of Appeal of Tillson *v.* McNeeley, Jud. Decs. 1090 (1889); Matter of Appeal of Van Vechten *et al.*, *Ibid.* 27 (1890); Matter of Appeal of Munger *v.* Pierce, Ann. Rept. Dept. Pub. Instn. 1892, p. 78 (1890).

[102] *Order condemning school buildings:* Flack *v.* Woods, Jud. Decs. 849 (1890); Matter of Appeal of Arnold *et al.*, 1 State Dept. Repts. (official) 537 (1914). *Accuracy of minutes of district meeting:* Matter of Appeal of Hawkins *et al.*, Ann. Rept. State Ed. Dept. 1913, p. 445 (1912); Matter of Appeal of Folmsbee, 7 State Dept. Repts. 575 (1915). *Local tax assessment:* Anonymous, Laws of N. Y. etc. and Digest of Decs. 1868, p. 380 (1862); Matter of Equalization of Assessments of Real Property in Union Free School District, etc., Ann. Rept. State Ed. Dept. 1913, p 456 (1912). *Marking of examinations in teacher certification:* Matter of Appeal of Halbert, 7 State Dept. Repts. 581 (1916); Matter of Jurisdiction of Board of Examiners, etc., 25 State Dept. Repts. 275, 290 (1921). *Appointment and removal of teachers:* Matter of Charges of General Inefficiency Against Reardon, Ann. Rept. State Ed. Dept. 1913, p. 472 (1912); Matter of Appeal of Mack, 30 State Dept. Repts. 154 (1923); Matter of Application of McQuade, Ann. Rept. State Ed. Dept. 1913, p. 432 (1912). *Orders altering and consolidating districts:* Reedy *v.* Commissioners of Com. Schs., Decs. Supt. Com. Schs., 35 (1829); In the matter of White, Jud. Decs. 641 (1887); Matter of Appeal of Chubbuck *v.* Barnum, *Ibid.* 738 (1888); Matter of Appeal from Order of District Superintendent, etc., 9 State Dept. Rept. 600 (1916).

[103] Matter of Appeal of Middlemist, Jud. Decs. 350 (1895). See also: Anonymous, Laws of N. Y., etc. and Digest of Decs. 1868, p. 298 (1860); Anonymous, Jud. Decs. 1045 (1886); Matter of Charges Against Depan *et al.*, Ann. Rept. N. Y. Ed. Dept. 1913, p. 428 (1911).

It is perhaps well to note that the rules of evidence before the commissioner are not nearly so technical as before the usual judicial tribunal. The very paucity of cases dealing with questions of evidence will indicate that this part of the judicial process before the commissioner is not very important. Yet problems of "relevancy" of the evidence [104] and "parole evidence" [105] do occur. The evidence of school children is somewhat at a discount.[106] In the Matter of the Appeal of Mufson *et al.*, the commissioner allowed a board of education to consider the bearing of a witness on the stand as a part of the evidence.[107] After all, rules of evidence were designed to guide juries untutored in weighing evidence, and not judges. No more, then, should they be a restriction on this technically competent tribunal.[108]

Question has arisen whether the many reports which are made to the commissioner every year both by members of his staff and by local school officers may be considered part of the evidence before him even though not mentioned in the appeal papers of either party. The rules of practice published in 1856 seem to have precluded this by stating that,

> No decision can be based upon any facts except those which are stated in the appeal, and which the opposite party has had the opportunity to controvert, although such facts may have been brought to the superintendent in some other way.[109]

Since then, however, the rules of practice permit the commissioner to take "judicial notice" of the records in his own department.[110]

The form of the commissioner's decision has been the subject matter of at least one appeal. In an application for a rehearing of an appeal it was pressed upon his attention that the previous

[104] Matter of Dismissal of Glassberg, 33 State Dept. Rept. 261 (1925).

[105] Matter of Appeal of Board of Education, etc., Ann. Rept. Dept. Pub. Instn., 1887, p. 848; Matter of Appeal of Gregg *v.* Thompson, Jud. Decs. 1087 (1890); Matter of Appeal of Roberts *v.* Board of Education, *Ibid.* 1163 (1902); Matter of Appeal of Edwards *v.* Board of Education, *Ibid.* 1193 (1888); Matter of Appeal of Wolford *v.* School District, *Ibid.* 687 (1891); Matter of Appeal of Douglass *v.* Martin, *Ibid.* 686 (1890).

[106] Matter of Appeal of Folts *et al. v.* Knapp, *Ibid.* 792 (1888); Matter of Appeal from the Action of the Board of Education, etc., 28 State Dept. Rept. 145 (1922).

[107] 18 *Ibid.* 393 (1918).

[108] Wigmore, J. H., Administrative Boards and Evidence Rules, 17 Illinois Law Review, 263.

[109] Code of Pub. Inst., 1856, p. 320.

[110] *Ante*, p. 28. *Justifying it,* see, People *ex rel.* Woodward *v.* Draper, 67 Misc. 460, 470 (1910). *Applying it,* see, Matter of Appeal of Butler, 3 State Dept. Repts. (official) 509, 511 (1914); Matter of Appeal of Coft *v.* Board of Education, Jud. Decs. 533 (1887); Matter of Appeal of King, *Ibid.* 1333 (1905).

decision was not correct in form. To this Superintendent Van Dyck answered,

> If it be objected that this decision was not in form and under seal, it is sufficient to answer that the statute does not prescribe the manner or form in which these decisions shall be expressed. That is left to the judgment of the Department itself. The seal, or other forms commonly attending the rendering of a decision are proper as evidences to third parties of the authenticity of the proceedings. But they are of no importance to the Department itself which is cognizant, at all times, of its own decisions.[111]

In no case will the commissioner's decision and order based thereon contain an allowance for costs of the suit to either party.[112] For one thing, the statutes do not authorize it. Even more important is the fact that awarding costs would tend away from making appeals to the commissioner the inexpensive remedy they were intended to be. Again, to incur such a money loss in many cases would add to the embitterment of local quarrels.

It has already been explained how any official act of a subordinate school body or officer may be the subject of appeal to the commissioner of education.[113] Not in every instance, however, may the appeal be direct to him. Where he is asked to relieve a grievance which a subordinate official might have corrected, and at least has not refused to remedy, it has been a precedent of long standing that the commissioner will refuse to take original jurisdiction and will direct the appellant to seek relief first from this subordinate officer, whose act or refusal to act may then become the proper subject of appeal. Thus, if the commissioner is asked to remove a teacher from service, he will remit the appellant to a remedy from the board of education which employs the teacher.[114] The same principle applies to the formation of districts and the alteration of their boundaries.[115] Vice versa, there are certain instances where no one but the commissioner is entitled to make a decision in the first instance. This is the case where the validity

[111] Anonymous, Jud. Decs. 23 (1859).

[112] Dibble *v.* Trustees of School District, Jud. Decs. 692 (1906).

[113] Section 2 of the present chapter.

[114] Matter of Appeal of Hill *et al.* *v.* Wickham, Jud. Decs. 1138 (1887); Matter of Rose *v.* Armstrong, 3 State Dept. Repts. (unofficial), 342 (1913); Matter of Appeal of Breslow, 4 State Dept. Repts. (official) 631 (1915); See also Matter of Appeal from the Action of the Board of Education etc., 29 State Dept. Repts. 504 (1923).

[115] Inhabitants, etc., *ex parte,* Decs. of Supt. of Com. Schs., 184 (1834); Matter of Appeals of Riebennacht and McDonald, 21 State Dept. Rept. 569 (1919); Matter of Appeal of Kellogg *et al.* *v.* School District, Jud. Decs. 664 (1887).

of district elections or proceedings is at issue.[116] It will later be pointed out how the commissioner exercises original rather than appellate jurisdiction when he initiates proceedings for the removal of malfeasant subordinates.[117]

After an appeal has been taken, and pending a final determination of it, the present rule of practice is that there will be no stay of the proceedings complained from unless it is requested or the commissioner deems it necessary.[118] In an early appeal from the commissioners of common schools' alteration of a district's boundaries, the commissioners made a still further change while the appeal was pending. The superintendent of common schools was quite indignant over this, remarking that,

> The whole design of the law, which authorizes the appeal, was that the authority in relation to the points in controversy should be taken from the commissioners and transferred to the superintendent from the time of taking the appeal. The appeal would be a mockery, if, in the meantime, the commissioners could go on and make anew all the alterations which were appealed from as a grievance.[119]

On the other hand, the commissioner will not allow mere pendency of an appeal so to hold up proceedings as to interfere with the educational interests of the locality.[120]

A few cases may be in place here to illustrate procedure which will have the sanction of the commissioner in local proceedings for the removal of a teacher or the annulment of her certificate. Even before the present teacher tenure law, which quite adequately guarantees the interests of a teacher in the permanency of her position, decisions of the department were made in her protection. The import of the decisions at the end of the nineteenth century seemed to be that justice and fairness required a preferment of charges and a hearing at which time and opportunity should be given to the teacher to defend and to confront and cross examine witnesses of the moving party.[121] Apparently, however, the trial

[116] Anonymous, Code of Public Instruction, 1856, p. 1 (1837); Matter of Election of School Officers, Jud. Decs. 254 (1895); Matter of Appeal of Merrill, *Ibid.* 1269 (1888); Matter of Election of Trustee, etc., 6 State Dept. Repts. 591 (1915).

[117] *Post,* p. 60.

[118] For an illustration of the practice rule, see: Matter of Appeal of Bortle *et al. v.* Trustees of School District, Jud. Decs. 463 (1890).

[119] Trustees of School District No. 12 *v.* Commissioners, etc., Decisions of Supt. of Com. Schs., 69 (1830); Acc.: Anonymous, Code of Public Instn. 1856, p. 70 (1852).

[120] Matter of Appeal of Rood, Jud. Decs. 955 (1886).

[121] Anonymous, Jud. Decs. 1045 (1886); Matter of Appeal of Barnard *v.* Board of Education, *Ibid.* 1201 (1894).

of the charges need not be a formal one.[122] When a board of education sits on such proceedings, it must be kept in mind that it does not sit as a court,[123] even though the commissioner is inclined to treat its decision as the verdict of a jury is considered in court.[124] An appellant has no legal standing before the commissioner, because the evidence in his case was taken before a committee of, and not the full board.[125]

5. The General Nature of the Decisions of the Commissioner

While the authority of the courts of the State of New York depends on the constitution and their jurisdiction to decide controversies is general, it must be remembered that the commissioner's authority rests upon statute and that his jurisdiction, therefore, is specific. His judicial discretion on this account must always be exercised within the limits set down by the legislature in the statutes relating to education.[126]. Even though the relief sought from the commissioner may seem reasonable to him, yet, if the statute does not authorize it, he is powerless to act in the premises.[127] In a rather striking case, where the issue to be decided was the right of a district to establish separate schools for white and negro children, the commissioner said:

> The Commissioner of Education is only concerned with the proper enforcement of, and compliance with, the statutory requirement as to the separation. He may not legitimately impress upon the situation his personal views as to the desirability of such separation, so long as ample provision is made for the educational needs of the colored children.[128]

[122] Matter of Appeal of Addis, 13 State Dept. Repts. 390 (1917). Similarly, a pupil may be suspended from school without the formality of a trial: Matter of Appeal of Ash, Jud. Decs. 509 (1907).

[123] Matter of Appeal of Mufson *et al.*, 18 State Dept. Rept. 393 (1918).

[124] Matter of Charges Against Weick, 10 State Dept. Repts. 459, 462 (1917). But see Matter of Appeal of Walrath *v.* Board of Education, Jud. Decs. 1026, 1027 (1906).

[125] Matter of Appeal of Pignol, 21 *Ibid.* 270 (1919).

[126] Matter of Board of Education *v.* Tuttle, 125 Misc. 230, 234 (1925); Matter of Appeal of Board of Education, etc., 21 State Dept. Repts. 681 (1919); Matter of Appeal of Riley, *et al.* *v.* Lounsbury *et al.*, Jud. Decs. 666 (1890).

[127] Anonymous, Jud. Decs. 1037 (1833); Matter of Appeal of Riley *et al.* *v.* Lounsbury *et al.*, Jud. Decs. 666 (1890); Matter of Application of Rau, 1 State Dept. Repts. (unofficial) 420 (1912); Matter of Appeal of Hasbrouck *v.* Clingan, Jud. Decs. 420 (1891).

[128] Matter of Appeal of Colored Residents, etc., 2 State Dept. Repts. (official), 613, 615 (1914). Where the commissioner would not set himself up in opposition to the legislature, see, Matter of Appeal of Decker *v.* Kenney, Jud. Decs. 661 (1890). In Matter of Appeal Relative to Consolidation of Certain Districts, 25 State Dept. Repts. 448 (1921), an order for extensive consolidation of common school districts was refused till the legislature could act on a new law relating to consolidation.

So careful is the commissioner to stay within his statutory jurisdiction, that, in the Matter of Appeal of Conger, he refused to allow the wisdom of the policy adopted by the legislature in enacting certain laws regulating teacher tenure to become an issue in the proceeding before him.[129] Yet one should not think that the statutes relating to education allow the commissioner no discretion at all in writing out his decisions, for, when Andrew S. Draper was Superintendent of Public Instruction, he stated it as his opinion that:

> It was impossible to provide by statute for all exigencies which might arise, and it was necessary to vest some discretion in the superintendent for the purpose of meeting these exceptional cases.[130]

Although by far the majority of appeal cases easily lend themselves to determination by an application of the statute or precedents already established, nevertheless some of the possibilities in the direction of a liberal application of the law by this administrative tribunal, individualized to the educational need of the particular situation, may be in place here. The state education law has provided for some time that a teacher's failure to complete her contract will be deemed sufficient cause for the revocation of her certificate. A board of education sought to enforce this section of the law against a teacher in its employ who had failed to gain her release from them before leaving for a higher position. Commissioner Draper's words are worth quoting in this case:

> The teacher did wrong in accepting a more desirable offer before being released from a prior engagement which she had made. But the temptation was too much for her. She made the effort to secure a release. She was not met with immediate refusal, or with decisive action of any kind, and she presumed upon a very common usage of trustees to grant releases in such cases rather than endure the consequences of disappointment. Doubtless teachers ought to be required to abide business contracts as sharply as other people, and women as well as men teachers. It is difficult to do it, but if it was a question of enforcing or assuring the results of a contract the Commissioner would try to do it. But that is not it. He is asked to punish a woman teacher for a frailty. He will do it to the extent of telling her she did wrong and must not repeat the offense, but

[129] 8 State Dept. Repts. 616 (1916).

[130] Matter of Appeal of Cunliff *et al. v.* Wood *et al.,* Jud. Decs. 771, 784 (1888). The court of appeals disagreed with the discretion he exercised in this case, but did not deny his right to exercise it within limits: see, People *ex rel.* Trustees *v.* Town Auditors, 126 N. Y. 528 (1891). See, *post* p. 165 f.

he must decline going to the length of revoking her certificate and putting a dark mark upon her life.[131]

In another case, a parent petitioned the commissioner to compel the district of which he was a resident to furnish transportation for his child. One of the defenses offered was that the petitioner's child had not yet reached compulsory school age, and, therefore, the district could not be compelled so early to provide transportation to school for him. But the commissioner answered that the schools were open to all between the ages of 5 and 21, and directed that transportation be provided. A final instance is most interesting. Five members of a union free school district board of nine resigned, because they were opposed to the selection of a school site favored by the majority of the community. The statute prescribed that the school commissioner might fill the vacancies of such a board, if the latter itself did not do so within thirty days. The attempt of the remaining four to act within this period in order to fill the vacancies was resisted in an appeal to the superintendent of public instruction, on the ground that being less than a majority they had no power to act in the premises. If this was taken as true, the board could, then, do nothing; and the result might be a failure of school administration for a gap of thirty or less days. Superintendent Draper was quick to assert that it was against the policy of the school law to have the schools fail to "carry on." Sound as this policy may be, his statutory route to it was rather devious. First he pointed out that two of three trustees in a common school district might perform all the functions of the three. Next he cited a section of the statute giving boards of education of union free school districts all the powers which trustees of common school districts had. From this it would follow that four members certainly could do what two could! Apparently even Superintendent Draper thought this was pretty free construction for he also rested his decision on the fact that the new members, if not *de jure,* were at least *de facto* trustees.[132]

If anything, the commissioner probably is even more generous in the individualized application of his own precedents. For a long time, it had been settled policy in the department not to dissolve a district and add it to another for the sole purpose of

[131] Application of Board of Education of Union Free School District No. 12, Jud. Decs. 1220 (1905).

[132] Matter of Appeal of Howard *et al. v.* Union Free School, District No. 2, Jud. Decs. 435 (1889).

increasing the taxable valuation of the latter so that it might more easily maintain a school of academic or secondary grade. Then came a case which did not fit the rule—or rather a case where the invocation of the rule did not spell justice for the districts concerned. The City of New York bought a large area for reservoir purposes. This purchase increased the taxable value of a common school district much beyond its own educational needs. The local school commissioner, believing that all the surrounding neighborhood should profit by this increased valuation and not just one small common school district, dissolved the district and annexed it to a union free school district which was supporting education beyond the elementary level. When the usual principle governing this sort of case was cited to the commissioner, he decided that justice required an exception to the rule.[133] Some decisions the commissioner expressly limits to individual cases. Superintendent Skinner, in being called on to review a school commissioner's refusal to endorse a teacher's certificate, remarked, in sustaining the commissioner: "Nor must this decision be construed as a precedent to guide the action of other commissioners under like circumstances."[134] Another precedent of the department from which the commissioner only most reluctantly digresses is to stand for the affirmance of a local board's judgment in proceedings for the removal of a teacher where fairly conducted. Yet this unusual case occurred in Buffalo. The board of education locked horns with a local teachers' association there over the alleged non-coöperation of the latter, and dismissed two teachers who were among its leaders. On an appeal of these teachers the commissioner practically affirmed the cause of removal, but, nevertheless, directed that the teachers be reinstated because both had been of long and acceptable service and would suffer too heavy losses in being cut off from their pension and retirement rights.[135] It is the rule in most judicial tribunals to grant no relief which the petitioner or appellant does not ask for. Nevertheless, the commissioner went out of his way to direct that a district provide transportation for the appellant's children even though they had not asked for it.[136]

[133] Matter of Appeal of Ganung, Ann. Rept. State Ed. Dept., 1912, p. 464 (1911). Acc.: Matter of Alteration of Districts, etc., 1 State Dept. Repts. (unofficial) 408 (1912).

[134] Matter of Appeal of Tucker *v.* Flint, Jud. Decs. 1067, 1070 (1899).

[135] Matter of Appeal of Shea *et al.*, 26 State Dept. Repts. 469 (1921).

[136] Matter of Appeal of Abrams, *et al.*, Jud. Decs. 156 (1909).

In harmony with the generous spirit indicated, it should be further noted that the commissioner will not often allow himself to be delayed in reaching his conclusions by complicated technical hurdles of law set up by opposing counsel. Rather will he prefer to go direct to the merits of the controversy.[137]

This whole broad-minded policy has been cast in most statesmanlike fashion by Andrew S. Draper in a decision rendered shortly after his accession to the commissionership. There he said:

> There is a different relation between the Commissioner of Education and a proceeding before him from that which obtains between a court and a proceeding before it. A court is disinterested in all questions except the facts and the law. The Commissioner of Education is the administrative or supervisory officer of the whole educational system of the State. He is bound to have an interest in the equity, right, and justice of all questions having a bearing upon the administration of the educational system. He must determine judicial questions with a view to the general effect upon the school system as well as to the technical requirements of the law.[138]

Having at heart the interests of education in the state not only explains the commissioner's liberality in his administration of the law, but it also indicates something of an initial bias which he has as a quasi judge. A word or two further will bring this latter point out in greater detail. It is very unprofessional etiquette for a member of the bench to express an opinion on controverted questions of the day, especially if there is any possibility of his later having to speak judicially on the same matter. The commissioner of education, because he is an administrator as well as a judge, is not similarly restricted. Being responsible to the state for its educational welfare, his executive function frequently must come ahead of the judicial both in point of time and importance. The commissioner thus frequently commits himself on questions of educational policy which may later be the subject of an appeal for his later judicial determination. Only two of many instances need be cited here. Take the following sentence from the superintendent of public instruction's annual report in 1903 on religious instruction in the public schools:

[137] Matter of Appeal of Cady *v.* Maxson *et al.*, Jud. Decs. 618 (1888); Matter of Appeal of Karker *v.* School District No. 4, *Ibid.* 488 (1891); Matter of Appeal of Turner, *Ibid.* 1234 (1905); Matter of Appeal of Knight, *Ibid.* 715 (1907). The commissioner's liberality in matters of procedure has already been noted, *ante* p. 29 ff.

[138] Election of Member of Board of Education Union Free School District No. 6, Jud. Decs. 175, 183 (1905).

> Wherever the practice thus established shall violate the provisions of the constitution, and the opening exercises or course of study as prescribed by them shall include the teaching of any sectarian tenet or doctrine, I should feel impelled, in case of appeal, to prohibit such exercises.[139]

Again, in affirming the order for consolidation of several common school districts, Deputy Commissioner Finegan expressed very frankly a bias when he said, "This Department has adopted the policy of centralizing school interests and of eliminating smaller and less efficient schools in adjoining districts, etc."[140] Objection is only seldom taken to this practice.

This bias, so unbecoming to the regularly constituted judiciary of the state and yet so necessary to an administrative tribunal, has a further important angle. As will be pointed out more fully later on, American courts are not in the habit of rendering advisory opinions.[141] They cross no bridges till they come to them. Where, however, an officer like the commissioner of education is charged with getting things done, he must frequently render *ex parte* advice on the administration of the school law without waiting for a formal appeal.[142] In fact, stating his opinions in this fashion takes almost as much, if not more, time than the determination of formal appeals. Since no finality attaches to *ex parte* decisions,[143] there is nothing to prevent the controversy coming before the commissioner again in the form of an appeal. But if it does, then the question arises whether, having expressed his opinion in advance, the commissioner is judicially competent to sit on the appeal. This actual point was raised in a controversy in New York City. There the board of education asked the commissioner's opinion on the propriety of the appointment of a Miss Anne Nicol to a district superintendency. The commissioner's opinion being averse to the appointment, Miss Nicol made a formal appeal of the case to the commissioner so that her side of the case might also be heard. Being disappointed in the appeal, she resorted to the courts where, among other things, she contended that the commissioner had really been disqualified from hearing her appeal because he had prejudged it. The appellate

[139] P. xxiv.

[140] Matter of Appeal of School Districts, etc., 6 State Dept. Repts. 525 (1915). See also Matter of Appeal of Maxwell, 3 *Ibid.* official 539, 553, 1914.

[141] *Post,* p. 61.

[142] If the formality of an appeal is relied on, the commissioner will no more give opinions on acts not yet committed than will the courts. Matter of Appeal of Edson *v.* Board of Education. Jud. Decs. 1222 (1887).

[143] *Post,* p. 61.

division of the supreme court held that the commissioner had a legal duty both to give *ex parte* opinions and to hear appeals and that "He could not by the performance of one (duty) be ousted from the performance of the other." [144] Probably the same reasoning would apply to the kindred situation where the commissioner has authority to initiate proceedings for the removal of delinquent subordinates and at the same time judge of the merits of the removal. For the same tribunal to combine the offices of both prosecutor and judge may at first seem a bit startling, but, again, when seen from the view of the efficient administration of the educational interests of the state, it is quite appropriate and necessary. While the commissioner's judicial function is and ought to be colored by his administrative functions, this is not exclusively so. Not infrequently in an appeal, one of the parties cites the opinion or direction of one of the commissioner's supervisory officers as binding and conclusive upon the commissioner's decision. He will not, however, be so bound although he will give the conduct of his subordinates its usual weight of a favorable presumption.[145]

The decisions of the commissioner have another characteristic that mirrors American judicial practice. Just as the Supreme Court of the United States has never yet given a general statement of what "due process" is, but has contented itself with determining that difficult question for each case coming before it, so, too, the commissioner refuses to commit himself in advance on certain phases of school administration till a concrete situation is put before him. Thus, when the statute required the establishment of a branch school, if a "considerable number" of children would otherwise be deprived of school privileges, the commissioner not only said that three was not a considerable number, but he further said, "It is not necessary for a determination of this appeal to decide what number would be a 'considerable number' within the meaning of the statute." [146] In a similar fashion he refused to set two miles as an arbitrary distance beyond which transportation had to be furnished for school children.[147] Another decision shows that

[144] Matter of Nicol *v.* Commissioner of Education, 212 App. Div. 216, 218 (1925). The court of appeals denied an application for an appeal.

[145] Matter of Appeal from the Order of King, 6 State Dept. Rept. 577 (1915); Matter of Dissolution of School District No. 2, Jud. Decs. 717 (1908). On presumptions, see *ante*, p. 33.

[146] Matter of Appeal of Sherman, Jud. Decs. 143, 144 (1909).

[147] Matter of Appeal of Sackett *et al.*, *Ibid.* 915 (1906).

this principle had been established as early as 1833.[148] In problems which require elasticity of treatment, this policy of limiting himself to the case at bar is invaluable for the individualized administration of the school laws.

The commissioner's judicial decisions are to be kept distinct from his administrative regulations. The importance of doing so will be illustrated by the following. A board of education employed a teacher who wore a garb peculiar to her religious order. Residents of the community objected to the superintendent of public instruction and on appeal were sustained. The teacher refusing to discard the dress of her order, the board dismissed her. Since she had a contract running to the end of the school year, she sued for breach of contract in the courts. There the board set up the decision of the superintendent as its defense. To this the plaintiff answered that, not having been a party to the action before the superintendent, she was not now bound by his adjudication. The court of appeals recognized the validity of this contention but, nevertheless, held her bound by the decision because:

> Although a decision in form, it was in fact a regulation in regard to the management of the common schools which the superintendent had a right to establish provided only that it was reasonable in its character and not in conflict with the laws of the state or public policy.[149]

Some significance attaches to the fact that the cases brought before the commissioner are designated "appeals."

> The word "appeal" comes from the civil law, and its nature and office is to substitute the appellate tribunal for that whose acts are examined; and, if the case be one involving discretion, then the appeal invokes that very discretion in the superior, in the same manner and to the same extent that it was possessed by the inferior. . . .[150]

It would have been less fortunate, of course, had the commissioner's appellate jurisdiction been of the common law nature where he could merely have reversed or affirmed the proceedings below. It is for this reason, as has already been pointed out,[151] that the commissioner can afford practically complete relief in his

[148] Inhabitants school district No. 7, Town of Freetown *v.* Commissioners of Common Schools, Decs. Supt. Com. Schs., p. 114 (1833).

[149] O'Connor *v.* Hendrick, 184 N. Y. 421, 426 (1906). See also, Anonymous, Jud. Decs. 598 (1855). Probably Superintendent Skinner meant no more than this when in Matter of Appeal of Kennedy *et al. v.* Board of Education, Jud. Decs. 554, 556 (1897) he said his decisions "have all the force and effect of statutes, etc." See Matter of Appeal of Putnam *v.* Trustees, *Ibid.* 1211, 1217 (1896).

[150] Anonymous, Jud. Decs. 7, 8 (1840).

[151] *Ante*, p. 23.

determination of controversies within his jurisdiction. Not only can he reverse a wrongful act or decision, but he can, also, if he sees fit, direct the institution of the correct proceedings. Not of the least advantage is the fact that he can dispose of all phases of the case as it regards all parties concerned in one decision.[152] The remedy or relief for each situation will therefore be peculiar to it. In most cases this is simple enough and requires no extended mention.

The method of disposing of some cases, however, is unusual enough to deserve attention here. To state one of them paradoxically, the commissioner's decision is to make no decision at all. Sometimes the point upon which a decision may turn is so doubtful or so difficult to determine that the commissioner will let the district itself decide at its next annual meeting. An illustration is the case where the removal of a trustee was asked. The cause alleged was his neglect of duty to repair the school building. On the other hand, it was doubtful that the trustee had ever been directed by the voters to make repairs. In as much as the annual election of trustees was to occur soon, the commissioner decided to let the decision of the remissness of this trustee go over till that time when the inhabitants of the district could elect the trustee who would reflect the wishes of the community.[153] The knotty problem of the choice of a school site has been solved by this same strategy.[154] It is difficult to say that this is shifting responsibility; on the other hand, it rather seems a fine respect for the local interest in education and a self-restraint against too highly centralized an autocracy in the state organization of education. A sterner variant of this type of case occurs where the commissioner lets it clearly be known what his opinion in the matter is, but, rather than directly order the respondent to act accordingly, he merely shakes a judicial finger at him to let him know what is in store for him if he does not voluntarily exert himself in the cause of righteousness. In one case the superintendent of public instruction sustained an appeal against consolidation of a common school

[152] Appeal of La Farge *v.* Board of Education, Jud. Decs. 1288 (1887); Matter of Appeal of Frink *v.* Haswell, Ann. Rept. Dept. Pub. Instn. 1893, p. 136 (1892).

[153] Matter of Appeal of Mason *v.* Butler. Jud. Decs. 483 (1888).

[154] Matter of Appeal of Vandenburgh *v.* Farrington, *Ibid.* 973 (1887). For other illustrations, see: Anonymous, Code of Pub. Instn. 1887, p. 779 (1881); Matter of Appeal of Lynch *et al.* *v.* Gibney, Jud. Decs. 1248 (1891); Matter of Appeal of Austin *et al.* *v.* Humphrey, *Ibid.* 1291 (1891); Matter of Appeal of Childs, *Ibid.* 328 (1888).

district, but threatened the affirmance of such an order sooner or later if the district did not pick up and maintain an adequate school of its own.[155] In another instance, there was strong evidence that the selection of a superintendent had been befogged by intoxication among the directors. In considering whether the evidence was sufficient to require disciplinary action against them, the superintendent, in finally deciding against such a step, earnestly hoped that mere reference to it would be sufficient to correct the error.[156] The commissioner appears in somewhat softer vein where, after deciding that a teacher was entitled to damages for a breach of her contract, he suggested that an effort be made to compromise the claim.[157]

Other cases, in addition to those just cited, might be adduced to indicate the commissioner's willingness to give local initiative every opportunity to operate before summoning state aid. The extent to which the commissioner's decision may go at the other extreme —strong centralized control—has been brought out by a series of more recent cases. The leading case is one which was before both the commissioner and the court of appeals. After consolidation proceedings, a new district failed to provide transportation for certain school patrons who desired it. The facts were set forth in an appeal as a result of which Commissioner Graves ordered transportation to be furnished and a tax raised for that purpose.[158] But even in the very face of this decision and order the district by majority vote refused to comply. The commissioner then directed that the state moneys be withheld from this community. In an attempt further to contest the education department's power, the board of education applied to the courts to review the proceedings had before the commissioner. The significance and implications of the decision of the court of appeals will perhaps best be brought out by first referring to the progress of the case in the court below. The appellate division sided with the board of education's conten-

[155] Anonymous, Code of Pub. Instn. 1887, p. 617 (1873); Matter of Appeal of Donel *et al.* *v.* Knapp. Jud. Decs. 706 (1890); Matter of Appeal of Lewis, *Ibid.* 643 (1910). See also Appeal from Order Dissolving District, etc., 23 State Dept. Repts. 640 (1920).

[156] Matter of Charges Against Depan *et al.*, Ann. Rept. State Ed. Dept. 1913, p. 428 (1911).

[157] Matter of Appeal of Barringer, 8 State Dept. Repts. 599 (1916).

[158] Matter of Appeal Relating to the Transportation of Certain Children, etc., 31 State Dept. Repts. 85 (1924). For similar instances, where the commissioner substituted his judgment for that of local body, see: Matter of Academic Instruction, etc., 10 State Dept. Repts. 449 (1916); Matter of Site of Schoolhouse, etc., 4 *Ibid.* (official), 636 (1915).

tion that providing transportation was left by statute to the discretion of the local electorate. Counsel for the commissioner endeavored to meet this argument by citing the usual rule of law that, although a statute appear permissive, it may be interpreted to be mandatory where the public interest demands it. The majority opinion swept this by with the remark that that rule of statutory construction might apply to the discretion of public officers and bodies but never to citizens' exercising of the franchise. Why, the court asks, put the district to the trouble of voting on this matter if the commissioner may overrule it? Reviewing the order for raising a tax and pointing to the fact that the commissioner was not a popularly elected officer, Justice Kellogg expressed great alarm that, "If he (the commissioner) may impose local taxation, an exception heretofore unknown in the law will have been made and a striking example of taxation without representation will be permitted to take place."[159] There was a dissenting opinion in the appellate division of the supreme court thus smoothing the way to an appeal to the court of appeals itself. The state's highest court had no difficulty at all in sanctioning the substitution of the commissioner's judgment for that of the community. It further overruled the lower court on the question of taxation. Pointing out that the state constitution requires the legislature to provide for the maintenance and support of a system of public schools, the court went on to state:

> The Education Law was enacted to the end that this constitutional provision might be fully and fairly carried out. Such law cannot be complied with unless means are furnished for transporting the children mentioned in the petition to and from the school building. Under such circumstances the Education Law provides that the Commissioner has the power to compel a board of education to act, the district meeting having previously refused to.[160]

It is a long way from People *ex rel.* Owen v. Masters[161] to the Brookhaven case. It is all the distance from a judicial power which was compelled to defer to local control to a judicial authority dominating the whole state. It is the difference between a department that could not overrule a subordinate on a question of teacher certification and one that could substitute its judgment for

[159] Matter of District No. 2 Town of Brookhaven, 214 App. Div. 40, 47 (1925).

[160] People *ex rel.* Board of Education *v.* Graves, 243 N. Y. 204, 208 (1926). Even before this decision, the legislature had made no doubt of the result of a future case by expressly conferring this power on the commissioner, Laws of N. Y. 1925, ch. 634.

[161] *Ante*, p. 13 ff.

the will of the majority on a point left by the legislature for determination by popular suffrage. Yet it is a power tempered with respect for the values of local initiative for it will only act when the latter fails.

6. Enforcement of the Decisions of the Commissioner of Education

As excellent an innovation as the legislature of 1822 made in conferring jurisdiction on the superintendent of common schools to put school controversies finally at rest, the effort lacked the vital sanction of vesting power in the superintendent to enforce the statute law and his decisions thereunder. Superintendent Dix, in reporting to the legislature in 1836, singled this out as the one point at which his judicial power was defective.[162] In a few instances, litigants had been able to defy the superintendent's decisions because of this weakness. One case in particular was appealed to him twice. The circumstances not having changed in any material connection, he just rendered the same decision over, admitting to the two-time appellant that he had no legal power to see to the execution of his decisions and urging him to appeal to the courts for an appropriate order to enforce his disposition of this case.[163] The court in the early decision of Easton v. Calendar seemed to recognize this deficiency by remarking *obiter* that it might be resorted to where the superintendent's powers "were inadequate to give the relief to which the party was entitled." [164] In the same report in which John A. Dix complained to the legislature of the shortness of his judicial arm, he also remarked that the superintendent's decisions were generally submitted to without objection. Perhaps for this reason, and surely because of the distrust of the times in a strong executive, this armorless condition continued for some time to come.

The middle of the century had almost been reached before the superintendent was given control over refractory subordinate school officers. He was then given a very effective instrument for enforcing his decisions in the power to remove any school officer who was guilty of embezzlement of public moneys, who had been

[162] Ann. Rept. Supt. Com. Schs. 1836, p. 32.

[163] Trustees of Joint School District No. 6 Town of Tyrone *v.* Commissioners, etc., Dec. of Supt. Com. Schs. p. 248 (1835); Ann. Rept. Supt. Com. Schs. 1836, p. 32.

[164] 11 Wendell 91, 95 (1833).

guilty of any "willful" violation of law or neglect of duty, or who had disobeyed any order or decision of the department.[165] In such strong and inclusive terms was this power lodged and so strong a prejudice in favor of localism did it have to overcome that Superintendent Van Dyck himself felt anxious about its exercise. In his annual report in 1860 he recounted to the legislature how he had removed a school commissioner, and then he asked that august body whether such action of his were within the purview of the act, especially as the school commissioner was a popularly elected officer.[166]

A very important element of the commissioner's present powers was mentioned for the first time in the consolidation of the laws in 1864. Two subdivisions there enabled him:

> 2. To determine whether an appeal shall stay proceedings, and prescribe conditions upon which it shall or shall not so operate. . . .
>
> 4. To make all orders, by directing the levy of taxes or otherwise, which may, in his judgment, be proper or necessary to give effect to his decision.[167]

One would ordinarily think that the second of the subdivisions cited would be the last word and that the legislature would not again feel the need of adding powers of enforcement to the superintendent. But add it did, and that by making definite in one very important direction the broad general powers just mentioned. In addition to all the foregoing, the superintendent was now empowered to withhold a district's share of the public moneys where the district willfully refused to obey the superintendent's orders or decisions.[168]

The instances where this last accession of power has been exercised are fewer than those of the other powers mentioned. It is a severe power because it operates on innocent parties, the children, as a leverage. Consequently, it is invoked usually only where state money might otherwise be spent illegally, as, for instance, for the

[165] Laws of N. Y. 1849, ch. 382, sec. 15. See also *Ibid.* 1894, ch. 556, title 1, sec. 13; *Ibid.* 1910, as amended to July 1, 1925, ch. 140, sec. 95. The present act extends to orders and decisions of the regents or those pertaining to any other act on education. Section 26 of title 9 ch. 555 of laws of 1864 made members of boards of education removable only on notice of preferment of charges and granting of an opportunity for defense. This is continued in sec. 309 of the present law.

[166] Ann. Rept. Dept. Pub. Instn. 1860, pp. 28-29.

[167] Laws of N. Y., 1864, ch. 555, title 12, sec. 2. Continued without change in Laws of 1910, as amended to 1925, ch. 140, sec. 891.

[168] Laws of N. Y., 1894, ch. 556, title 1, sec. 13; continued in Laws of 1910, as amended to 1925, ch. 140, sec. 95, subdiv. 2.

salary of a teacher wearing a distinctive religious dress,[169] or where an officer or district openly resists the commissioner and other remedies have been, or would be unavailing.[170]

Where the commissioner's decisions or orders are disobeyed, the usual remedy is to remove from office the recalcitrant party.[171] The instances of local officers resisting the commissioner and thinking that they can be successful at it have been less numerous latterly than formerly. This fact alone is mute evidence of the position of power and respect to which the state department of education has grown. But this club of removal from office is not only wielded by the commissioner to enforce his will, it may also be set in motion by any aggrieved party to fall upon any school officer who has been guilty of violating the school law or been neglectful of other duties. Thus, a district trustee who fails to maintain educational opportunities for the children of his district,[172] or is remiss in repairing the school building[173] will be removed. Another trustee who did not enforce the compulsory attendance law, especially in the case of his own children, was relieved from his official duties.[174] While a school officer may not follow his own judgment on such a matter as that, yet he may aid in the support of a private school by sending his children to it and yet not be removable as trustee of a public school.[175] Nevertheless, to keep his office, a trustee must be cautious in taking sides in his district for, after all, his duty is to ascertain the will of the majority of lawful voters and then to execute it.[176] A district clerk's refusal, accompanied with abusive language, to give residents access to the official records, books, and other papers belonging to the district, has been sufficient to occasion his ousting.[177] Mere profanity, however, even though indulged in before the school under his charge, and even though reprobated by the

[169] Matter of Appeal of Kennedy *et al.* *v.* Board of Education, Watervliet, Jud. Decs. 554 (1897).

[170] Matter of Removal of Harder, 5 State Dept. Repts. 592 (1915); Matter of Appeal Relating to the transportation of children, 31 *Ibid.* 85 (1924).

[171] Anonymous, Code of Pub. Instn. 1887, p. 762 (1871); Anonymous, *Ibid.* p. 762 (1872); Matter of Appeal of Hasbrouck *v.* School District, Jud. Decs. 418 (1891); Anonymous, Code of Pub. Instn. 1856, p. 58 (1851); Matter of Removal of Austin, 3 State Dept. Repts. (official), 576 (1914).

[172] Anonymous, Code of Pub. Instn. 1887, p. 762 (1879).

[173] Anonymous, *Ibid.* p. 762 (1881).

[174] Application to remove Roe, Jud. Decs. 443 (1906).

[175] Anonymous, Laws of N. Y. etc. and a Digest of Decs. 1868, p. 423 (1858).

[176] Anonymous, Code of Pub. Instn. 1887, p. 761 (1869).

[177] Petition of Casey, Jud. Decs. 438 (1893).

superintendent of public instruction, oddly enough did not cause a trustee's dismissal because the superintendent could find no provision in the law which would enable him to take cognizance of such an offense against decency.[178]

Instead of multiplying the samples of circumstances which have merited removal proceedings, it will be well to point out a common factor to them all, namely, that the wrongful conduct, which is made the occasion of this remedy, must have been "willful"![179] Unless it be so, in spite of the fact that the act is clearly an improper one, no ousting will take place.[180] What is "willful" misconduct? It very simply means "acts intentionally done with a wrong purpose."[181] But something less than actual affirmative "willful" or "intentional" misconduct, however, will suffice to put the removal machinery into operation. If reasonable diligence and circumspection in the execution of one's office would have easily brought to light the impropriety of the circumstances relied on for ousting, the respondent officer will not be heard to say that he had no actual knowledge that he was violating the law or neglecting his official duties.[182]

Once the remedy of removal from office has been exercised, it is irrevocable. The superintendent of public instruction was once asked to reopen such proceedings because the respondent was under a misapprehension that led him to fail to defend against his ousting. Although inclined to grant the application, the superintendent reluctantly had to say that the matter had passed beyond his jurisdiction because, although he had the power to remove, he had not the authority to appoint and the latter would be necessary since the appellant had once been actually removed.[183]

In some respects the power to remove local officials has seemed rather high handed. Should a non-popularly elected commissioner

[178] Anonymous, Code of Pub. Instn. etc., and Decs. relating to Com. Schs., 1887, p. 762 (1875). Cf. Anonymous, Jud. Decs. 470 (1869).

[179] *Ante*, p. 48 f.

[180] Matter of Appeal of Board of Education, etc., Ann. Rept. State Ed. Dept. 1912, p. 472 (1911); Petition of Warner *et al.*, 2 State Dept. Rept. (official) 616 (1914); Proceedings for Removal of Member of Board, etc., 33 *Ibid.* 7 (1925).

[181] People *ex rel.* Clingan *v.* Draper, 63 Hunt 389 (1892); Petition of Sweet *et al.*, Jud. Decs. 464 (1899); Petition for removal of Stark *et al.*, *Ibid.* 95 (1905).

[182] Matter of Charges Against Board of Education, etc., 2 State Dept. Repts. (official) 628 (1914). Dicta inferring the same result can be found in: Petition of Warner *et al.*, 2 *Ibid.* (official) 616 (1914); Anonymous, Code of Pub. Instn. etc. and Decs. Relating to Com. Schs. 1887, p. 760 (1868); Matter of Removal of Miller, Jud. Decs. 441 (1905).

[183] Anonymous, Code of Pub. Instn. 1887, p. 760 (1868); Application of Zipfel, 26 State Dept. Rept. 427, 428 (1921).

have power to remove popularly elected subordinates? This is a delicate question. The department was early sensitive to it,[184] and still has a natural reluctance to interfere except for imperative cause.[185] In one outstanding case the commissioner was made a defendant in an action in the courts to determine whether proceedings had before him for removal of a school commissioner did not infringe constitutional guarantees.[186] In the argument there the chief contention of the school commissioner's counsel was that the statute conferring powers of removal upon the commissioner did not provide notice or hearing for this popularly elected school official, while, at the same time, these advantages were specified in the statutory removal proceedings against members of boards of education. The court justified this summary power of the commissioner's in the following language:

> The Department of Education was at the time of the passage of the Education Law well known to the Legislature to be one of the most important departments, if not the most important, of the State, entrusted to the supervision of a commission. There are nearly 11,000 school districts in the state over which the Commissioner of Education exercises control, having upwards of 30,000 school officers. . . . It may be fairly said, after an examination of these provisions, that the Legislature, having full knowledge of the condition of affairs that existed in the State of New York, intended in that class of cases that no notice or opportunity of defense should be given. . . . It is not too much to say that the Legislature assumed that the Commissioner of Education had other duties to perform besides sitting at formal trials of such of the 30,000 school officers removable by him against whom charges may be preferred.[187]

Hardly less impressive than the foregoing, however, are the remedies and orders for enforcement that the commissioner has devised from time to time under the broad authority to "make all orders, by directing the levy of taxes or otherwise, which may, in his judgment, be proper or necessary to give effect to his decisions."[188] One of the outstanding examples where this power was invoked occurred in Elmira. The special school act for Elmira provided that the taxes for school purposes should be collected in the same manner, by the same collector, and at the same time that other city taxes were. Because the local political

[184] *Ante,* p. 49.

[185] Matter of Charges Against Depan *et al.*, Ann. Rept. State Dept. Ed. 1913, p. 428; Ann. Rept. Dept. Pub. Instn. 1860, p. 56.

[186] People *ex rel.* Woodward *v.* Draper, 67 Misc. 460 (1910). Affd. 202 N. Y. 612.

[187] *Ibid.* pp. 465-69. See also: Ann. Rept. Dept. Pub. Instn. 1880, p. 26.

[188] *Ante,* p. 49.

parties were in a deadlock over the rest of the municipal finances and therefore no taxes had been appropriated nor collected to carry on the city government, the future gave every promise that there would be no funds on hand to open the schools at the commencement of the term. An appeal was at once taken to then Superintendent Draper. There was no dispute over the amount needed for schools; the amount adopted in the budget of the board of education had been ratified by the common council. The chief contention was that the superintendent was powerless to act in the premises, for the act of the legislature had provided one and only one way to collect school taxes, and that had been cluttered up by a political brawl. Deciding that the schools must be opened regardless of local party strife, Superintendent Draper solved the problem of collecting the taxes by citing and relying on his power to direct the levy of taxes. The order accompanying the decision consequently directed the city clerk to apportion the appropriation for the schools, the city chamberlain to collect the same, and both officers to act without the formal authority of the mayor and common council but to depend upon the order of the superintendent of public instruction as their warrant.[189] This is a striking assumption of power in behalf of the state's interest in education and yet one not easy to quarrel with.

Only a few years later another case arose in Watervliet which was to tax the superintendent's ingenuity as much, if not even more, than the Elmira one. In that community the board of education was of bipartisan constitution. It became so deadlocked over the appointment of teachers and other wrangles of long standing, that it found itself unable to open the schools on the date set for that purpose. Upon an appeal being taken to the state superintendent, he directed the schools to be opened by a set time. The board, however, was so hopelessly deadlocked that even the decision of this official failed to change the *status quo*. At the expiration of the time limit, Superintendent Skinner exercised the most drastic power at his command by issuing an order directing one of the officials of the state department to go to Watervliet as temporary superintendent of schools to put the system in operation. The order was further completed with specifications as to the appointment of teachers, librarians, janitors, their salaries,

[189] Matter of Appeal of Citizens of Elmira *v.* Board of Education, Jud Decs. 585 (1891).

school apparatus, supplies, etc.[190] It is not surprising that such a bold step as Superintendent Skinner's was contested in the courts. Almost at once application was made for an injunction against the operation of this last order. The superintendent was upheld at every point, the court saying in part,

> The paramount object of the decision was to procure the opening of the schools. The schools could not be opened without teachers and other employees. The appointment of the persons named in the subsequent order of the superintendent, as teachers, janitors, and truant officers, was but the incident of the main object to be accomplished. The superintendent undoubtedly had power to withhold the public funds instead of making the order he did, but that would not have caused the schools to be opened. He might have removed the members of the board from office, but that would not have accomplished the desired result. He had the right to make the order which in his judgment was necessary to make his former order effective, and if he had jurisdiction to make the order he did, as I think he had, the propriety of the exercise by him of his discretion is not subject to question by the court.[191]

The statutes and the decisions of both the courts and the education department already cited clearly leave no room for difference of opinion as to the supreme authority of the commissioner of education in enforcing his orders and decisions. Considering the wide range of powers conferred upon him, no less complete an armory of weapons would be commensurate with his office.

7. Finality of the Decisions of the Commissioner of Education. Review of His Decisions by Other Tribunals

Closely connected with the problem of the respective spheres of concurrent and exclusive original jurisdiction of the courts and the commissioner of education is [192] the further one of the degree to which any decision of the commissioner's is final. The original act merely provided that the superintendent's decision on the matters entrusted to him should be "final." [193] This word "final" must be considered from two aspects: whether it precludes review by other tribunals in the state, notably the courts; and whether it is conclusive within the department itself. Since the latter phase is more easily disposed of, perhaps it should receive first attention.

One of the very earliest litigants before the superintendent of

[190] Matter of Appeal of Flewwellin *et al.* *v.* McLeese *et al.*, Jud. Decs. 121 (1897).
[191] Hutchinson *v.* Skinner, 21 Misc. 729, 735 (1897).
[192] *Ante*, section 3 of this chapter.
[193] *Ante*, p. 10.

common schools was brought there for having dissolved a district and annexed it to another in the very face of the fact that five years earlier the superintendent had rendered a final determination against proceedings identical with these. Just why the respondents in the latter case laid themselves open to an appeal involving no different circumstances than the former is not clear from the report of the case. Perhaps they expected a different result from Superintendent Flagg, the successor of Superintendent Yates who sat on the first appeal. At any rate, in clear-cut language that has remained the policy of the department to the present time, Superintendent Flagg said:

> If the word "final" were construed to mean only that the question should not be carried up to a higher tribunal, it would not reach the main object for which the act of 1822 was passed; which was the establishment of a tribunal where, on an appeal, the controversies and litigations in districts should be finally settled and put at rest; and that the parties should not only be protected from the expense of an appeal to the courts, but that the districts should not be harassed by the same question at another meeting of the commissioners.[194]

This decision must not, however, be taken so literally as to preclude the commissioner's granting a rehearing of an appeal decided earlier by him. In 1856 an application for a rehearing was opposed on the ground that the superintendent had no statutory authority to grant one, but Superintendent Van Dyck held that the power was inherent in his office, "without special legislative designation." [195] But an applicant for rehearing will be unsuccessful if he fails to show a change of circumstances, such as new evidence,[196] or some misapprehension or other matter prejudicing a fair disposition of the first appeal.[197] At the same time it should be borne in mind that the commissioner may grant a rehearing without at the same time granting a motion to set aside the former decision and order based thereon.[198]

[194] Safford *et al.* *v.* Commissioners, Decs. Supt. of Com. Schs. p. 44, 45 (1829); Anonymous, Code of Pub. Instn. 1856, p. 9 (1840); Anonymous, Jud. Decs. 598 (1855); Anonymous, Code of Pub. Instn. 1887, p. 501 (1884); Matter of Appeal of La Rone *et al.*, 1 State Dept. Repts. (unofficial), 411 (1912); Matter of Site of Schoolhouse, etc., 4 State Dept. Repts. (official), 636 (1915).

[195] Anonymous, Jud. Decs., 23, 25 (1859).

[196] Anonymous, Code of Pub. Instn. etc. and Decs. relating to Com. Schs., 1887, p. 500 (1879); Coon *et al.* *v.* Sprague, Jud. Decs. 26 (1886). See also: Matter of Charges of General Inefficiency Against Reardon, Ann. Rept. State Ed. Dept. 1913, p. 472 (1912).

[197] Application of Zipfel, 26 State Dept. Rept. 427 (1921); Rehearing of Matter of Appeal of Raymond, 21 *Ibid.* 268 (1919).

[198] Matter of Appeal of Griswold, 9 State Dept. Rept. 567 (1916).

In view of what has been said so far on the "finality" of the commissioner's decisions and in view of what was earlier pointed out as the commissioner's policy of a liberal and individualized application of the education law,[199] it may well be wondered by this time what his attitude toward the policy of *res judicata* is, the usual policy of the courts to be bound by the precedents of their own prior adjudications. The early publications of decisions [200] all seem to have had as one of their main purposes the cutting down of the number of appeals by informing people of a body of decisions which would enable them to predict the probable outcome of any appeal which they might take to the superintendent. In initiating in 1887 the policy of printing his decisions in the annual reports of the department, Superintendent Draper made a clear-cut statement for the policy of *res judicata*. In a foreword to the first collection of decisions so published, he said,

> While it is undoubtedly important to the interests of the school system that there should be provided such a method for procuring an easy, speedy, and final determination of local controversies, it also seems important that so great a power should be exercised in conformity with a line of .precedents to which the public should at all times have free access. Moreover, it is believed that the publication of these decisions will serve to lessen controversy and, perhaps, to some extent, avoid the necessity of so frequently reasserting principles which have long since been well settled.[201]

Looking forward, as well as backward, some decisions have a distinct ring as a guide to future controversies of a similar nature.[202]

But what is the proper conclusion from the following:

> It is usual to give consideration to decisions by former superintendents of public instruction on appeal involving the same or similar questions of law and fact. But such decisions are not controlling, and may be departed from where there has been a change of educational policy in respect to the matter under consideration, or it has been made to appear to the satisfaction of the Commissioner of Education that the former determination was erroneous.[203]

[199] *Ante*, p. 38 ff.

[200] For a description of them see. *post*, p. 62 ff.

[201] Ann. Rept. Dept. Pub. Instn. 1886, p. 826.

[202] Matter of Appeal of Stafford *et al.*, 21 State Dept. Repts. 144 (1919); Matter of Appeal of Van Tassell *et al.*, 26 *Ibid.* 675 (1921).

[203] Matter of Appeal of Trustees, etc., 6 State Dept. Repts. 557, 563; Matter of Appeal of Lichterman, etc., 7 *Ibid.* 593, 599 (1916).

It is here submitted that there is no assertion of an arbitrary discretion in this statement. Even the courts have been known to overrule their former decisions. And as for changes in educational policy, with whatever fickleness it may seem to veer in the cross currents of educational theory, there is no evidence of a similar wavering in the long line of the department's decisions. Changes and overrulings have occurred, but it is here further submitted that an examination will show that in each instance the change was due to an alteration of the educational law by the legislature. Only a few of a number of possible illustrations will here be cited to the reader. In an anonymous case in 1886, acting Superintendent Morrison held a teacher's license was conclusive evidence of her ability to teach. In doing so, he overruled a precedent in the department to the effect that the certificate was only *prima facie* evidence. The difference between the two cases can be traced to a change in statute.[204] Again, while Superintendent Draper sanctioned a community's action in engaging a teacher, discharging him before his term of service commenced for no other reason than it preferred another candidate, and voting money to meet any legal action of his against the district, a later decision under the teacher tenure law arrived at the opposite result on identical facts because such a discharge had no excuse sanctioned by the statute.[205] More outstanding, probably, are the decisions on the consolidation of districts. The change of front in the department toward openly favoring consolidation is very marked in the judicial decisions after 1913 and 1914. But why should it not be, when in those years the legislature showed its hand by increasing financial aid for consolidating districts?[206] It is, after all, only logical to expect change from the direction of the legislature, for, as already indicated, the judicial power is quite entirely statutory.[207]

While putting controversies at rest within the school system may have been the main purpose of the inclusion of the word "final" in the act of 1822, as Superintendent Flagg said, and while putting their determination beyond the reach of any other tribunal may have been only a secondary purpose, as he implies, it is the

[204] Jud. Decs. 1046 (1886).

[205] Matter of Appeal of Stafford *et al.*, 21 State Dept. Repts. 144 (1919).

[206] Matter of Bonner, 9 *Ibid.*, 611 (1916); Matter of Dissolution of Common School Districts, etc., 4 *Ibid.* (official), 614 (1915); Matter of Appeal from the Dissolution of District No. 4, etc., 13 *Ibid.* 401 (1917).

[207] *Ante*, p. 37 f.

latter implication of the word "final" which has consumed by far the largest part of attention from recent legal talent. While the public interest in schools was small, this characteristic of finality in the superintendent's decisions, though of value to the common school system, did not take on much, if any, importance in the courts. The best, and practically only, early exposition of this aspect of the word is to be found in an *ex parte* decision of Superintendent John A. Dix in 1835. He stated it as his opinion that:

> The superintendent of Common Schools has no power to interfere with the determination of other tribunals. His decisions are final with regard to the special cases in which they are pronounced. Other tribunals have an equal right with the superintendent to put their own construction upon the provisions of the statute, and in matters coming within their jurisdiction to lay down principles at variance with those which govern him in his determinations. That his decisions should be treated with some deference on account of the special supervision which the law gives him over controversies arising in school districts, and indeed in all matters arising under the title of the statute relating to "common schools," may reasonably be expected; and, while they ought to be set aside by other tribunals, it will doubtless be deemed desirable, if not proper, to sustain his constructions of the statute referred to, in all cases where there is any just ground for a difference of opinion.[208]

It is doubtful whether this particular opinion had any influence on present-day interpretation, but, surprisingly enough, it rather well pricks out the line of reasoning adopted at the present time.

In the consolidation and revision of laws in 1864, this aspect of the commissioner's present judicial power was stated much more emphatically; it provided that his decisions "shall be final and conclusive, and not subject to question or review in any place or court whatever." [209] With the truly tremendous growth of the state interest in education, commencing in the latter half of the nineteenth century and increasing to the present time, decisions have come to be pronounced on public interests of exceeding importance. Naturally, a final and non-reviewable determination of matters of such quality by a tribunal primarily non-judicial has become a source of no small concern. But even so, no challenge was seriously raised before the turn of the century. Up to that time it had apparently been the opinion of superintendents of public

[208] Trustees of School District No. 7 *v.* Spencer, Decs. Supt. of Com. Schs., p. 241 (1835).

[209] Laws of N. Y., 1864, ch. 555, title 12. Continued in the present law, as amended to 1925, Laws of N. Y., 1910, ch. 140, sec. 890.

instruction—such as Van Dyck,[210] Ruggles, and Skinner—that their judicial power was well-nigh absolute. In his last annual report Superintendent Ruggles, in a rather lengthy analysis and review of the superintendent's judicial power, says:

> I am not aware of the existence of any other judicial tribunal in this State which is intrusted with such absolute judicial power over matters within the scope of its jurisdiction. Even the decisions of our highest State appellate court—the Court of Appeals—in a large number of cases, are subject to be reviewed and reversed by another court.[211]

With respect to the attention paid to appeals by the department, Superintendent Skinner said that, "more careful examination and consideration are given than would be if there existed any tribunal in which such decisions could be reviewed." [212] In his annual report four years later, he gives evidence of thinking that the remedy for any abuse of the superintendent's judicial power lay in an appeal to the legislature—not the courts, let the reader mark —and he takes pride in the fact that the legislature had never seen fit to curtail this power.[213]

In spite of the clear and strong language used in the statute, the legislative fiat that the commissioner's decisions are beyond review really barks more menacingly than a procession of court decisions in the twentieth century have let it bite. These cases have come to the court of appeals in various ways, sometimes by *certiorari*, to review the commissioner's decisions; sometimes by a writ of prohibition, to prevent the commissioner from enforcing his decision; and other times a review becomes necessary when the superintendent's decision is presented as a bar to the relief sought by the plaintiff. Whether and to what degree the courts will allow this provision to have full literal operation has come to follow much the same reasoning employed in determining the question of concurrent and exclusive original jurisdiction.[214] If the commissioner's decision concerns matters of internal administration of the school system of the state, and only incidentally, if at all, property rights, the general policy of the courts is not to review it.[215] But the courts do not seem to think themselves excluded

[210] Anonymous, Jud. Decs. 23, 25 (1859).

[211] Ann. Rept. State Supt. of Pub. Instn. 1886, p. 11.

[212] Ann. Rept. State Supt. of Pub. Instn. 1896, p. xxxiv.

[213] Ann. Rept. State Supt. of Pub. Instn. 1900, p. 30.

[214] *Ante*, section 3 of this chapter.

[215] Board of Education *v.* Finley, 211 N. Y. 51 (1914); Bullock *v.* Cooley, 225 N. Y. 566 (1919); People *ex rel.* Peixotto *v.* Board of Education, 212 N. Y. 463, 465 (1914);

from reviewing even this type of case, at least where it appears that the commissioner has acted illegally, with "gross abuse of authority," or without jurisdiction.[216]

One such case deserves more than passing attention here in showing the growth of the judicial power.[217] While Skinner was superintendent of public instruction, he initiated proceedings for the removal of a member of a board of education for malfeasance in office. After being removed, the board member sought a writ of *certiorari* to review Superintendent Skinner's decision. The superintendent contended that his decision was final and not reviewable. An able decision of the court of appeals decided that his removal of the relator was not an exercise of appellate, but rather of original jurisdiction by the superintendent, and that the statute only made his decisions final in the former case. This defect in the commissioner's judicial armor was repaired in 1910, when it was enacted that his decisions in proceedings initiated by him should be final just the same as where he exercised appellate jurisdiction.[218]

If, however, the case before the commissioner involves matters in which the schools are only incidentally interested and in which important property rights are concerned, or in which a question of jurisdiction is involved, the court will feel entitled to review the commissioner's decision since it never does relinquish jurisdiction in such cases.[219] But in any event the court of appeals takes the view that "much weight should be given to the practical construction of a statute by the officers whose duty it is to enforce it,"[220] and will therefore be in no haste to overrule a decision of the commissioner.

Naturally this character of "finality" attaches in no way to the commissioner's disposition of *ex parte* cases, that is, cases arising

People *ex rel.* O'Reilly *v.* Finley, 175 App. Div. 204, 206 (1916); Matter of O'Neil, 71 Misc. 469 (1911); People *ex rel.* Clingan *v.* Draper, 63 Hun 389 (1892); People *ex rel.* Woodward *v.* Draper, 67 Misc. 460 (1910); affd. 202 N. Y. 612; Hutchinson *v.* Skinner, 21 Misc. 729 (1897); People *ex rel.* Yale *v.* Eckler, 19 Hun 609 (1880).

216 People *ex rel.* Merrall *v.* Cooley *et al.*, 75 Misc. 188, 191 (1912); People *ex rel.* Bowers *v.* Allen, 19 Misc. 464, 467 (1897).

217 People *ex rel.* Light *v.* Skinner, 159 N. Y., 162 (1899).

218 Laws of N. Y., 1910, ch. 140. Citing this law and overruling People *ex rel.* Light *v.* Skinner, *supra*, see, Matter of O'Neil, 71 Misc. 469 (1911).

219 People *ex rel.* Hylan *v.* Finegan, 227 N. Y. 219 (1919); Bennett *v.* Burch, 1 Denio 141 (1845); People *ex rel.* Light *v.* Skinner, 159 N. Y., 162 (1899); O'Connor *v.* Emerson, 196 App. Div. 807, 810 (1921), affd. 232 N. Y. 561. But see Matter of Levitch *v.* Board of Education, 243 N. Y., 373 (1926).

220 Bullock *v.* Cooley, 225 N. Y. 566, 571 (1919); Application of McQuade, Ann. Rept. State Ed. Dept. (1913), p. 432 (1912).

on the representations of only one party. Although the handling of this sort of case forms a very considerable part of the department's business, it is contrary to the usual American practice to attach the significance of a precedent to opinions that are, after all, only advisory. A very early decision of Superintendent Flagg's brought the decisions of his office in accord with this custom.

> The fact of establishing a tribunal from which there is no appeal, does not consequently give the Superintendent unlimited jurisdiction. So far from this it ought to be an admonition to exercise this authority with great caution and circumspection, and not until after a hearing of both parties, and an examination of all the facts in the case. In this case, the opinion of the Superintendent appears to have been given on an *ex parte* representation, and must be considered merely advisory, and applicable to that special case, based upon the representations made. It is only in cases of appeal that the decisions of the Superintendent are declared by the law to be final; and in such cases the law presupposes that there will be a hearing of both sides and a full investigation of the rights of both parties, preparatory to making such a decision. The daily opinions of the Superintendent given in reply to abstract questions and *ex parte* representations cannot be classed among those decisions alluded to in the act of 1822, and which are declared to be final. It would be unjust to allow the opinions thus given, in reply to abstract questions, to affect the rights of individuals beyond the cases in which they were specially given.[221]

Since the best theory and practice of state educational administration requires that the state educational executive propose and execute policies and that the state educational legislative body adopt policies,[222] it becomes pertinent to inquire into the effect of the Unification Act of 1904 [223] on the judicial power, especially its finality. At first, apparently, Commissioner Draper entertained doubt as to whether his judicial power should remain so final as under the department of public instruction. In the annual report of the State Education Department for 1905, he suggests that perhaps the enlargement of the educational system would produce questions that ought to be settled by a tribunal higher than the commissioner. He even indicated the Appellate Division of the Supreme Court as an appropriate appellate tribunal.[224] What the final status of the judicial power came to be in the new State Education Department is best explained in Commissioner Draper's

[221] Allen *v.* Trustees, Decs. Supt. Com. Schs., p. 4 (1826).

[222] Cubberley, E. P., Public School Administration in the United States, pp. 32-33; Houghton Mifflin Co., 1922, 479 pp.

[223] *Ante*, p. 6.

[224] Ann. Rept. State Ed. Dept., 1905, p. 609.

own words in submitting to the regents the rules which he and the regents' law committee drew up for carrying into effect the new statutes reorganizing state education:

> In the drafting of the mentioned rules, it has been clearly recognized and kept in mind that the Commissioner of Education is charged with, and has a responsible, exclusive, and final judicial jurisdiction over the appeals which the law provides may be made to him, as likewise over the rules of practice relating thereto, and your committee has, therefore, given no consideration to such rules which, to avoid possible misconceptions, are expressly excepted from the operation of the repealing section of the said code.[225]

While thus the commissioner's judicial power is not expressly reviewable by the regents, yet it does seem that his holding office at their pleasure is one sort of review.

The State Departments Law of 1926 has given this question a new direction. In describing the office of Commissioner of Education it states:

> He shall continue to exercise the judicial functions conferred by law upon the commissioner of education and, subject to rules of the regents, to make, execute, and issue in the name of the department such determinations, decisions, orders, notices, and certificates as may be required for the exercise and performance of the functions, powers, and duties conferred or imposed upon the department.[226]

Does this statement of the law give the regents any more control over the commissioner's decisions than they had under the rules reported by Draper and his committee? As will be seen later, many of the questions which come before the commissioner for adjudication involve very considerable problems of educational policy. In arriving at his decision, and thus determining the educational policy of the state, would it not be quite in line with good educational administration that the commissioner discuss with the regents a decision about to be handed down? It seems so. In Matter of Appeal of Certain Members of Board of Examiners, Commissioner Graves withheld judgment on certain parts of an appeal before him since they might involve changes in the statute law and hence should first be dealt with by the commissioner acting with the regents.[227] But it is submitted that a type of review by the regents which would involve an appeal from the commissioner's decision to the regents and a hearing before them

[225] Ann. Rept. N. Y. State Educational Dept. 1907, p. 393.
[226] Consolidated Laws of N. Y., 1926, ch. 78, art. xi, sec. 311.
[227] 34 State Dept. Repts. 183 (1926).

would fall within that part of the law earlier cited,[228] namely, that the commissioner's decision "shall be final and conclusive, and not subject to question or review in any place or court whatever," for this is still as much the law as the new State Department's Law.

In spite of the fact that the commissioner's decision is not so completely beyond the reach of review as one would infer from the wording of that law, nevertheless, there still has been no inconsiderable number of critics who characterize even what is left of the "finality" of the commissioner's jurisdiction as "arbitrary" and "autocratic." The high tide of this complaint came with a bill twice presented in the lower house of the legislature which proposed to amend and curtail the judicial provisions. The bill read that the commissioner's decisions were to be final and not subject to review "unless a justice of the supreme court in the judicial district in which the petitioner resides allows an appeal, and certifies that one or more questions of law have arisen which, in his opinion, ought to be reviewed by *certiorari*."[229] The enactment of such an amendment would prevent the commissioner's decisions from being final even in matters which pertain wholly to the internal administration and supervision of strictly professional problems of education. Fortunately, this bill on both presentations was read once and then referred to the committee on public education out of which it was never reported. When one stops to consider the vastness and complexity of the present State Department of Education—take just one example: that there are about 10,000 school districts in the state each with its trustee or trustees, its teacher, school building, school elections, taxes, etc., all regulated by state law and under the supervision of the commissioner of education—it must become evident that some degree of finality and conclusiveness must cling to the commissioner's decisions if any real degree of effectiveness in educational administration is to be obtained. Some have feared that the very size and technical intricacy of the system of which he is head will prevent the commissioner's decisions from rendering more than offhand justice and that certainly such decisions should not carry finality. In answer to this apprehension the court of appeals itself has said:

[228] *Ante*, p. 57 ff.

[229] Bill No. 963 in the Assembly, introduced Feb. 13, 1924, by Assemblyman Carlin and again Jan. 14, 1925, as bill No. 158.

> It is not to be assumed that the commissioner of education will lightly or erroneously decide the complicated questions of school administration which will be presented to him, but we are entirely justified in presuming that he will consider them deliberately and carefully and that his decision will command respect and carry much influence.[230]

It is here submitted that the enemies of the commissioner's judicial power in its present status should be able to find no comfort in the hiatus which occurred therein from 1849 to 1853. The repeal of his judicial power during those years was due to a clerical error in the engrossing of the laws of 1849 which included Section 16 of Chapter 382—the one conferring appellate jurisdiction—among those repealed by that session of the legislature. No complete explanation exists why the legislature waited four years to enact Chapter 78 of the laws of 1853 and thus correct a clerical error. An apparently adequate and satisfactory one, however, can probably be inferred from Chapter 388 of the laws of 1847 which was in effect during this period. Up to the latter year all appeals were heard by the county superintendent in the first instance and appeals to the state superintendent were only authorized from the decisions of the county officer.[231] In 1847 the post of county superintendent was abolished and all appeals formerly brought to him were directed to be taken to the state superintendent. This account reckons the repeal of section 16 of Chapter 382 above, no significant setback to the onward march of the judicial power.[232] In any event, it should be noted that the superintendent of common schools exercised judicial functions throughout the interim without any serious exception ever having been taken.[233]

8. The Law Division of the State Education Department

When Gideon Hawley became the state's first superintendent of common schools, he was practically the whole personnel of the state's enterprise. As education has come to command more and more of the state's attention, a necessity has arisen for division and specialization of the superintendent's labors. Whereas in the infancy of his office he was administrator, judicial tribunal, supervisor, and clerk, he has now come to delegate more and more of

[230] People *ex rel.* Board of Education *v.* Finley, 211 N. Y. 51, 59 (1914).
[231] See *post,* p. 66 f.
[232] Code of Pub. Instn. 1856, pp. 317-18.
[233] Ann. Rept. Supt. Com. Schs., 1853, p. 13.

these duties to deputies and subordinates. The sharing of his judicial function has been particularly imperative. The growing, technically legal aspect of his office and the tremendous press of business have been largely responsible for this. Indicative here, we have the word of Superintendent Yates himself, the first superintendent to wield judicial power, that in the first six months of his new power he settled over one hundred fifty appeals![234] And that is nothing at all compared with the figures that Superintendent Flagg set forth in his report two or three years later. He is authority for saying that within the preceding two years and eight months no less than one thousand, seven hundred and forty appeals had been heard and decided under his official seal![235] Such figures seem impossible. They would mean the settlement on the average of two or three appeals a day every day in the week, every week in the year, for the more than two-and-one-half-year period. And in addition to that, the superintendent would have his other duties in connection with the common school fund and the secretary of state! The only possible explanation of the figures is that perhaps the superintendent did not clearly distinguish between appeals and *ex parte* actions. But presuming that a proportionate share of the one thousand, seven hundred and forty appeals mentioned were really *ex parte,* even yet the burden of work on the superintendent's shoulders must have been considerable enough. Superintendent Dix thought his most laborious duty was his judicial duty.[236] Add that he could derive no aid from subordinates except in registering his letters and orders,[237] and it will be easily seen why the same superintendent said that the post of superintendent of common schools "is essentially judicial."[238]

Some relief from this situation was attempted as early as 1827 when grievances from the acts or decisions of district meetings and district trustees were made appealable to the commissioners of common schools whose determination after hearing was to be "final."[239] The only appeals to the superintendent of common schools under the statute of that year became those where the

[234] Ann. Rept. Supt. Com. Schs., 1823, Appendix A, p. 2.

[235] Ann. Rept. Supt. Com. Schs., Assem. J. 1826, Appendix G, pp. 3-4.

[236] *Ibid.* 1835, document No. 8, p. 34.

[237] Ann. Rept. Supt. Com. Schs., 1856, p. 31.

[238] *Ibid.*

[239] Laws of N. Y. 1827, ch. 15, sec. 110. In Storm *v.* Odell, 2 Wend. 287 (1829), there is a dictum that a writ of *certiorari* would "probably" lie if the school commissioners should err in their decisions.

school commissioners' proceedings with reference to formation and alteration of districts and distribution of state school moneys were complained of.[240] This arrangement only lasted several years when the superintendent was reinstated as the ultimate appellate tribunal in all matters arising under the school laws. It seems that this resulted from the fact that commissioners of common schools were too close to local quarrels to escape imputations of bias from one or the other of the parties.[241]

For approximately the next decade nothing was done to relieve the state superintendent of any of the burden of his judicial labors. But in his report to the legislature in 1843,[242] Superintendent Young suggested that the county superintendents be directed to hear all controversies in the first instance with an appeal from their decisions to the state superintendent. Apparently the idea occurred to him because he had already been in the habit of occasionally employing county superintendents to visit the actual scene of local disputes and make a report to him on which he could base a satisfactory decision. In pressing this proposal, Superintendent Young pointed out that at that time he was sitting on an appeal on the average of at least one case every two days in addition to which he had his voluminous correspondence requiring *ex parte* advice. Further, the multiplication of districts due to the expanding population gave him every reason to expect his judicial duties would increase in the future rather than decrease. Much of this work he thought could very satisfactorily be channeled through the county superintendent. It is interesting to see this local officer recommended for this duty for exactly the same reasons that Superintendent Dix had praised the withdrawal of judicial functions from the commissioners of common schools. Superintendent Young anticipated not only greater expedition and less expense in such a handling of appeals, but, on the whole, a more equitable settlement of disputes because the county superintendent was on the spot and was more familiar with local circumstances than the state superintendent in Albany could be. The legislature lent a favorable ear and imposed this new duty upon the county superintendent.[243] One has but to turn to the annual

[240] Laws of N. Y. 1827, ch. 15, sec. 111.

[241] Ann. Rept. Supt. Com. Schs., 1835, Assem. J., document No. 8, p. 34; See also, Laws of N. Y. 1830, ch. 320, sec. 7.

[242] Randall, S. S., History of the Common School System of the State of New York, pp. 169, 172.

[243] Laws of N. Y. 1843, ch. 133, sec. 7.

reports of the superintendents of common schools for the next few years to see with what success the new system operated. Superintendents Young,[244] Benton,[245] and Morgan [246] were loud in their encomiums of the system. But in spite of this administrative success the legislature abolished the post of county superintendent in 1847.[247] Apparently this period of the nineteenth century was not a suitable one for this administrative sprout to grow. Extreme localism was still too malignant a weed. For a number of years after the abolition of the office the superintendents of common schools addressed themselves to the legislature for the reëstablishment of the office. Superintendent Morgan pointed out that in the four years of the operation of the county superintendent as a judicial officer only one hundred ninety-two appeals reached the state superintendent, while in just the two or three months after the abolition of the office already one hundred forty appeals had been carried to him.[248] But the legislature did not have a sympathetic majority for the superintendents' recommendations. Nor has it to the present time ever attempted a similar delegating or sharing of the state superintendent's or commissioner's judicial function.

Apparently, but it is not altogether certain, as the superintendent of public instruction emerged out of the superintendency of common schools in 1854, a new avenue of escape from the pressure of judicial duties was attempted. After this date one increasingly finds decisions handed down by the deputy superintendent. This deputancy had been created as early as 1841.[249] Its incumbent was enabled to perform all the duties of the superintendent himself during the latter's absence or a possible vacancy in the office. But whether he actually decided disputes under the school law before the office became deputy superintendent of public instruction does not appear. Yet even this seemingly justifiable practice was eventually discontinued. In the edition of the school laws and decisions thereunder that was published in 1887, the editor has inserted a footnote to the effect that for several years there had

[244] Ann. Rept. Supt. Com. Schs., 1846, p. 9. Of the fifty-four appeals carried from the county to the state superintendent in the first year and a half, only five were reversed.

[245] *Ibid.* 1847, p. 46.

[246] *Ibid.* 1849, p. 36.

[247] Laws of N. Y. 1847, ch. 358; *Ibid.* ch. 388.

[248] Ann. Rept. Supt. Com. Schs., 1849, p. 36. A sampling of the 192 is contained in Code of Pub. Instn., 1856.

[249] Laws of N. Y. 1841, ch. 260, sec. 41.

been doubt about the authority of the deputy superintendent to render decisions, and, therefore, the earlier practice of the department was to be discontinued.[250] No reason was assigned and the writer can think of none.

Since the consolidation of the old board of regents with the department of public instruction in the present State Education Department, the whole educational administrative organization at Albany has been overhauled. Out of this reorganization has come the present law division. This expression of the specialization and division of the commissioner's labors has quite solved the problem which has confronted the office since its very inception. But even this unit had its antecedents. The editor of the volume of school laws and decisions of 1887 was James Kirk, a law clerk in Superintendent Draper's office. Whether such a clerk had been employed for some time previous is doubtful. In the preface to the edition of laws and decisions of the department in 1866, Superintendent Rice makes acknowledgment of the legal services of A. G. Johnson, Esq., but whether he was a permanent subordinate in the department or outside talent called in especially for this work does not appear anywhere. But, at any rate, from that time down to the Unification Act of 1904, there was continually in the office of the superintendent of public instruction someone entitled to practice before the bar of the state. Superintendent Skinner specifies this man's function as the "law department." [251] James Bentley is mentioned as the next law clerk and Edwin Holbrook served in that capacity to the end of the old department of public instruction. Holbrook also continued his services after 1904 as the first chief of the law division, but the period was shortened by ill health. The next incumbent of the office was Thomas E. Finegan. Draper promoted him from the examination division rather than open the post to competitive examination with the probable result of getting either a young man or one not successful in practice, and in either event running the risk of getting a man little familiar with the administration of the school system.[252] This at once set a high standard for this function of state educational administration and the office has ever since been filled by men of more than usual distinction. Dr. Finegan later became deputy, and then acting commissioner of education in the state.

[250] Code of Pub. Instn. 1887, p. 498.

[251] Ann. Rept. Dept. Pub. Instn. 1900, p. 29.

[252] Ann. Rept. State Ed. Dept. 1906, p. 425.

His successor was Frank Gilbert, the author of several very useful legal works. The most recent appointee to this office, which has now become that of counsel of the department, is a former state senator, Mr. Cole, a lawyer of parts. So important does the state hold the work of this official that it pays him a salary of $9,000 a year.

Humble as was the beginning of this division of the commissioner's duties, it has increased very considerably in size. Before the State Education Department was ten years old, there were two subordinates in the office of chief of the law division. At the present time, in addition to the counsel for the education department, there are also two other fully qualified members of the bar, one of them, Mr. Irwin Esmond, retaining the old designation of chief of the law division. Besides these, there is an appropriate clerical force. The size of this division is not at all disproportionate. Superintendent Ruggles, writing just before Andrew S. Draper became superintendent, stated that the number of letters coming to the department for one sort of advice and another varied between 40 and 80 daily.[253] In 1922 the number of contracts alone which was examined by the law division was 900.[254] The number of actual appeals has varied considerably, but since the beginning of the century it has averaged over 100 a year. Together with these duties the law division represents the education department when the latter is involved in any litigation in the courts.[255] It also has important offices to perform in examining the form and effect of educational bills appearing in the legislature.[256] Finally, it acts as legal adviser to the boards of veterinary, medical, dental, and other professional examiners.[257]

The evolution of so large a unit to look after the judicial functions of the commissioner of education must not lead the reader to think that the delegation of duties has been so complete as to put the commissioner out of personal contact with this part of educational administration. As a matter of fact, he personally sits at the hearing of the majority of the appeals if there is an oral argument. In any event the memoranda on the law and facts of each case, prepared by the law division, go through his hands before any decision is handed down. He may, if he

[253] Ann. Rept. Dept. Pub. Instn. 1886, p. 13.

[254] Ann. Rept. State Ed. Dept. 1922, p. 191.

[255] *Ibid.* 1905, p. 37.

[256] *Ibid.*

[257] *Ibid.* 1913-1914, p. 22.

sees fit, make alterations in these or, as was pointed out earlier,[258] confer with the regents before making a final determination. When there is an oral hearing, members of the law division see to the pleadings, arrange the case for hearing, and one of them will himself sit in at the hearing. In recent years there has been a revival of the practice of having the deputy commissioner of education sit on some of the cases. Many cases never get so far as a formal appeal, these being settled before they ripen into such serious consequences.

The matters which are most frequently handled by the law division in an informal way are those related to "the organization of school districts, appropriations for the erection and improvement of school buildings, the issuance and sale of bonds, the preparation of tax budgets, the levy and assessment of taxes and contractual obligations incurred or about to be incurred by school districts." [259]

Due to one circumstance and another the original records of the law division are not complete. Evidently Superintendent Yates, the first superintendent of common schools to hand down decisions under the law of 1822, did not consider his determinations worth his own careful record,[260] for his successor in office lamented the absence of any record of them which might enable him to maintain some sort of uniformity in the administration of the school laws.[261] The legislature did not speak on this matter till 1839, and then only to provide that copies of decisions deposited or filed in the office of the superintendent of common schools would be evidence equally with the originals when authenticated under the seal of the secretary of state.[262] This enactment was enlarged and made mandatory in 1864, and remains without change the statement of the law at the present time. It reads as follows:

> The superintendent shall file, arrange in the order of time, and keep in his office, so that they may be at all times accessible, all the proceedings on every appeal to him under this title, including his decision and orders founded thereon; and copies of all such papers and proceedings authenti-

[258] *Ante,* p. 62.

[259] Ann. Rept. State Ed. Dept. 1922, p. 191.

[260] It was the custom of Superintendent Yates to send his decisions for record in the town where the dispute arose and, apparently not to keep a record in his own office—Decs. Supt. Com. Schs., Preface, p. vi.

[261] Ann. Rept. Supt. Com. Schs., Assem. J. 1827. Appendix G, p. 34.

[262] Laws of N. Y. 1839, ch. 330, sec. 7.

cated by him under his seal of office shall be evidence equally with the originals.[263]

Even before this statute more care was taken in recording decisions, for, with the inception of the department of public instruction in 1854, a practice of numbering cases was commenced.[264] From that time to the present by actual count the department has adjudicated approximately sixty-five hundred cases. Unfortunately, the original record of the first fifty-five hundred was almost completely destroyed in the fire which gutted the state capitol in 1911.[265] Some of the appeal papers between 1868 and 1884 are to be found in wooden boxes in the stacks of the State Library, but none of the many examined contained the final decision and order based thereon. The decisions for an extended period, but no appeal papers, of Superintendent Skinner can be found in the vault of the education department. Since the date of the fire, the records are complete and on file in the State Education Building at Albany.

It is fortunate that, while the original records of the division are in this state, there is, nevertheless, a convenient and fairly complete report of the important cases from the superintendency of Andrew S. Draper to the present. When he came into office he found only manuscript volumes of his predecessor's decisions. Holding that so important a power as his judicial one should be exercised in conformity with a line of precedents accessible at all times to the public, he commenced the custom in 1887 of publishing in the annual report of the department all the cases decided in the preceding year which established principles not hitherto determined. This practice was maintained down to 1912, when decisions came to be reported in the State Departments Reporter, a volume containing decisions of the Attorney General, the Public Service Commission, and other *quasi*-judicial tribunals. The first four volumes were undertaken unofficially, but the enterprise proved so successful that the publication has since become an official one. Commencing approximately at the same time that the commissioner's decisions came to be reported in the State Departments Reporter, the numbering of cases was

[263] Laws of N. Y. 1864, ch. 555, title 12, sec. 3; continued in Laws of N. Y. 1910 as amended to 1925, ch. 140, sec. 892.

[264] Perhaps numbering commenced even earlier, for a case reported in 1833 refers to a prior decision number "81." Anonymous, Decs. Supt. Com. Schs., p. 121.

[265] Ann. Rept. State Ed. Dept. 1912, p. 942.

started all over with the number one. While the earlier practice was to publish only important cases, latterly it has been the habit to publish them all.

While the reporting of cases annually is invaluable, yet, since they are published in order of determination, there is always need for a digest of decisions with subject indices and the like. The commissioner and his predecessors have undertaken a number of these. The first one of which there is any record at all must have been published in 1822 by Superintendent Yates,[266] but the writer has never been able to lay his hands on a copy of it.[267] In 1837 the legislature directed a publication of the statute law on common schools and the decisions of the superintendent thereon.[268] Shortly afterward Superintendent Dix got out a volume entitled Decisions of the Superintendent of Common Schools.[269] The volume collects the more important decisions in chronological order but contains also a fair index to facilitate reference. A large portion of the cases reported were *ex parte,* but were included to show "what would be the issue of an adjudication by the superintendent in a similar case." [270] Such of them as find their way into these pages are included for the same reason. The report of each case was assimilated to the usual court practice by the inclusion at the beginning of a brief statement of the rule which the decision laid down. So far as possible, legal verbiage was avoided so that the volume would be intelligible to the average lay reader of the day. A copy of this volume was given to every district in the state and another to each town clerk. In 1854 a similar volume was again authorized by the legislature,[271] but nothing was forthcoming till 1856. The Code of Public Instruction [272] of that year unfortunately omitted the names of the parties to the actions reported, thus affording no convenient handle for referring to them. An improvement, though, was the annotation for the first time of the statutes on education. Superintendent Rice's reference to this in the preface

[266] Decs. Supt. Com. Schs., Preface, p. vi.

[267] Careful search was made for this volume in the New York State Library at Albany, the Columbia University Libraries, the New York City Library, and the New York County Bar Association Library.

[268] Laws of N. Y. 1837, ch. 298.

[269] Croswell, Van Benthuysen & Burt, Albany, N. Y., 1837, 479 pp.

[270] Decs. Supt. Com. Schs., Preface, p. iii.

[271] Laws of N. Y. 1854, ch. 397.

[272] Weed, Parsons & Co., Albany, N. Y., 1856, 492 pp.

of the edition affords an interesting inference as to the pettiness of the times which, if for no other reason, practically necessitated vesting judicial power in the superintendent if the state was to be successful in its support of education:

Greater facility of reference was thus secured, and the opportunity offered of giving such instructions as may serve to anticipate and prevent the most common occasions of difficulty. These may seem to the intelligent reader as in many instances unnecessarily minute, and as presupposing an almost incredible inattention on the part of school officers to the ordinary forms of business and to the precautions against litigation, which every prudent man is in the habit of observing. The experience of the department, however, suggests the apprehension that the error will be found rather on the side of omission than in giving information that is not required. The changes in the law affecting local administration of district affairs have been very trifling, but the constant repetition of inquiries in regard to the modes of proceeding under it indicates that the exposition cannot be made too specific or minute for the practical wants of a class of officers so frequently changing, and so destitute of facilities for obtaining legal advice, as those of the school districts.[273]

Apparently a good deal of trouble had been experienced with Superintendent Dix's edition in its frequent loss and its inaccessibility to many because someone borrowed it and kept it an excessively long time. Precautions against this sort of thing were taken by the insertion of a fly-leaf giving distinct directions in regard to the custody of the volume and the manner of its use.

The next similar publication came in 1868 under the title of Laws of New York Relating to Common Schools with Comments and Instructions and a Digest of Decisions.[274] This had the advantage over its predecessors in that the cases were grouped according to subject indices. A far smaller proportion of the opinions reported here were *ex parte* as compared with the edition of 1837. It is impossible to tell, whether any of the decisions in the volume of 1856 are such. Still no titles were given cases, and, in spite of the fact that the practice of numbering cases had been commenced in 1854, no numbers were given, so that these cases had to be referred to by date of decision. The next publication containing decisions of the superintendent of public instruction was published privately in 1879; but of this work, too, the writer has been unable to find any trace in spite of a search as wide as that for the 1822 edition.[275] The most complete of the

[273] Code of Pub. Instn. 1856, Preface, pp. iii-iv.

[274] Weed, Parsons & Co., Albany, N. Y., 1887, 1070 pp.

[275] *Ante*, p. 72.

publications containing annotations of the school law and decisions of the superintendent was published right after Superintendent Draper took office. This work was done largely by James Kirk [276] under Draper's personal supervision, and resulted in a volume known as Code of Public Instruction of the State of New York Containing the Laws and Decisions Relating to Common Schools [277] with Comments and Instructions. In a few instances numbers of cases are appended, which was an improvement. The volume covered so large a field, however, that for compactness many of the decisions reported were pared down to just the important essence of the case, this sometimes not even being a direct quotation.

The best and latest collection of cases appeared as the second volume of the State Department's annual report in 1914, and goes commonly by the title of Judicial Decisions, although its more complete description is Judicial Decisions of the State Superintendent of Common Schools, State Superintendent of Public Instruction, State Commissioner of Education from 1822 to 1913.[278] Only a selection of cases prior to 1887 is made, but from that date on nearly everyone reported in the annual reports is included in the collection. The cases are grouped according to the matter with which they deal, and the volume is by far the most useful that has been published to date. No other collection or digest of decisions has been brought out since the Judicial Decisions.

A copy of the school law was not included in the volume of Judicial Decisions, as it had been in previous collections. That is now published as a separate pamphlet though without its former annotations. The Education Department also publishes a little handbook which includes the rules of practice before the commissioner, and a copy of the sections of the education law dealing with the commissioner's judicial powers.

[276] *Ante,* p. 68.
[277] Weed, Parsons & Co., Albany, N. Y., 1887.
[278] University of the State of New York, Albany, N. Y., 1914, 1508 pp.

CHAPTER III

DECISIONS OF THE COMMISSIONER OF EDUCATION ON TECHNICALLY EDUCATIONAL ASPECTS OF THE STATE EDUCATION LAW

It has already been pointed out in the preceding chapter that the commissioner's jurisdiction is a special and not a general one and that, therefore, his discretion must operate within the limits set down by legislative enactments.[1] Thus far, in addition to other sources, these enactments have been an object of study in themselves, where they have specifically concerned the judicial function itself. Naturally, all of them were examined in detail to complete the general description of the commissioner's judicial power. But in the commissioner's decisions about to be studied now—those illustrating his exposition of technically educational questions, in contrast to those pertaining more to the technically judicial aspects of his power—the statutes of the legislature will not, as hitherto, be such an object of study by themselves. Of course, they must still be the point of departure, but the aim of the following pages will be, not so much to study the statutory evolution of New York's present school system as to ascertain the contribution of the commissioner's determinations under and in addition to the statutes. It may readily be surmised, for instance, that many of the disputes brought to the commissioner are "open and shut" cases, that is, they do not involve any intricate point of statutory interpretation, but fall clearly under one section or another of the legislative enactments. To examine this sort of case, where the commissioner does hardly more than apply the law, would amount to little further than a study of the statutes on education from 1822 to date. This might be interesting to the reader to show what the statute law of the state on particular professional questions of education has been at different times. Yet, not only would this require a more lengthy and more extensive treatment than is possible here, but it is further submitted that,

[1] *Ante*, p. 37 f.

even if undertaken, it would not amplify an understanding of the judicial power in any significant and useful manner, save, perhaps, to show how many appeals are brought with little forethought or previous study of the legislative enactments on education. It is proposed, therefore, to omit reporting this sort of case so far as possible. While it will be the endeavor of the writer to include types of all important decisions, yet no claim will be laid to a complete collection of all the cases on a particular subject. If the reader is annoyed by the absence of links that are necessary to a more perfect understanding of the legal status of technically educational points in the state school system than is presented here, he is urged to turn to the statutes on education.

1. Preëminence of the State Interest in Education

Some evidence of the preëminence of the state interest in education has already been presented.[2] In reviewing the controversies which have become appealable to the commissioner of education, it was pointed out that an early provincialism in the state at first strongly contested the state superintendent's jurisdiction to hear appeals on any and every matter arising under the education laws. It was noted further, however, that by the end of the nineteenth century this localism had, through careful reasoning, been fairly well ruled out, and that the inclusiveness of the state superintendent's jurisdiction had gained recognition as being no less extensive than the pronouncements of the legislature itself on education. Penetrating deeper into this jurisdictional problem, it may be of interest here to expand on the issue of state versus local control, which lay at the root of the matter. In the Matter of the Appeal of Edson v. Board of Education, it will be remembered that the question at issue was whether the board's vote on textbooks came under the state superintendent's jurisdiction as "any other official act or decision concerning any other matter under this act or any other act pertaining to common schools." [3] Superintendent Draper was also confronted with the objection that the local charter of the city of Binghamton did not confer jurisdiction on the state superintendent of public instruction to hear grievances arising out of that city. While Superintendent

[2] *Ante,* pp. 13 ff.; 46 ff.

[3] Matter of Appeal of Edson *v.* Board of Education, Jud. Decs. 1222 (1887). Also *ante,* p. 15 f.

Draper intimated that he might have rested his jurisdiction on the charter itself, yet he preferred the broader and firmer ground that "the State Superintendent does not get jurisdiction from local acts but from the general school law." [4] The merits of the Binghamton controversy further illustrate the advisability, even necessity, of resting the superintendent's jurisdiction on state, rather than local authorization. The appellant complained there that the board of education had changed the textbooks more frequently than the state law allowed. Said the superintendent:

> The determination of this question may involve the construction of the provisions of this general law, rather than of the special laws relating to Binghamton. It will hardly be contended that the legislature meant to leave it to the board of education or trustees in each city or district having a special school act to place such construction as it would see fit upon this general law, and to suit its acts to its views of the meaning of the law, without affording a means of redress to persons differing with it in opinions and aggrieved by its acts. Such a view would result in as many different constructions of the meaning of this statute as there are different localities having special acts, and would defeat the purpose and intent of this general law.[5]

Ten years later, when the city of Watervliet was unable to open its schools at the appointed time in the fall because the local bipartisan board of education was hopelessly deadlocked, Superintendent Skinner was forced to seek a formula to cut this local Gordian knot. He, too, found this to lie in the preëminence of the state interest in education. In the Matter of the Appeal of Flewwellin *et al.*, v. McLeese *et al.*, he stated the proposition as follows:

> The common school system of the state is a state and not a local system. The citizens of the most remote section of the state have an interest in the schools of this city. They assist in maintaining them and they have a direct interest in their efficiency.[6]

By 1917 these precedents had become so firmly set that Commissioner Finley remarked, "It is not necessary to cite authorities sustaining the power of the State as to the school system." [7]

[4] *Ibid.* p. 1224.

[5] *Ibid.* p. 1225. Of course the legislature may except a community from the operation of the general law—Matter of Appeal of McCann, 30 State Dept. Rept. 626 (1923).

[6] Jud. Decs. 121, 124 (1897). Acc.: Matter of Appeal of Citizens, etc. *v.* Board of Education, *Ibid.* 585 (1891); Matter of Appeal of Mann, *Ibid.* 12 (1908). For the same case in the courts with a like result, see, Matter of Harris, 58 Misc. 297 (1908); Matter of Appeal of Covern, 21 State Dept. Rept. 486 (1919).

[7] Matter of Board of Education, etc., 14 State Dept. Rept. 434 (1917).

Dominant as is the state's interest in its educational affairs it is very necessary to add that local initiative is not in complete eclipse. A dictum in the Appeal of King clearly declares that, "In the management of their local affairs school districts should be accorded the greatest independence possible and consistent with sound educational policies." [8]

2. The State Common School Fund, Taxation, and Other Kindred Financial Matters

It should be remembered at this point that though the state's first interest in a system of common schools extended no further than to a money subvention, it was not long before, as patron of the piper, it was calling the tune.[9] It should further be recollected that, calling the tune, it was laying down specifications for the expenditure of the state moneys, which so complicated the early administration of the school laws that judicial functions were recommended for the superintendent of common schools.[10] But, while the state wields its regulatory power largely through its subsidies—gives financial aid for assertion of local initiative beyond minimum requirements and threatens to withhold it where the latter are not yet reached—yet in only a comparatively limited number and variety of cases is the common school fund itself the direct and principal subject of appeal.

Realizing that the teacher was the weak point in the early common school system, the state ordered its apportionment of public moneys to go in support of salaries. But nothing less than payment in hand would suffice; a teacher's "debts due the district, or bought by the trustees, cannot be offset against wages. Nothing but payment to, or on the order of, the teacher, is a compliance with the law." [11] It is of historical interest to note that the local division of money between two teachers in the same district was not equal, as on a teacher quota basis, but depended on the number of pupils in the teacher's charge. This was necessary to equalize the local rate bills.[12] When it was still customary to hold summer and winter terms of school so as to serve the children who could

[8] Jud. Decs. 1333, 1335 (1905).

[9] *Ante,* p. 6 f.

[10] *Ante,* p. 6 f.; ch. II. sec 2.

[11] Anonymous, Code of Pub. Instn. 1887, p. 594 (1839); Acc.: Anonymous, Code of Pub. Instn. 1887, p. 708 (1881).

[12] Allen *et al.* *v.* Trustees, etc., Decs. Supt. Com. Schs. 4 (1826).

attend at only one or the other, it was enjoined on communities to make a fair division of the state's contribution to local school support between the two sessions.[13] If a new district is created, it is generally necessary to wait a year before it can share in the state school moneys, for, until the lapse of such a period, it will be impossible to gain statistics on which to base an apportionment. Yet, where the new district was formerly a branch school and ample data were in existence for fixing its share, the superintendent has ordered the old district to pay over to the new a proportionate share of what it had received on the mistaken basis that no division of the district had occurred.[14] But for a new district to bargain away its right to state school funds would be distinctly against public policy.[15] Curious *ex parte* proceedings in 1833 had as their object the requirement that local officers in possession of state school moneys either lend them at interest or pay interest thereon themselves.[16] Surprisingly, as late as 1916 argument was pressed upon the commissioner's attention that high, evening, and trade schools were not entitled to participate in the common school funds of the state. To this antiquated and narrow view of "common schools" the commissioner replied:

> Under the Constitution, it is mandatory upon the State to establish and maintain a system of free common schools appropriate to the needs of the people of the State. There is nothing in the language of the Constitution or the statutes which have been enacted pursuant thereto limiting or prescribing the extent or character of courses of instruction to be given in the common schools of the State. The Legislature has full power, in its discretion, to determine the courses of instruction which shall be provided in the public school system. In pursuance of this power the Legislature has, from time to time, in common with the policy in the country at large, greatly extended the work of the public school system in order to meet the demands of our educational development. At the present time, therefore, there are many phases of public school activities now maintained by public taxation which were not maintained at the time the Constitution was enacted. . . . High schools, being publicly maintained for the free instruction of all children, are free common schools, within the meaning of the Constitution. Common schools are generally accepted in this country to mean public schools, schools supported by public taxation, schools which are open to all children within certain ages and meeting certain qualifications for admission, high schools as well as ele-

[13] Budd *v.* Inhabitants, etc., Decs. Supt. Com. Schs., p. 162 (1834).

[14] Anonymous, Jud. Decs. 782 (1886).

[15] Commissioners of Common Schools, etc., *v.* Commissioners, etc., Decs. Supt. Com. Schs., p. 55 (1829).

[16] Inhabitants of School District No. 7, Town of Carlisle, *ex parte, Ibid.* 127 (1833).

mentary schools. The courts have sustained this view as the following cases show. . . .[17]

Of importance to the distribution of the common school fund and also to the burden of local tax support of schools is the handling of non-resident pupils. Even before judicial power was put in the hands of the superintendent of common schools, Superintendent Hawley had made an administrative ruling that children who were not domiciled in New York could not benefit by the distribution of the state's common school fund.[18] The principle of domicile applied to states is also the rule between districts. So much of general policy is clear; what constitutes domicile is more difficult to determine. The abstract definition of domicile, as developed in the courts, is echoed in the Matter of the Appeal of Patterson v. Board of Education.[19]

> To acquire a domicile two things are necessary, the fact of residence in a place, and the intent to make it indispensable, but it is retained by the mere intention not to change it or adopt another, or rather, by the absence of any present intention of removing therefrom. . . . A domicile once acquired remains until a new one is acquired. In legal contemplation every person must have a domicile somewhere, and he can have only one domicile at one and the same time. Mere intention to remove, without the fact of removing will not change the domicile, nor will the fact of removal without the intention to change the residence change such residence.

From this statement it will readily be seen that domicile will almost always be a question of fact. Because a child is a minor he cannot generally obtain an independent domicile of his own, and, therefore, the presumption is that his domicile is that of his father.[20] If a child's father dies, his domicile is taken to be that of his father at the latter's death. Yet this fact should not prevent the child from getting free tuition where a guardian, appointed for him, takes him to live in his own district.[21] Since the domicile of a ward does not follow that of his guardian, as it would his parents, the child is free to return to his former district and domicile at any time and be entitled to free instruc-

[17] Matter of Appeal of Pettebone *v.* Board of Education, 7 State Dept. Rept. 617, 625 (1916).

[18] Trustees School District No 4, Town of Orangetown, *ex parte,* Decs. Supt. Com. Schs., p. 11 (1826).

[19] Jud. Decs. 1311 (1893).

[20] Trustees School District No. —, Town of Hammond. *ex parte,* Decs. Supt. Com. Schs., p. 33 (1829); Matter of Appeal of Ellis *v.* Board of Education, Jud. Decs. 1308 (1894); Matter of Appeal of MacFarran, 5 State Dept. Rept. 639 (1915).

[21] Anonymous, Jud. Decs., 1296 (1871).

tion there.[22] Probably the most difficult question of fact as to domicile is raised where a child goes to live with another family.

The decisions have always inclined to the side of liberality. If a child of school age moves in a district for the sole purpose of securing the benefits of the school in the district, and intends to remain there only temporarily, it is to be deemed a non-resident and required to pay tuition fees. But when it comes into the district to take up its abode permanently therein, even though its parents may be living, it is entitled to the school accommodations of the district. The residence of a minor child is presumed to be with its parents, but it may be elsewhere by their consent.[23]

Families whose domicile in a district is only transitory present another knotty problem of domicile. Such is the case of a family which tarries in a locality only so long as employment lasts there, as in the construction of public improvements, canals, highways, and the like. There is a balance of interests to be struck here. At first the locality was favored; a temporary overcrowding of schools made local income somewhat unsteady and even capricious, to say nothing of the lessened efficiency of overcrowding. Consequently no domicile was accorded and full tuition was charged.[24] Later, however, it was felt that the interest of the state in the education of all its children and in the prosecution of public works outweighed that of the locality, and public funds were apportioned to defray educational expenses for the transients.[25] In the early history of the state, children in charge of the superintendent of the poor were not entitled to have state moneys put toward their education in the district where the state home was.[26] Children attending night school, on the other hand, were entitled to benefit from the local apportionment if the night school was under the control of the trustees and if the child did not attend day school.[27] Finally, children living on a United States reserva-

[22] Watkins *v.* Board of Education, *Ibid.* 1300 (1890).

[23] Matter of Appeal of Thayer *v.* Board of Education, *Ibid.* 1302, 1303 (1889); Acc.: Anonymous, Laws of N. Y., etc., and Digest of Decs., p. 91 (1855); Anonymous, *Ibid.* 353 (1857); Anonymous, Jud. Decs. 1296 (1865); Anonymous, *Ibid.* 1298 (1884); Moore *v.* Board of Education, *Ibid.* 1298 (1890); Matter of Appeal of Tiernan *v.* Board of Education, *Ibid.* 1320 (1897); Matter of Appeal of Carr *v.* Board of Education, *Ibid.* 1324 (1900); Matter of Appeal of Davis, *Ibid.* 504 (1908); Matter of Appeal of Greeley, 7 State Dept. Rept. 606 (1916).

[24] Commissioners of Common Schools, *ex parte,* Decs. Supt. Com. Schs., p. 208 (1835).

[25] Anonymous, Code of Pub. Instn. 1856, p. 16 (1842). See also, Trustees School District No. 1, Town of Nauticoke, Decs. Supt. Com. Schs., p. 293 (1836).

[26] Commissioners of Common Schools, etc., *Ibid.* p. 25 (1828); Anonymous, *Ibid.* 303 (1836).

[27] Trustees School District No. 8, Albany, *ex parte, Ibid.* p. 211 (1835).

tion within the state are not on that account to be required to pay full tuition.[28] If it turns out on appeal that a child who has been attending school free of charge should have been paying tuition, the decision of the commissioner requiring it will not operate retroactively to allow trustees reimbursement for back tuition.[29] In any instance where a child of admittedly foreign domicile seeks admittance to school other than his home district, he must enter on the terms laid down by the local authorities.[30] Of course the terms must be reasonable.

The aid received from the state common school fund and the determination of a pupil's domicile were, perhaps, the more important before the common schools were made entirely free in 1867, for then they very directly affected the rate bill. Although the rate bill now is a thing of the past, it, nevertheless, may be of some historical interest here to note some of the department's judicial pronouncements on it. A word of description in regard to the rate bill will probably be in place for the uninitiated. Before there was any state aid at all, each family in the community shared the expense of maintaining the local school in proportion to the number of children it sent and the number of days each child attended. With the coming of state aid in 1812, directed to the chief element of expense, the teacher's salary, the rate per child dropped. This of course was due to the fact that localities exhausted the state subsidy before making out the rates. But since the state aid was relatively small, the schools were not yet made entirely free. An early decision points out the distinction between tax support and support through the rate bill; the former of course would rest on the shoulders of every taxable inhabitant while the latter would only affect those who sent children to school.[31] While the rate bill thus set up a financial hurdle to be overcome before one could be admitted to school, the common school, nevertheless, was considered a "public" school because every child was entitled to the opportunity to attend by paying rates.[32] The "public," though perhaps not democratic, nature of the school was further carried out in that no child could be ex-

[28] Anonymous, Jud. Decs. 514 (1869).

[29] Matter of Appeal of Ellis *v.* Board of Education, *Ibid.* 1308 (1894).

[30] Anonymous, Code of Pub. Instn. 1856, p. 10 (1841); Anonymous, *Ibid.* p. 95 (1855).

[31] Anonymous, Decs. Supt. Com. Schs., p. 87 (1831).

[32] Inhabitants School District No. —, Town of Cairo, *ex parte, Ibid.* 119 (1833).

cluded on account of poverty.[33] Probably no system of school administration better illustrates education on the *quid pro quo* basis than does the rate bill. If school was maintained for a month longer than usual, only those attending could be required to provide the extra support.[34] If a child attended only a half day, his bill was later to be made out accordingly; but less than a half day the superintendent refused to recognize.[35] If one wanted advanced instruction he paid accordingly.[36] For instruction in the common branches no distinction in subjects was allowed in the rate bill.[37] The principle of the rate bill was extended to the provision of fuel for the school stove in winter,[38] and if anyone defaulted on his aliquot share, the trustee was supported in tacking an addition on his tuition bill.[39] The purpose of the rate bill was applied, however, to no other expenses than the teacher's salary and fuel,[40] and consequently items for transporting the teacher home,[41] paying his board.[42] or providing premiums for meritorious students [43] were ruled out. One of the difficulties in the administration of the rate bill was that of collections. Because it was made out on the basis of the number of children attending and the number of whole or half days attended, the bill could not be made out till the end of the term's work. By that time the children had benefited from the performance of the teacher's side of the contract, and, as a result, some parents were very dilatory in executing their part of the bargain. Some trustees tried to avoid the difficulties involved in collecting the rates by transferring to the teacher the power to collect, but the state superintendent held that an unfair procedure.[44]

Since the rate bill applied only to making up that part of the

[33] *Ibid.* The trustees had discretion in determining whether a child was indigent. It is natural that they should have been urged to incline to the side of liberality: Trustees of School District No. 19, Town of Pompey, *ex parte, Ibid.* 56 (1829); Anonymous, Code of Pub. Instn. 1856, p. 31 (1848).

[34] Anonymous, *Ibid.* p. 52 (1845).

[35] Anonymous, Decs. Supt. Com. Schs., p. 162 (1834).

[36] Appeal of Baker *v.* Board of Ed., Jud. Decs. 1330, 1332 (1889).

[37] Anonymous, Decs. Supt. Com. Schs., p. 47 (1829); Trustees School District No. 1, Town of Castile, *ex parte, Ibid.* 207 (1835).

[38] Anonymous, *Ibid.* 39, (1829).

[39] Anonymous, *Ibid.* 77 (1831).

[40] Anonymous, Code of Pub. Instn. 1856, p. 49 (1849).

[41] Anonymous, Decs. Supt. Com. Schs., p. 313 (1836).

[42] Trustees School District No. —, Town of White Creek, *ex parte, Ibid.* 206 (1835).

[43] Hoskins *v.* Trustees, *Ibid.* 124 (1833).

[44] Trustees School District No. —, Town of Walkill, *ex parte, Ibid.* 31 (1828); Anonymous, Jud. Decs. 1294 (1836).

teacher's salary which was not defrayed by an apportionment of the state common school fund, other school burdens, notably securing a schoolhouse and site, had to be met by taxation. Public taxation for school support was therefore in vogue before 1867. But it was a difficult principle to sell to some narrow-gauge minds. A case appealed to Superintendent Flagg makes an excellent statement of the situation. Due to the decease of the head of the house, a family was about to remove from a district. It alleged these circumstances in attempting to evade a tax levied on the deceased's estate for the erection of a schoolhouse:

> As to the hardship of paying for a schoolhouse from which the family, in consequence of their removal, will derive no advantage, it is similar in character to the apparent hardship to which all those persons are subjected who are assessed to erect schoolhouses when they have no children to send to school, and consequently receive no direct equivalent for their money. The law, however, for supporting common schools is based upon the principle that all property shall be assessed for the support of schools whether the owner has children requiring school accommodations or not. And if the persons thus situated receive no direct equivalent for their money, and they are nevertheless interested in and benefited by every measure which tends to ameliorate the condition and enlighten the minds of those around them. Property is valueless unless the owner is protected in the quiet enjoyment of it, and it is better to pay a tax to give instruction to the rising generation, and thus train them to usefulness, than to pay a tax to punish them for crimes from which an education might have protected them. Persons of property have the greatest interest in whatever concerns the peace and welfare of the community; and they have an interest in supporting the common schools proportioned to their property. If the child of their neighbor becomes intelligent and grows up a useful citizen, he is a safeguard to them, and secures them in the quiet possession of their property. If he grows up in ignorance and vice, and becomes a depredator upon society, the man of property is exposed in proportion to the extent of his possessions, and in addition to this his property is taxed for the punishment of the depredator. County and town taxes are paid with a less gratifying equivalent than that received for taxes paid for schools.[45]

While a taxpayer has this definite interest in the support of schools, his interest is not to be weighed more heavily than that of those whose suffrage qualifications rest, not on property, but on parenthood.[46]

[45] Executors, etc., *v.* Trustees, etc., Decs. Supt. Com. Schs., p. 66 (1830).

[46] Matter of Appeal of Randall *v.* Union Free School District. Jud. Decs. 1024 (1888); Matter of Appeal of Mills, *Ibid.* 501 (1906); Anonymous, Code of Pub. Instn. 1887, p. 638 (1886).

With the above general observations about taxation, it is proposed to conclude the

Several matters of financial administration apart from taxation and income from the state treasury are worthy of reporting here. Under no circumstances will the department sanction the indiscriminate mingling of public funds with the private ones of the local financial officer.[47] Confusing the two accounts is bad enough, but using the public moneys for private ventures, even though ultimately returned to the district, is much worse.[48] The practice of reporting to the district meeting each year only the balance in favor of the district has been held a vicious one. Nor will the department excuse it when the local trustee pleads a local custom of keeping out of the report an amount equal to the outstanding indebtedness of the district. Nothing less than the complete financial statement should be reported.[49] Further, "A report which does not show in detail the purposes for which expenditures are made, the names of persons to whom orders were drawn for the payment of district money, and the amounts paid to such persons, does not comply with" the education law.[50] Again, handing over vouchers will not be a sufficient account in writing of moneys received, appropriated, etc.[51] In one case, at least, the commissioner has taken upon himself to review a local budget and lop off excessive items therein.[52] In yet another case the commissioner reviewed the method by which a community arrived at its charge for academic instruction for non-residents, and, after some corrections in depreciation and debt service, reduced the charge fifteen dollars per pupil.[53]

The passage from private rate bills to public taxes, from almost exclusive local effort to generous state aid, and from unequal distribution to state equalization has been a tortuous one, but the general direction is unmistakable. The coördinating force of

subject. How and to whom real and personal property should be assessed, the levy and collection of taxes, and associated concerns are matters more than usually carefully covered by statute and administrative regulation. To examine the commissioner's decisions under them in adequate manner would entail a more extended study of the tax policies of the legislature and courts than time or space allows here, and in many instances would carry quite beyond the professional educational interest of these pages.

[47] Matter of Appeal of Gormly *et al. v.* Montgomery *et al.*, Jud. Decs. 1267 (1891); Matter of Appeal of Dempsey *et al.*, *Ibid.* 1398 (1908).

[48] *Ibid.*

[49] Matter of Appeal of Gormly *et al. v.* Montgomery *et al.*, Jud. Decs. 1267 (1891).

[50] Matter of Appeal of Steele, Ann. Rept. State Ed. Dept. 1912, p. 429 (1910).

[51] Commissioners of Common Schools, etc., *ex parte,* Decs. Supt. Com. Schs., p. 189 (1834).

[52] Appeal of Board of Education, etc., 13 State Dept. Rept. 410 (1917).

[53] Matter of Appeal of Board of Education, etc., 28 *Ibid.* 710 (1923).

a central appellate tribunal in the educational system has been almost indispensable to the whole process.

3. Teacher Certification

In New York State the licensing of teachers is quite distinctly under the control of the state department of education. That its authority on this point of state educational administration has not always been respected, the decision of People *ex rel.* Owen v. Masters, noted earlier,[54] will bear witness. While the localism of the first half of the nineteenth century begrudged the state superintendent an authority even on appeal in matters of certification, yet, one of his early *ex parte* opinions will indicate what were his ideas on the subject. On an application of one of the local licensing officers inquiring what equipment a teacher should have, he answered that he should be "well instructed in reading, orthography, penmanship, English grammar, geography, and arithmetic, including vulgar and decimal fractions."[55] Of course the department has pushed far beyond these merely academic requirements to-day, but as that has been done through statute and regulation rather than judicial interpretation it can receive no further attention here.[56]

The issuance of certificates has always been dependent on the applicant's possession of moral character. As early as 1829 the superintendent of common schools expressed an *ex parte* opinion that the local licensing officer might take moral character into account in the issuance of a certificate and also its annulment.[57] Addiction to profanity has been held such an objection to a teacher as to justify the withholding of a license.[58] On the other hand, the qualification of moral character may not extend to the question of the applicant's religion. An *ex parte* opinion early settled that by stating:

> Every person has a right to the enjoyment of his own religious belief without molestation: and the inspectors should content themselves with inquiries as to the moral character of the teacher; leaving him to the

[54] *Ante,* p. 13 ff.

[55] Inspectors of Common Schools, Town of Ripley, *ex parte,* Decs. Supt. Com. Schs., 42 (1829).

[56] But see Matter of Appeal of O'Brien *et al.,* 27 State Dept. Rept. 334, 341 (1922) where examination for teacher licenses could be graded for the quality of English used.

[57] Inspectors of Common Schools, Town of Guilderland, *ex parte,* Decs. Supt. Com. Schs., 46 (1829).

[58] Anonymous, Code of Pub. Instn. 1887, p. 700 (1874).

same liberal enjoyment of his religious belief that they ask for themselves. If a person openly derides all religion, he ought not to be a teacher of youth.[59]

The coming into vogue of an examination set by the state department has been interpreted as intended to certify to a teacher's qualities of intellect but not to his character and tact.[60]

When and where school commissioners have been required to indorse a certificate already issued "unless a valid reason exists for withholding such indorsement, etc.,"

A valid reason means a "good reason," "sound reason," existing in the mind of the school commissioner, based upon information obtained by him from trustworthy sources and which he believes to be true, relative to the abilities of the holder of the certificate properly to impart instruction to, and govern, the pupils attending the school which he is employed to teach, and his moral character has not been questioned; as distinguished from mere caprice, prejudice, bias, or absence of good faith, or proper inquiry on the part of such commissioner.[61]

Several interesting cases have arisen involving the extent to which a state certificate is entitled to recognition throughout the length and breadth of the state. May a local board of education select only a particular class of teachers possessing a state certificate? The leading case on this point is the Appeal of Masten.[62] In that instance the board of education passed a resolution to employ only college graduates unless impossible to obtain them. A minority member of the board appealed. On first examination it would seem that the board was entitled to commendation for setting such a high standard for its teachers. The reasoning of Superintendent Skinner, however, points out implications of such a resolution which, if valid, certainly cannot be tolerated. If a locality is allowed to set up such artificial lines of selection among candidates, all of whom are certified as eligible by the state department, then there is nothing to prevent their narrowing the selection down to a particular college, or, in a *reductio ad absurdum,* to simply the possessors of third-grade certificates. For the state to submit to such procedure would amount to losing

[59] Inspectors of Common Schools, Town of Monroe, *ex parte,* Jud. Decs. 1036 (1830).

[60] Matter of Appeal of Williston *v.* Knapp, Jud. Decs. 1059 (1889).

[61] Matter of Appeal of Tucker *v.* Flint, Jud. Decs. 1067 (1889). A certificate cannot be withheld merely because a community dislikes a teacher: Anonymous, Laws of N. Y., etc., and Digest of Decs. p. 410 (1859).

[62] Jud. Decs. 1075 (1902).

much of the ground it had won away from the local control of certification. A second undesirable result of this board's resolution would have been the practical nullification of the state's teacher-training policy which even at that time was costing nearly a half-million dollars. None of the state normal school graduates would find an entrance into this community. Finally, of course, there is no guarantee that college graduates are the best teachers. For these reasons Masten's Appeal was sustained. It is difficult, however, to get over the first inclination to lend approval of this board's resolution. So far as can be calculated, it seems reasonable to conclude that the teacher with the longer and broader preparation will be more successful than one with fewer qualifications in these respects. Instances of the contrary will occur, but in the majority of cases this conclusion must be correct. It seems, therefore, that fundamentally the board was oriented in the right direction. While, of course, no one would wish to see the state spend $500,000 in vain, yet there appears no overpowering reason to think that many communities in the state would adopt similar resolutions because of the sheer expense involved in engaging all teachers with so long a period of training behind them. The principle of the logic in the first ground of Superintendent Skinner's opinion is sound enough. But is he not too logical? He admits that a board may recognize financial limits in its employment of a teacher. If a board should decide that it could afford all teachers holding first-grade state certificates, would it not be disregarding the community's interests to do otherwise? Should not the state department look on its certificates as minimum requirements and encourage communities to exceed them? Where the state has empowered cities through their charters to set examinations in addition to those of the state, this is exactly the view that the commissioner himself has taken in appeal cases.[63] There are, of course, limits to the classifications that can be superimposed upon the state department's. Thus, to discriminate in favor of teachers of a particular religion has quite meritoriously drawn the censure of the commissioner in several of his decisions.[64] Let the commissioner in his discretion determine what are advantageous requirements beyond the state

[63] Matter of Appeal of Oppermann, 7 State Dept. Rept. 584 (1916); Matter of Appeal of Lichterman, etc., 7 *Ibid.* 593 (1916).

[64] Anonymous, Jud. Decs. 1210, 1211 (1886); Matter of Appeal of Colt *v.* Board of Education, *Ibid.* 533, 537-38 (1887). See also, *post*, p. 119 f.

minima, and it is submitted that Masten's Appeal might well have been overruled.

The revocation of a teacher's license is undoubtedly a more serious censure of a teacher than her formal removal for cause from a particular teaching position. An early opinion of Andrew S. Draper's sets this thought out more at length:

> The annulment of a license is a severe penalty to inflict upon a teacher. It ought not to be imposed except for a cause sufficiently grave to justify a public and permanent revocation of the right to teach. It is not to be resorted to for the purpose of removing a teacher from the school because people in the district are dissatisfied with her. Moral delinquency or a deliberate infraction of school laws, or the wilful defiance of the proper suggestions or directions of supervisory officers, or utter inability to follow them, may be sufficient ground for annulling licenses.[65]

Drunkenness,[66] "scurrilous and obscene language" to a school commissioner,[67] patronizing a house of ill fame,[68] cruel punishment of pupils,[69] and palpable neglect of work,[70] have all been held sufficient cause for the revocation of a teacher's license. Falsifying examination papers and grades, and aiding students to pass who did not deserve to struck so vitally at the respectability of the teaching service and the moral welfare of the parents and children of the state that the state commissioner annulled a teacher's diploma as well as his license on these grounds.[71] On the other hand, "it is very difficult to annul the certificate of a successful teacher, and one whose moral character is shown to be now good, for acts committed some time ago." [72] Again, the investigation of moral character is not to be carried to such personal and non-professional matters as a teacher's repeated failure to pay his debts.[73] Once a license has been issued by a local officer, it cannot be revoked by his successor in office just because the latter voluntarily takes it into his head to regrade the papers, and, as a result, finds a discrepancy in his predecessor's valua-

[65] Matter of Appeal of Wells, Jud. Decs. 1049, 1050 (1887). Acc.: Matter of Morris, 24 State Dept. Rept. 713, 715 (1921).

[66] Anonymous, Laws of N. Y., etc., and Digest of Decs. p. 410 (1860).

[67] Matter of charges against Utter, Jud. Decs. 1051 (1890).

[68] Matter of charges against Craw, *Ibid.* 1053 (1890).

[69] *Ibid.*; Anonymous, *Ibid.* 1042 (1843). In Matter of Application of Daniels, *Ibid.* 1040 (1909) not only did the commissioner require evidence of cruel punishment but also that the teacher had been "habitually" brutal.

[70] Peckham *v.* Francis, *Ibid.* 1054 (1890).

[71] Anonymous, Ann. Rept. State Ed. Dept. 1912, p. 485 (1911).

[72] Anonymous, Jud. Decs. 1043 (1876).

[73] Matter of Appeal of Durfee *v.* Thyne, *Ibid.* 1048 (1888).

tions.[74] A very important precedent in the revocation of teachers' certificates is one having to do with inefficiency in teaching. One observation of the teacher at work has been held hardly sufficient to justify a school commissioner's revocation of a teacher's license on this account.[75] In fact, a school commissioner will find it difficult to justify a revocation until he has made some attempt at constructive supervision of the teacher's work.[76] And even then the superintendent of public instruction has held that a young teacher's lack of success would merit no more than a school commissioner's withdrawal of his endorsement, for the teacher must have room to improve with maturity and experience.[77] A decision has already been noted under that part of the statute law of the state which authorizes the cancellation of a teacher's certificate if he fails to complete his contract without good cause.[78] On the other hand, if the contract provides for liquidated damages in such an event, and the teacher is willing to pay them, the commissioner will not add the further penalty of the statute.[79] A board of education which seeks to invoke this statute will not get far in its purpose if it becomes clear that the breached contract was itself an improper one for the board to exact from the respondent. In such a case the commissioner will apply the equitable doctrine that those seeking relief in equity must do so with clean hands.[80] Resignation on the advice of a qualified physician will also satisfy the statute.[81]

Cities of a million population and over, notably New York City, present some special problems. By statute[82] New York City has a board of examiners which examines and prepares eligible lists of all teachers in the city's schools. One matter and another in connection with this board have formed the bulk of all the appeals that are carried to the state department from this city. Had not the commissioner forestalled it, the rating on examinations alone would have constituted a veritable flood of appeals

[74] Matter of Appeal of Hunter *v.* West *et al.*, *Ibid.* 1060 (1894).

[75] Anonymous, *Ibid.* 1043 (1886); Anonymous, Code of Pub. Instn. 1856, p. 24 (1848).

[76] Matter of Appeal of Wells, Jud. Decs. 1049 (1887).

[77] Matter of Appeal of Smith *v.* Harkness, *Ibid.* 1071 (1891).

[78] *Ante,* p. 38 f.

[79] Matter of Board of Education, 26 State Dept. Rept. 79 (1921).

[80] In the Matter of Board of Education of Union Free School District, No. 4, Town of Salamanca, Jud. Decs. 1081 (1908).

[81] Matter of Sohnker, 25 State Dept. Rept. 617 (1921).

[82] Laws of N. Y. 1910, amended to 1925, ch. 140, sec. 871.

to Albany. Such an outcome he at first headed off by refusing to entertain appeals from ratings unless "fraud or gross abuse of discretion" were shown.[83] Although disgruntled parties frequently utilized the opportunity to appeal to the board of examiners, yet there were many who urged the commissioner to "assume full and complete jurisdiction of all appeals from ratings of the examiners, whether based on fraud, gross abuse of discretion, or manifest error in judgment, however honestly made." [84] Admitting that perhaps the access to his appellate jurisdiction was not free enough in this type of appeal, the commissioner thereupon suggested that it might be well to amend the rules of appeal so that if the superintendent of schools should represent to the commissioner that there was a reasonable basis for complaint as to an appellant's rating upon examination for license, he would make determination of it on its merits.[85]

From examinations held by it, the board of examiners has been in the custom of preparing lists of candidates eligible for a particular position. When one list becomes exhausted a new examination is held and another list drawn up, but the former list must be exhausted before steps toward a new one can be taken. This simple statement becomes complicated when two eligible lists for a single type of position are made up, one for men and one for women, as in the case of elementary school principalships. The problem has arisen here whether both must become depleted before a new examination can be held. The commissioner has very soundly decided in the negative. It would seriously interfere

[83] Matter of Jurisdiction of Board of Examiners, 25 State Dept. Repts. 275, 290 (1921). Cf. Matter of Appeal of Halbert, 7 *Ibid.* 581 (1916).

[84] Matter of Jurisdiction of Board of Examiners, *supra.*

[85] *Ibid.* No change in the printed rules of appeal has as yet occurred. In Matter of Appeal of O'Brien, decided the following year, it appeared as a matter of fact that, before bringing the appeal, the indorsement of the board of education had been obtained. Assuming that this was due to an actual change in practice, if not in the formal rules, it is interesting to note that the commissioner made no radical departure in his previous policy in hearing appeals from examination ratings. As might be expected (*ante,* p. 33), he inclined decidedly in favor of a presumption that the board of examiners had made a correct ruling. He said: "The Commissioner of Education must, in determining appeals relating to the rating and standing of candidates, be very reluctant to substitute his judgment for that of the board. If it is shown that the board acted arbitrarily or that the examination has been conducted fraudulently, or that there have been gross irregularities in vital matters, or that the board or some of its members in the performance of their duty have unjustly discriminated against an individual candidate or a group of candidates, the Commissioner may set aside the examination or direct that the errors or irregularities be corrected and that the aggrieved candidates be granted their just rights. The results of the examinations as conducted by the board must, however, have finality in the absence of affirmative proof of such defects." (27 State Dept. Repts. 334, 338 (1922)).

with the administration of the school system to hamper the board's choice of a man or woman according to the needs of a particular school situation.[86] There is some authority in the Matter of Appeal of Maxwell for saying that the mere existence of an undepleted eligible list will not be allowed to embarrass the city educational administration in initiating a new one for that position carrying with it higher qualifications.[87] It is, perhaps, also worth while to note in connection with these eligible lists that they are not finally made up till all appeals from examinations have been heard. For this reason, a teacher can have no legitimate complaint if someone receives a rating senior to his own after the first composition of the list.[88] Having different eligible lists for different positions and correspondingly varying salary levels has led to the commissioner's recognition in a typical appeal from New York City that, "The transfer of a teacher who has been employed in the grades of the first six years to the grades in the seventh and eighth years is to be regarded as an advance in grade promotion." [89] How far this view of a moot question, equal pay for equal work, represents the state department's view, and how far it is the necessary respect for the local opinion of a great city is difficult to tell.

4. Teachers' Contracts

As might be imagined, teachers' contracts form one of the most frequent subjects of litigation before the state department. At the same time they comprise a field where the commissioner has ample guidance from precedents laid down in the courts of the state. The law of offer and acceptance is illustrated, for instance, where a board gave a teacher ten days in which to accept a contract. At the meeting when the teacher's acceptance was received, the board voted to rescind their offer, but the acceptance having preceded the rescission, the commissioner decided against the board.[90] An offer and acceptance may take place through the fulfillment of a condition of a prior contract. Thus a second term of employment may hinge on whether satisfaction is ren-

[86] Matter of Appeal of Davidson *et al.*, 17 State Dept. Rept. 448 (1918).
[87] 3 State Dept. Repts. (official) 539 (1914).
[88] Matter of Board of Examiners, 27 *Ibid.* 684 (1922).
[89] Matter of Appeal of Cooke *v.* Board of Education, 15 *Ibid.* 480, 488 (1918).
[90] Matter of Appeal of Fairman, Jud. Decs. 1162 (1899). Where circumstances produced an opposite result, see, Matter of Appeal of Foster *v.* Board of Education, *Ibid.* 1086 (1904).

dered in the first. If nothing is said at the expiration of the first and the teacher commences a second term, a binding contract will have been formed without further formality.[91] Like an offer and acceptance, a resignation once tendered and accepted cannot be withdrawn as a matter of right.[92] Contracts by duly authorized agents of the board will be enforced just as if made by the board itself.[93] If a member of a board, acting as the board's agent, fails to reveal a limitation of his authority to contract, namely, that the six months' contract offered could be terminated at the pleasure of the board, the state department will see to it that the teacher is not prejudiced thereby.[94] The fact that a teacher may not have reached her majority will not make her contract void but only voidable, and that at her election rather than the board's.[95]

To obviate much of the misunderstanding attendant on oral contracts, the legislature has made it mandatory for local officers to give teachers employed by them a written memorandum of their bargain at the time of its consummation.[96] The fact that no memorandum is made, however, will not invalidate any oral contract that may have been entered into.[97] Reducing the contract to writing has the further important consequence that it supersedes all previous oral negotiations and stipulations so that these cannot be cited to contradict the written evidence of the contract.[98] No doubt the parties to the contract can modify it by later agreement, for example, as where the board votes an increase of pay on the request of a teacher whose burdens have been increased.[99]

[91] Matter of Appeal of Roberts *v.* Board of Education, *Ibid.* 1163 (1902).

[92] Matter of Appeal of Woodhull, 6 State Dept. Rept. 599 (1915).

[93] Matter of Appeal of Stiles *v.* McAloon, 18 *Ibid.* 434 (1919).

[94] Anonymous, Jud. Decs. 1116 (1862).

[95] Matter of Appeal of Barnard *v.* Board of Education, *Ibid.* 1201 (1894).

[96] Laws of N. Y., 1887, ch. 335; continued as section 561, subdiv. 1, of ch. 140 of the law of 1910 as amended to 1925. The Law Division has drawn a model contract which it recommends.

[97] Matter of Appeal of Roe *v.* Snyder, Ind. Decs. 1189 (1890); Matter of Appeal of Foster *v.* Board of Education, *Ibid.* 1086, 1087 (1904).

[98] Matter of Appeal of Gregg *v.* Thompson, Jud. Decs. 1087 (1899); Matter of Appeal of Parttro *v.* Hale, 1 State Dept. Repts. (unofficial) 383 (1912); Matter of Appeal of O'Brien, 21 *Ibid.* 477 (1919).

[99] Matter of Appeal of Peirson, 16 *Ibid.* 332 (1918). But compare this with Matter of Appeal from Action of Board of Education, etc., 7 *Ibid.* 560 (1915), where the commissioner held that the board could not raise teachers' salaries voted by their predecessors in office unless some change of circumstance had occurred justifying it. Extra compensation for summer school attendance will be enforced: Matter of Appeal of Taylor, 27 State Dept. Rept. 346 (1922).

The present statute law on education, although brief on teachers' contracts, has two further provisions in regard to them which have stopped one source of litigation. Section 561 prevents districts of three or more trustees from contracting with teachers for terms longer than a year in advance, and districts with a sole trustee from contracting with a teacher for a period longer than his term of office.[100] Before this section was incorporated into the law, outgoing trustees had frequently been in the habit of selecting the teacher for the next year. This often provoked the incoming trustee to try to avoid the contract and so, in one way and another, an appeal would result. One of the earliest cases shows an inclination to discountenance any policy tying the hands of the incoming trustee.[101] Later cases, on the contrary, took an opposite view and upheld just such contracts,[102] although not if made by the outgoing trustee after he had vacated his office.[103] As for contracts running for more than a year in advance, a decision of Superintendent Draper's commends them, probably because of the unhappy state of affairs obtaining before the passage of a tenure law.[104]

A variety of special provisions in contracts have been pressed upon the commissioner's attention. For instance, there is no uniform practice in regard to vacations. If the contract calls for consecutive weeks of teaching, the local authorities will not be able to deduct salary for a vacation which it forces on the teacher against her protest.[105] On the other hand, if the space in the contract relating to vacations is not filled in, the appellant teacher cannot recover salary for a vacation in which he does acquiesce.[106] Vacations should be arranged for the convenience of the community and not the teacher,[107] although a trustee cannot avoid a teacher's pay during an institute week by setting the vacation for that period.[108] Money earned by a teacher during winter vacation will not decrease a district's liability for the teacher's

[100] Laws of N. Y. 1910, ch. 140, as amended to 1925, subdivs. 2 and 3.

[101] Anonymous, Laws of N. Y., etc., and Digest of Decs. p. 400 (1859).

[102] Matter of Appeal of Woodward *v.* Hill, Jud. Decs. 1151 (1894); Matter of Appeal of Rowe *v.* Hamilton, Ann. Rept. Dept. Pub. Instn. 1897, p. 124 (1896); Matter of Appeal of Griffin, Jud. Decs. 1103 (1906).

[103] Matter of Appeal of Saltsman *v.* Fox, *Ibid.* 1181 (1891).

[104] Matter of Appeal of Dougall *v.* Board of Education, Ann. Rept. Dept. Pub. Instn. 1888, p. 927 (1887).

[105] Matter of Appeal of Deming, 34 State Dept. Rept. 454 (1926).

[106] Matter of Appeal of Marsh, 17 *Ibid.* 468 (1918).

[107] Matter of Appeal of Wilson, Jud. Decs. 1098 (1905).

[108] Matter of Appeal of Hinman *v.* Caywood, Jud. Decs. 1174 (1890).

contracted salary.[109] Where the salary arrangements cover the vacation period, at least the summer one, the money paid during that period has properly been held a part of the consideration for the services rendered during the previous term's work, and not a bonus.[110] Similarly, a teacher's resignation has been held directed to the succeeding year's work and, therefore, should not deprive her of her twelve monthly salary installments which fall due during the summer after the resignation.[111] The question of building fires and doing other janitorial work was the subject of appeal till finally put at rest by an unequivocal statute. In an early case a teacher sought to reimburse himself for having been put to the trouble of building fires, but he was unsuccessful because his contract carried no provision allowing pay for it.[112] At a later time it was held that teachers could not be compelled to do janitorial work against their consent.[113] This trouble all seems to have arisen because the statute of 1864[114] merely provided that trustees "may" make provision for fires and like conveniences. This uncertainty of responsibility was ultimately disposed of, first by a decision holding that the permissive nature of the law might be interpreted to be mandatory since the public interest demanded that this service be performed,[115] and second by a legislative enactment which in no uncertain terms made the duty mandatory upon the trustees.[116] Where a teacher is employed for a certain number of months, a "month" to the commissioner means a "calendar month."[117] It has been further held that where no time of payment is mentioned in the contract a teacher is entitled to be

[109] Anonymous, Jud. Decs. 1114 (1886).

[110] Anonymous, Code of Pub. Instn., 1887, p. 707 (1879); Matter of Appeal Relative to Salary, etc., 27 State Dept. Rept. 649 (1922); Matter of Brownell, 29 *Ibid.* 603 (1923).

[111] Matter of Appeal of Cornell *v.* Denison, Ann. Rept. Dept. Pub. Instn. 1892, p. 81 (1890).

[112] Anonymous, Code of Pub. Instn. 1887, p. 705 (1868). The appellant in this case made a claim for other services which the superintendent of public instruction put aside with rather unusual and choice language: "Concerning the exhausting efforts attending the care of the district property, supposed to have been exercised in keeping the pupils from picking up and running off with a red hot stove, or overturning the schoolhouse before the opening and after the solemn and soul-subduing exercises of the school" no claim can be recognized.

[113] Matter of Appeal of Patterson *v.* Paff *et al.* Jud. Decs. 1158 (1894); Matter of Appeal of Barnett *v.* Stanton, Ann. Rept. Dept. Pub. Instn. 1895, p. 184 (1894).

[114] Laws of N. Y. 1864, ch. 555, title 7, sec. 50.

[115] Matter of Appeal of Barnett *v.* Stanton, Ann. Rept. Dept. Pub. Instn. 1895, p. 184 (1894).

[116] Consolidated Sch. Law, 1894, title 7, sec. 50.

[117] Matter of Appeal of LeRoy, Jud. Decs. 1101 (1905).

paid at least by the calendar month and, if the contract specifies "monthly," then at the end of each school month.[118] It is hard to find a distinction here to justify the difference in treatment. In at least one decision the superintendent of public instruction refused to recognize a custom, which is common in some localities, of giving an absent teacher the right to select and pay her substitute.[119] Of course the commissioner will not sanction a contract gained under duress by a principal who threatened to quit at a critical time unless paid extra for completing his regular contract.[120] While the teacher may not so force the hand of her employer, neither may a trustee of a school district force the teacher's by requiring her to board with him.[121] Doubt has been expressed whether a trustee could require a teacher to recruit pupils for the school or raise money for it by holding an exhibition even though the same were parts of the contract.[122] To what other incidental activities such a precedent might extend lies in the lap of the future.

With the above sketch of the formation of contracts and some of their provisions, it is in place now to examine into appeals pertaining to the performance of the contract by the parties thereto. If the trustee or board of education is unable to perform its side of the contract because an epidemic requires the closing of the school,[123] because the school building was destroyed by fire,[124] or because the wrangling of the board of education prevented the opening of the school,[125] the teacher will nevertheless be entitled to her salary if her enforced idleness was through no fault of her own. Presumably, if a trustee failed to keep a building warm enough, a teacher would be justified in closing it, and would be able to claim her salary for such time as the school

[118] Matter of Appeal of Townsend *v.* Turck *et al.*, Jud. Decs. 1178 (1896).

[119] Matter of Appeal of De Bevoise *v.* Board of Education, *Ibid.* 1035 (1891).

[120] Matter of Appeal of Barker, Jud. Decs. 1032 (1907).

[121] Matter of Appeal of Griswold *v.* Rossman, *Ibid.* 1142 (1887).

[122] Matter of Appeal of Kimm *v.* Board of Education, *Ibid.* 594 (1889).

[123] Matter of Appeal of Miller *v.* School District, Jud. Decs. 592 (1888); Matter of Appeal of Vernooy *v.* Slater, *Ibid.* 1169 (1889); Anonymous, Code of Pub. Instn. 1887, p. 708 (1883); Matter of Appeal of Becker, 2 State Dept. Rept. (unofficial) 388 (1913). A contract with a teacher to make up time lost by an epidemic will be binding even though state department excuses the loss; Matter of Appeal of Braman, 22 State Dept. Repts. 315 (1920).

[124] Matter of Appeal of Voorhies *v.* Board of Trustees, Jud. Decs. 1168 (1890). This conclusion follows even though a district did everything possible to provide temporary quarters and at the end of more than a month was still unsuccessful; Appeal of Bennett *v.* School District, etc. *Ibid.* 1194 (1889).

[125] Matter of Appeal of Robinson *et al.* *v.* Board of Education, *Ibid.* 1171 (1888).

was not fit to occupy.[126] During the privation of school facilities, a teacher cannot be compelled to remain idle; in fact, the state superintendent has thought that she should earn what she reasonably could in the meantime, presumably to mitigate the board's loss.[127] When the shoe is on the other foot, and it is the teacher who is unable to perform her part of the contract because of illness, she cannot recover for time lost even though she is incapacitated through no fault of her own.[128] Not only that, but she cannot insist that the board keep the position open for her until her return.[129] Of course this is sound policy, because the teacher's inability to teach is such a breach of contract as will justify her employer, if not in suing her, at least in treating the contract as at an end so that he may engage another teacher and thus keep the school open. How grave the illness must be to justify such an abrogation of contract, or how grave an epidemic or destruction of the schoolhouse need be to justify a teacher in treating the contract as terminated are questions which have not presented themselves in the commissioner's tribunal.

What are a teacher's remedies where her contract has been breached? If she has been unjustly dismissed she has two alternatives open; she may either seek specific performance of her contract and ask to be reinstated or she may sue for damages. The department's general policy toward the first alternative is exactly that followed in the courts, namely,

> It is well settled that one party to a contract can claim a specific performance of the same only when he can show that other legal remedy is inadequate, and that without such specific performance injustice or irreparable injury will be done him. A claim for such a performance is one which is always addressed to the equitable jurisdiction of the court. The relief sought by the claimant in such a case is not one which is asked as a right, but one which is addressed to the discretion of the court, after showing that legal remedies are inadequate.[130]

[126] Matter of Appeal of Williams, 21 State Dept. Rept. 570 (1919). In this case, however, the teacher was too quick to anticipate a failure of the trustee to provide heat.

[127] Matter of Appeal of Robinson *et al. v.* Board of Education, Jud. Decs. 1171 (1888).

[128] Matter of Appeal of Wensley, 26 State Dept. Repts. 92 (1921). Acting-Superintendent Morrison has held *obiter* that while the teacher may not recover salary for the period of his illness he may at least recover for the period of service prior thereto; Anonymous, Code of Pub. Instn. 1887, p. 723 (1886).

[129] Matter of Appeal of Wensley, 26 State Dept. Rept. 92 (1921).

[130] Matter of Appeal of Mapes *et al. v.* Board of Education, Jud. Decs. 1120, 1123 (1888).

Very few appellants are able to prove that money damages will not compensate them for their injuries suffered, so that the commissioner is most likely to remit them to their alternative remedy of an action for damages. Again, irreparable injury of the appellant is not the only problem the pros and cons of which the commissioner must balance in his discretion; he will also take into account the local situation as well. If he has cause to think that reinstatement of the appellant will merely irritate the old quarrel and interfere with the efficient conduct of the school, he will be even more likely to put the aggrieved party to his remedy in money damages.[131] But even this course is not free from difficulties, for the commissioner himself will only entertain an action for damages when these are liquidated or uncontroverted. If they are uncertain or indefinite, he will leave the appellant to an action in the courts as better equipped to determine such questions.[132] The court of appeals seems to think that the commissioner might settle these damages too, for in a case where he remitted an appellant to the courts, it said,

> Having assumed jurisdiction, I am of the opinion the commissioner might very well have ascertained the plaintiff's damage. Section 881 (now 891) would seem to indicate this was the proper practice to be pursued, since by this section he is given ample power to enforce his decision. While I think he had jurisdiction to assess the damages, I do not think it was exclusive. At least where all parties assented to that course it cannot now be questioned. He could, acting within the power given to him, do what he did—remit the plaintiff to an action at law to have the same ascertained.[133]

Where the commissioner will assess the damages he may and does award interest thereon as well.[134]

The teacher is entitled to bring her action for damages immediately upon occurrence of the breach. Thus it was held that an appellant, under contract for another year of service and dis-

[131] Matter of Appeal of Mapes *et al.* *v.* Board of Education, *supra.*

[132] Matter of Appeal of Tillson *v.* McNeeley, Jud. Decs. 1090 (1889); Matter of Appeal of Munson *v.* School District, *Ibid.* 22 (1891); Matter of Appeal of Mowell *v.* Sliter, *Ibid.* 139 (1905); Matter of Appeal of Keller *v.* Board of Education, Ann. Rept. Dept. Pub. Instn. 1912, p. 468 (1911); Matter of Appeal of Landel, 28 State Dept. Rept. 255 (1922). The same principle obtains where damages for other injuries than teachers' contracts are sought, e.g., Matter of Appeal of Feldman & Kretchmar, 4 State Dept. Rept. (unofficial) 394 (1913); Matter of Appeal of Sayre *v.* Stevenson, 6 *Ibid.* 589 (1915).

[133] Barringer *v.* Powell, 230 N. Y. 37, 43 (1920). Relative to section 891 of the Education Law, see *ante*, p. 49.

[134] Matter of Appeal of Hunt *v.* Vanderzee, Jud. Decs. 1170 (1889).

missed at the end of the instant year, could sue at once and did not need to wait for a possible change of heart and tender of performance by the board of education in the fall.[135] While it is usually incumbent upon the plaintiff to attempt a mitigation of damages by finding other employment, yet he need not make that part of his affirmative case before the commissioner.[136] But "there is no law that requires the appellant, in order to preserve her rights, to have sought or to have accepted employment, even in her profession as teacher, at a point distant from that where she had agreed to give her services, much less that would compel her to engage in any other occupation, however convenient to her residence." [137] If a teacher can show no actual damages, as where, since her dismissal, she has secured a position at a higher remuneration and where her dismissal was not the result of charges against her conduct or professional competence, her appeal will be dismissed.[138]

5. Dismissal of Teachers

Before there was a state-wide teacher tenure law, or even tenure in certain classes of schools, one type of teacher contract was all too frequent, namely, that whereby the trustee or board of education might discharge a teacher at its pleasure.[139] The scant protection that a teacher might get was that she should have two weeks' to a month's warning in advance.[140] Of course, in strict legal parlance, the teacher might just as easily avoid such a contract, because it would hardly be fair that she be bound for a definite term and not the trustees or board.[141] But even so, the advantage must have lain with the employer, as it generally does. With the accession of Andrew S. Draper to the state superintendency of public instruction conditions changed. In 1887 a case was presented to him in which the respondent made affidavit "that he informed said teachers when he employed them that he hired them for one day only and that their time would close every night, but that if they gave satisfaction he would keep them as

[135] Matter of Application of Lamson, *Ibid.* 1091 (1906).
[136] Matter of Appeal of Stiles *v.* McAloon, 21 State Dept. Rept. 264 (1919).
[137] Anonymous, Code of Pub. Instn. 1887, p. 720 (1869).
[138] Matter of Appeal of Wight, Jud. Decs. 1111 (1909).
[139] E.g., Anonymous, Code of Pub. Instn. 1887, p. 721 (1880); Anonymous, *Ibid.* p. 722 (1886); Anonymous, p. 725 (1886); Anonymous, *Ibid.* p. 726 (1886).
[140] Anonymous, *Ibid.* p. 726 (1886); Anonymous, *Ibid.* p. 725 (1886).
[141] Anonymous, *Ibid.* p. 721 (1880).

long as he remained trustee."[142] So hard and so cleanly did Superintendent Draper hit this contractual provision that his language must be quoted:

> I find myself unable to uphold such a contract because I think it was an unconscionable contract, without sanction of law or good usage and against sound policy. . . . Trustees may, undoubtedly, at times summarily dismiss a teacher for a palpable breach of contract or gross and open immorality, but such action must be taken, if at all, upon the personal responsibility of the officer. But these are exceptional cases, outside of the general rule. There can be no pretense that the case under consideration is one of that nature. Moreover, trustees ought not to be permitted to absolve themselves from the responsibility of making investigations and of exercising proper precautionary care and good judgment when employing teachers, but reserving the right to discharge them at any moment. A duly licensed and employed teacher ought to have security of position for a reasonable length of time, which should be long enough to prove himself successful or to demonstrate his inability to do so. It is humiliating to self-respecting teachers to be at all times liable to discharge from employment because others may want their places or because of the antagonisms which a vigorous and wholesome performance of their duties in the schoolroom may engender. To adopt this doctrine is only to drive the most self-respecting and the best-qualified persons from teachers' work. This is unquestionably against wise policy. Furthermore, if the trustee could discontinue these teachers at any time, they could abandon their places at any time. But the school must continue without interruption. Teachers must be under a legal and honorable obligation to so continue it. An agreement between trustee and teacher, which does not involve this is manifestly against the interests of the public school system.[143]

The superintendent held the determination of a reasonable minimum length of time to depend on local custom and circumstance. But the size of even this remaining loophole was cut down by a statute two years later, which made sixteen weeks a minimum term of employment unless for an unexpired term of school.[144]

This same statute also offered teachers a further protection which they had not enjoyed before, namely, that they were not to be removable in the future "except for reasons which, if appealed to the superintendent of public instruction, should be held to be sufficient cause for such dismissal.[145] The present

[142] Anonymous, Jud. Decs. 1112 (1887).

[143] *Ibid.* pp. 1112-13. Acc.: Matter of Appeal of Groom *v.* Hough, *Ibid.* 1188 (1888); Matter of Appeal of Burdick *v.* Board of Education, *Ibid.* 1189 (1890).

[144] Laws of N. Y. 1889, ch. 328, sec. 2. The present provision provides for a minimum of ten weeks: laws of 1910, as amended to 1925, ch. 140, sec. 561, subdiv. 2.

[145] *Ibid.* Continued in the present law as section 565, with the specified causes—"neglect of duty, incapacity to teach, immoral conduct"—added.

teacher tenure law has gone further and secured teachers in their positions "during good behavior and efficient and competent service" and from dismissal "except for cause."[146] What, then, are circumstances, which on appeal, the commissioner will hold sufficient cause for the removal of a teacher from his office? The absence or revocation of a teacher's license will occur at once as a valid cause for removal.[147] Hardly less serious as a disqualification is simple physical inability to administer the school.[148] While a delicate and difficult standard to judge by, want of tact and judgment has been held a justifiable cause for dismissal.[149] Yet a principal who writes a very offensive letter to his board of education seems to be clearly lacking in qualities of tact and judgment.[150] Necessary as excellent intellectual capacities are, they will not save a teacher from ousting if she cannot maintain discipline in the school.[151] Though a teacher is not altogether to blame if the trustee or board of education does not back him in his disciplinary problems,[152] the failure of either to do so will not be a complete defense for the teacher.[153] Persistent and apparently willful lack of punctuality will certainly justify a teacher's employer in disciplining her.[154] The charge of inefficiency, although a broad one, and presenting real difficulties in the presentation of proof, has been upheld by the commissioner on appeal.[155] Absence without leave is a serious charge at almost any public post.[156] A closely parallel case is that of a teacher dismissing school without permission from the authorities.[157] If

[146] Laws of N. Y. 1917, ch. 786, section 3.

[147] C. W. M., etc., *ex parte,* Decs. Supt. Com. Schs., p. 211 (1835); Matter of charges against Mulligan, Jud. Decs. 1195 (1890); Matter of Appeal of Clemens *v.* Stedman, *Ibid.* 1145 (1891).

[148] Matter of Appeal of Kennedy. 4 State Dept. Rept. (unofficial) 389 (1913).

[149] Matter of Appeal of Williston *v.* Wood, Ann. Rept. Dept. Pub. Instn. 1890, p. 143 (1889).

[150] Matter of Appeal of Smith, Ann. Rept. State Dept. of Ed. 1913, p. 452 (1912).

[151] Anonymous, Jud. Decs. 1118 (1886); Matter of Appeal of Roe *v.* Snyder, *Ibid.* 1189 (1890); Matter of Appeal of Porteus *v.* Rutherford, *Ibid.* 1129 (1895); Matter of appeal of Botsford, *Ibid.* 1101 (1907); Matter of Appeal of Stackpole, *Ibid.* 1125 (1910).

[152] Anonymous, Jud. Decs. 1118 (1886); Matter of Appeal of Groom *v.* Hough, *Ibid.* 1188 (1888).

[153] Matter of Appeal of Zeiner, 27 State Dept. Rept. 680 (1922).

[154] Matter of Appeal of Baldwin, Jud. Decs. 1127 (1910).

[155] Matter of Appeal of Streamer, 6 State Dept. Repts. 611 (1915); Matter of Appeal of Roberts *v.* Board of Education, Jud. Decs. 1163 (1902).

[156] Matter of Appeal of Town, 1 State Dept. Repts. (unofficial) 385 (1912); Matter of Appeal of Fotheringham, 15 Ibid. 498 (1918).

[157] Anonymous, Laws of N. Y., etc., and Digest of Decs., p. 406 (1860); Anonymous, *Ibid.* (1863); Matter of Appeal of Palmer, Jud. Decs. 1096 (1905).

ill health, as a cause for leave of absence, stretches into what may reasonably be anticipated to be permanent disability, a teacher may be regarded as dismissed although never formally notified.[158] Again, a teacher who fails to coöperate with the proper authorities to facilitate the enforcement of the compulsory attendance law certainly does not deserve clemency from the commissioner.[159] Of course the same applies to a more general insubordination to, and lack of coöperation with administrative officers.[160] It hardly needs mention that immorality cannot be tolerated and the teacher at the same time retain his position.[161] Finally, it should be noted that if the appellant wants to contest his removal for any cause he should force his dismissal rather than appeal from his resignation even though he claim the latter forced.[162]

In the cases where marriage and its natural consequences, maternity, have been at the bottom of dismissal, proceedings deserve special attention. The New York City Board of Education, with a rule against employing married teachers unless their husbands were incapacitated or had abandoned them, was about the first to become involved in an appeal to the commissioner. A young married woman signed her maiden name to an application for a teaching position and left unanswered, even though called to her attention, the question whether she was married. When it came to the notice of the board of education a year later that this teacher was married, charges of gross misconduct were preferred against her, her misconduct consisting in deceiving the board of education as to her true status. She appealed her eventual dismissal to the commissioner who sustained the board's discretion although he distinctly left open the validity of the board's rule, since that had not been raised as an issue in the appeal.[163] In the city of Buffalo a teacher, who was already in service and who married with full knowledge of a city ordinance

[158] Matter of Little, 19 State Dept. Rept. 301 (1919).

[159] Matter of Appeal of Gelder, 1 State Dept. Repts. (unofficial) 433 (1912).

[160] Matter of Appeal of Shea *et al.*, 26 *Ibid.* 469 (1921). Cf. Anonymous, Jud. Decs. 1132 (1893).

[161] Matter of Charges Against Wilson, Ann. Rept. Dept. Pub. Instn. 1891, p. 92 (1890); Matter of Dismissal of Bush, Ann. Rept. State Ed. Dept. 1912, p. 479 (1911). In the latter case it was further held that the fact that the principal was implicated as well as the teacher, but had not been ousted by preferment of charges, could hardly save the teacher. Cf. Matter of Appeal of Van Slyke, 3 State Dept. Rept. (unofficial) 330 (1913).

[162] Matter of Appeal of Richardson, 14 State Dept. Rept. 452 (1917); Matter of Appeal of Dent *v.* Thayer, Ann. Rept. Dept. Pub. Instn. 1891, p. 112 (1890).

[163] Matter of Appeal of Ortman, 4 State Dept. Rept. (official) 627 (1915).

which held a teacher's position to be vacated when she married, was successfully removed.[164] Both of the above cases arose under local city charters which, because they were specific in contradistinction to the state education law which is general, took precedence over the latter in the question as to what is a valid cause for removal.[165] Not till the enactment of the state-wide teacher tenure law did the commissioner gain an opportunity to express his own opinion on the validity of the status of marriage as a cause for removal from office. The leading case is the Appeal of Thomas, decided by Commissioner Graves.[166] The fact that in this case the appellant signed her maiden name to the payroll and had therefore opened herself to the accusation of deceit in office was quickly passed over as not alone sufficient to justify her dismissal. Coming down to the real merits of the case, whether marriage was a sufficient reason for discharge, Commissioner Graves said:

> It seems clear to me . . . that to declare either by a legislative act or an administrative rule that the marriage of a teacher unfits her for public school service would be opposed to existing public policy and would be an unfair discrimination against married women. If a married woman possesses the required qualifications and performs her duties with the same degree of competency and efficiency as an unmarried woman, it would not be only unjust but I think illegal to discriminate against her because of her marriage. As stated by the Supreme Court in the State of Oregon in the case of Richards v. District School Board, 153 Pac. 482, L.R.A. (1916C), 789, 78 Ore. 621: "If a teacher becomes inefficient or fails to perform a duty, or does some act which of itself impairs usefulness, then a good or reasonable cause for dismissal would exist. The act of marriage, however, does not, of itself, furnish a reasonable cause. . . . The act to which the instant rule relates does not involve a single element of wrong, but, on the contrary, marriage is not only protected by both the written and unwritten law, but it is also fostered by sound public policy. It is impossible to know in advance whether the efficiency of any person will be impaired because of marriage, and a rule which assumes that all persons do become less competent because of marriage is unreasonable because such a regulation is purely arbitrary. If a teacher is just as competent and efficient after marriage, a dismissal because of marriage would be capricious. If a teacher is neglectful, incompetent, and inefficient, she ought to be discharged whether she is married or whether she is single." [167]

[164] Matter of Appeal of Conger, 8 *Ibid.* 616 (1916).
[165] *Ibid.*
[166] 33 State Dept. Repts. 12 (1925).
[167] *Ibid.* pp. 17-18.

It remains now to note the commissioner's attitude to the fundamental problem, childbirth. The conclusion is practically foregone. A number of these cases arose about 1915, the Peixotto case being the best enunciation of the state department's policy.[168] The teacher in this case gave notice of absence but set forth a different reason from her impending maternity. The board of education, when it learned the true facts, preferred the charge of neglect of duty against her and dismissal followed in due course after a hearing had been had. The case was first carried to the courts where it finally reached the court of appeals.[169] It is to the credit of the board of education that it passed over the minor question of deceit, and in the course of the case in the courts rested the issue squarely on the problem whether absence on account of maternity was neglect of duty. The Court of Appeals was divided but the majority sustained the board of education. The issue was not presented to the courts, however, whether the board of education would have been unreasonable in denying maternity as a proper excuse under its policy of granting leaves of absence. The Court of Appeals passed only on the question of neglect of duty and specifically left this issue open. Because the decision of such a question was peculiarly within the province of the judicial power of the commissioner of education,[170] an appeal presenting it was soon carried to him. There was some opinion in the Court of Appeals that even the question of neglect of duty should have been left to the commissioner, at least in the first instance. After a careful and thorough examination of the papers in the case, Commissioner Finley came to the conclusion:

> That the board should have accepted the natural corrollary of its policy, voluntary or enforced, of employing or retaining married women teachers, and should have given at least as favorable consideration to an absence for childbirth as is normally given to absences asked for reasons of personal convenience, or minor or grave illness, or for purposes of study and travel, or of improving health. . . .
>
> Home duties should, doubtless, in some cases, suggest to the teacher withdrawal from the school after maternity. Dismissal for "general inefficiency" would be warranted if upon return a teacher was found to be

[168] Matter of Appeal of Peixotto, 4 State Dept. Repts. (official) 596 (1915). Acc.: Matter of Appeal of Weeks, 4 *Ibid.* 605 (1915); Matter of Appeal of Griswold, *Ibid.* 654; Matter of Appeal of Robbins, 3 *Ibid.* (official) 518 (1914).

[169] People *ex rel.*, Peixotto *v.* Board of Education, 212 N. Y. 463 (1914).

[170] *Ante*, ch. II, sec. 3.

unable after trial to perform school duties. But it is difficult to conceive how a reasonable, unwilful absence, due to a natural unavoidable cause, could be construed as neglect of duty; and it is difficult to understand why an absence for the most highly creditable social reason should be so treated.[171]

In another case decided at almost the same time the issue of the teacher's deceit in attempting to conceal her maternity was brought more to the front. While marking it as reprehensible conduct, the commissioner held it insufficient cause in itself to merit dismissal from office.[172]

One other group of cases may be of more than passing interest, those involving a teacher's freedom of thought and expression of opinion on social, political, and economic questions. These arose during the World War and during the aftermath of conservatism that swept over the state and nation in the succeeding two or three years. While they are to be read in that light, nevertheless the principles they lay down seem sound educational philosophy. The outstanding war case is the appeal of three men dismissed from the teaching service in New York City.[173] The charges against the appellant Mufson were that he insisted on maintaining strict neutrality in the classroom in the discussion of the relative merits of anarchism and the existing government of the United States and also in discussing the obligation of everyone to support the United States in its prosecution of the war. Asked on the trial of his case whether he felt it his duty to inculcate in his pupils respect for the president, sympathy with the American view of the war, and support of the government in its prosecution of the war, he refused to answer. After taking notice of the nation's crisis, Acting-Commissioner Finegan remarked:

Under this condition of the nation's affairs a teacher in the public school system will not be permitted to hide behind any claim of privilege when a question affecting his loyalty to the government is concerned. He must come out in the open and cheerfully and unhesitatingly stand up and make known to the entire community in which he is employed that he is giving his unquestioned support to the president and to the government in the prosecution of this war, and if he refuses to give such assurance he shall not be permitted to discharge the high office of teacher in an American school system. The public schools of any country should be the expression of that country's ideals, the purpose of its institutions and

[171] Matter of Appeal of Peixotto, 4 State Dept. Repts. (official), 596, 604 (1915).
[172] Matter of Appeal of Griswold, 4 *Ibid.* (official), 654 (1915).
[173] Matter of Appeal of Mufson *et al.*, 18 State Dept. Rept. 393 (1918).

its philosophy of life and government. The schools of America should be an expression of America's ideals, of her democratic institutions, and of her philosophy of life and of representative government. There has not been a time in the history of the country when the public schools should be engaged more persistently, scientifically, and patriotically in teaching the fundamental principles of America's philosophy of life and government than at the present time. A person who does not, without reservation, utilize all his intellectual powers and exert all his influence as a teacher in the public schools to make such schools an efficient and effective agency in the accomplishment of this great function of a school system is not a suitable person to be charged with the duties of the sacred office of teacher. A teacher who is unwilling to follow this course "fails to live up to his duty as teacher" and fails properly to support the government in this war.[174]

The appellant Schneer was charged with asserting that patriotism was not a fitting subject for discussion in the high school, that uniformed soldiers should not be permitted to address the school assembly, and that the board of education had no authority to institute military training in the school. His dismissal was sustained for much the same reasons as Mufson's. The appellant Schneer also came in for censure for having published and put on sale at school a book in which, among other really excellent literary selections, were included some with subtitles such as "The Wilder Fires of Sex," "Heart Throbs of the Midnight Hours," "Fragrant Kisses of Passion," etc. The commissioner held a man with such ideas as to good literature is hardly to be entrusted with the training of adolescents for citizenship.

The case against appellant Schmalhausen was similar. He was particularly criticized for permitting his pupils to write seditious letters to the President of the United States in connection with the war. An example of a typical pupil letter is included in the full report of the case and should be read in order to appreciate this appeal fully. In considering Schmalhausen's case, Acting-Commissioner Finegan remarked still further in regard to a teacher's intellectual freedom,

It must be held that teachers have the same right to form judgments and to express opinion upon public questions that other citizens possess. A teacher is not compelled to sacrifice his individuality, his personal liberties or his judgment upon social and public problems simply because he is a teacher. Upon questions on which citizens generally may express different opinions or judgments, a teacher has the right to express his opinion and to form his own judgment. The power conferred by law upon the Com-

[174] *Ibid.* pp. 407-08.

missioner of Education will be freely exercised to protect this right of a teacher whenever the authority over such teacher attempts to restrict or annihilate it. There is, however, no difference of opinion among the patriotic citizens of this county as to the duty of all Americans in supporting the President of the United States and the government in the prosecution of this war. . . . If a teacher cannot give that unquestioning support to the country that makes his own individual freedom in time of peace possible, his place is not in the school.[175]

The case of the teacher who was a Quakeress, and, therefore, whose religious scruples prevented her from teaching support of the war, will be reviewed in another connection. It may be forecast, however, that it reaches the same result as those already considered.[176]

In the Matter of the Appeal of Pratt,[177] arising since the war, a teacher's membership in the communist party became the subject of appeal to the commissioner. Addressing himself to this problem, he held close to his argument in dealing with Schmalhausen:

It has been suggested that a teacher may not be dismissed under the statute where the charges involve her rights and duties as a citizen and go outside of her duties as a teacher. It may be accepted as a general policy that a teacher should not be dismissed from the service on account of her political, religious, and social affiliations and activities outside of her employment. If, however, a teacher becomes a member of an organization, political or otherwise, which exists for the accomplishment of an unlawful purpose or object, or which advocates the use of unlawful means in such accomplishment, or if she becomes allied with such an organization and is actively engaged in carrying out its program, she should not be continued in the public schools. The public avowal or support, by a teacher, of the principles advocated by such an organization would show such a mental and moral condition as to make her unfit as an instructor of the children in our public schools.

The doctrines and principles of the Communist Party of America, as proclaimed by its constitution and program, declared in effect for the overthrow by force and violence of our existing constitutional government. The party is not in this respect a political party, in the sense that the Republican, Democratic, and Socialist parties are political parties. . . . A teacher in the public schools is a member of a State system and a servant of the people of the State. A teacher cannot properly perform the duties of her position and give expression, either verbally or by affiliation with any political or other organization, to her belief that our present government should be overthrown by revolution or by force and violence through direct action of any group or class. The teacher owes allegiance to

[175] *Ibid.* pp. 416-17.
[176] *Post,* p. 120.
[177] 25 State Dept. Rept. 65 (1921).

the State, and school authorities are required to insist upon absolute loyalty of the teachers to the government of the State.[178]

A number of the cases already considered arose under the teacher tenure law of the state. It remains, however, to note some further considerations as to the purpose of the tenure law and its administration. Its purpose was excellently stated within a year of the passage of the statute in the Matter of the Appeal of Mufson *et al.*[179] Counsel for the appellants who had been dismissed from service argued to the commissioner that the purpose of the law was to make teacher's tenure secure. In correcting this impression he said:

> The enactment of this provision of the law was not predicated upon that ground. This provision of law was enacted for the primary purpose of providing the schools with efficient and suitable teachers and of guaranteeing, so far as may be possible, to the children of the city their right to receive instruction from competent, experienced teachers. The theory is that permanent tenure will attract men and women of the best intellectual attainments to the teaching service; that teachers will make more thorough academic and professional preparation, will remain in the service longer, and thus bring to the support of the schools teachers whose training and experience will be a valuable asset. The primary interest, however, which the state seeks to protect is the right of the child. For this same reason the Legislature very properly provided for the elimination of inefficient, unworthy, and undesirable teachers.[180]

In the administration of the tenure law one or two problems have required exposition. For instance, is the abolition of the position which one holds to justify him in feeling aggrieved under the tenure law? This raises the very difficult question of what was the intent of the board of education in doing away with the position, a bona fide cutting down of offices or an indirect attempt to dismiss the teacher? This is a question of fact for the commissioner of education to determine in each case.[181] If the former, no question of the tenure law will be involved. It is equally clear, too, in that event, that the board is under no obligation to create a new position with equal remuneration to which it can transfer the teacher whose position has just been abolished.[182] Again, since the tenure law provides for a probation period of from one to three years, the question has arisen whether

[178] *Ibid.* pp. 69-73. Acc.: Matter of Glassberg, 33 State Dept. Rept. 261 (1925).

[179] 18 State Dept. Repts. 393 (1918).

[180] *Ibid.* pp. 399-400.

[181] Matter of Appeal of Leitzell, 12 State Dept. Rept. 406 (1917).

[182] *Ibid.* p. 410.

one to three years of service prior to the enactment of the tenure law will satisfy the statutory requirements. This proposition has been decided in the negative.[183] Nor can a teacher complain if, during her probationary period, the same is extended beyond what it was at the inception of her term of service.[184] A curious application of the law arises where a district was legally beholden to its principal for the next school year. It then ousted him and at that same meeting voted funds to defray any legal claim the principal might press in the courts. In the early Matter of Appeal of Mapes,[185] decided prior to the teacher tenure law, this procedure of the district was sanctioned on appeal to the state superintendent of public instruction. But when the same set of facts was presented in the Matter of Appeal of Stafford *et al.*, decided in 1919, the tenure law was held to bar the way to such proceedings.[186] Finally, does the law apply to night schools and the like? One can only conjecture. In a decision under a local tenure law before the state-wide law obtained, a negative conclusion was reached because such schools were not held to be part of the common school system of the state.[187]

6. Teacher Transfer, Professional Relationships, Retirement and Pension, etc.

Frequent as is the transfer of teachers from one position to another in a school system, there must be many more wounds inflicted on pride and pocketbook than are ever brought to the commissioner for healing. Fundamentally the commissioner entertains "no doubt of the authority of the board of education to transfer teachers in its employ from one position to another in any way which shall seem to such board best calculated to promote the efficiency of the schools in its charge." [188] If the board thinks that a teacher's health demands a reduction from the head of a department to the ranks, the chances are that the commissioner will sustain the board's discretion and overrule the teacher's protest.[189] Again, if friction demands a change in the headship

[183] Matter of Appeal of Fayette, 21 *Ibid.* 330 (1919).

[184] Matter of Appeal of Krebs, 26 *Ibid.* 353 (1921).

[185] Jud. Decs. 1120 (1888).

[186] 21 State Dept. Repts. 144 (1919).

[187] Matter of Application of McQuade, Ann. Rept. State Ed. Dept. 1913, p. 432 (1912).

[188] Matter of Appeal of Valentine *v.* Board of Education, Jud. Decs. 1110 (1890).

[189] *Ibid.*

of a department, a transfer will likely be sustained for the good of the service,[190] and, anyhow, one derives no legal right to a headship of a department when the only reference to its existence is a mention of it in a report of the board of education.[191] The transfer of a teacher, however, from high school work to elementary work as a mark of censure is not to be tolerated.[192] A different situation arises where the board transfers a teacher certified in one field to teach in another. Objection to this procedure has been upheld on appeal because it would let down the bars of certification for the entrance of all sorts of abuses.[193] The practice may also be unfair to the teacher. Not only may the transfer call upon her to do teaching different from her certificate, but it may also require teaching normally carrying an increase in pay. While equitably entitled to it, actually she will be unable to collect it because her license does not meet the requirement of that level of the salary schedule. Obviously, such a practice should be discontinued.[194]

In the last several cases preceding, there may be some implications for the conception of a single salary schedule. Some mention of this problem has already been made.[195] Very few cases have presented the single salary issue alone. In one of these the objection was made that different minima and maxima were in operation for men and women teachers of vocational subjects. The distinction was held justified on appeal because the vocational subjects taught by men were different from those taught by the women and, for all that appeared, were more exacting and required a difference in pay.[196] In somewhat like manner teachers of special subjects are entitled to be placed on levels of salary schedules appropriate to their training. Such is the case of a teacher of speech correction,[197] or such a one as does the "liaison" work of a "visiting teacher." [198]

The question of teacher rating is one very closely allied to the foregoing topics. Yet, it is seldom if ever the subject of

[190] Matter of Appeal of Allen, 14 State Dept. Rept. 465 (1917).

[191] *Ibid.*

[192] Matter of Appeal of Macomber, Jud. Decs. 1106 (1910).

[193] Matter of Appeal of Lichterman, 7 State Dept. Rept. 593 (1916).

[194] Matter of Appeal of Pettebone, 7 *Ibid.* 617 (1916).

[195] *Ante*, p. 92.

[196] Petition of Teece *v.* Board of Education, 27 *Ibid.* 652 (1922); Matter of Appeal of Simar, 32 *Ibid.* 604 (1925).

[197] Matter of Appeal of Foote, etc., 22 *Ibid.* 565 (1920).

[198] Matter of Appeal of Louderback, 32 *Ibid.* 588 (1925).

judicial appeal, probably because the commissioner would always be inclined to rest very heavily upon the discretion of local officers. One case, nevertheless, may deserve mention. A local board of education provided an extra salary increment for teachers of "superior merit" on their completion of twelve years of service. A teacher put in a claim for this recognition but was turned down. A year later her right to be recognized as a superior teacher was affirmed. Not content with winning this point, the appellant made a claim for the increment she alleged should have been paid her the year before. The board resisted this claim but on appeal was overruled because it was held that if the appellant was a superior teacher, entitled to the additional increment at all, she must have been so at the end of the twelve-year period, even though her merit was not recognized till a year later.[199]

Mutual loyalty is a *sine qua non* within the teaching corps, in fact within any profession. The Matter of the Appeal of Walrath v. Board of Education,[200] declares the obligation due a principal from his superintendent. It also gives warning to a board of education against looking upon a teacher as a "hired man" or making his position the "football of politics." The appeal is worth reading for its dignified conception of professional relationships. Of teachers' associations the commissioner has asserted:

> There is no legal objection to the organization of teachers' associations to promote mutual welfare, improve teaching conditions, and advance the interests of the public school system. Such associations of teachers may prove of great value in obtaining public support of, and coöperation with our public schools and in aiding school authorities in bringing about effective school administration. There is nothing to be criticized in a teachers' association becoming energetic in promoting the interests of its members and improving the teaching conditions in the schools of a city, but such an association must not be permitted to coerce teachers in the public schools who are not members of such association. Teachers who do not see fit to affiliate themselves with such an association should not be vilified and unjustly criticized by the official utterances of such association. The members and officers of such an association must be required to coöperate and work in harmony with teachers who are not affiliated therewith, and on this account school authorities will be compelled to prevent incrimination and abuse by such association, through its officers, or non-affiliated teachers.[201]

[199] Matter of Appeal of White, 22 *Ibid.* 669 (1920).
[200] Jud. Decs. 1026 (1906).
[201] Matter of Appeal of Shea *et al*, 26 State Dept. Rept. 469 (1921).

Finally, the spirit between the community and the schools is an important one. A most unusual case in this connection was an anonymous one arising in 1911.[202] In that instance the principal of the local school had been dismissed and his certificate and diploma annulled for having falsified examination papers. Ordinarily this should have provoked quite a moral storm in any community, but strangely enough the opposite result was produced here. The appointment of a new principal was greeted with a student strike. Student parades of protest were engineered in which the teachers who had divulged the information which indicted the principal were placarded as "snoopers." The student turmoil was aided and abetted by parents and citizens who themselves held indignation meetings. Nor did the flames beneath this pot of public excitement lack fanning from the bellows of the local press. When the appeal before the commissioner came on to be heard, a petition from the great body of the community was presented asking for leniency. Again, one must read at length the decision itself to appreciate the splendid way in which Commissioner Draper was sensitive to human frailties in such a situation and how soothingly he met them without the sacrifice of an iota of principle. Of course the former principal's appeal for relief was denied and the community urged to bury the hatchet in the best interests of the school.

Not many decisions are extant as yet in connection with retirement and pensions. The decision of the board in charge, while subject to review, will have the usual rebuttable presumption as to its correctness.[203] Upon adoption of the retirement and pension law a number of teachers who had earlier withdrawn sought reëmployment long enough to qualify under the benefits of the statute. While recognizing such cases as entitled to sympathy, the commissioner could concede them no further favor.[204] It is worth noting that a teacher is not entitled of right to retire when he has completed the number of years prescribed as a minimum by the statute. The purpose of the statute has been held to be to retire those whose physical condition is so impaired as materially to interfere with their further teaching. Many

[202] Ann. Rept. State Ed. Dept. 1912, p. 485 (1911).

[203] Matter of Appeal of Murphy, 8 State Dept. Rept. 608 (1916); Matter of Appeal of Stiles, 9 *Ibid.* 590 (1916); Matter of Appeal of Swaneman, 9 *Ibid.* 591 (1916). See also *ante*, p. 33.

[204] Matter of Appeal of Carpenter, 14 *Ibid.* 485 (1918).

teachers are at the zenith of their powers after twenty-five years of service, and the state is unwilling to lose the advantage of that ability and experience.[205]

7. Appeals Concerning Instruction, Curricula, Textbooks, etc.

It can readily be seen that the number of appeals which might possibly arise out of grievances against a teacher's method of instruction, a school's curriculum, or the textbooks adopted are limitless. The department does not encourage them. Where an appeal was taken involving a teacher's right to require left-handed children to write with their right hands, the superintendent said:

> It is not possible for me to lay down any general rule upon this subject, and I do not feel bound to determine the matter. . . . If the habit can be acquired, it ought to be acquired, and the teacher ought to insist upon it. At the same time, when a child has always used his left hand, and has come to be twelve or fourteen years of age, it seems very doubtful whether it is practicable to change the habit, and therefore doubtful whether the teacher should insist upon it.
>
> The Department cannot interfere in all small matters of school discipline, particularly where no charges are made against the character or competency of teachers, and where children have not been punished or deprived of the privileges of school.[206]

Appeals relating to the dismissal of teachers and methods of punishment employed by them have already been treated elsewhere as special topics.[207] A few other miscellaneous matters of internal school management may be considered together in this section.

Dropping a pupil from school on account of low mentality will probably gain the commissioner's attention because it is a deprivation of school privileges. "I suppose the true rule touching such a case is that the child should be permitted to attend the school unless his presence is obnoxious to others, and unless he is so weak-minded as to be incapable of caring for himself and receiving the elements of an education," is the way Superintendent Draper first spoke on the matter.[208] The teacher's convenience in having such a student in his class is distinctly secondary to the efficiency and success of the school.[209] While school authorities

[205] Matter of Appeal of Redmond, 3 *Ibid.* (official), 515 (1914).

[206] Matter of Appeal of Frink *v.* Haswell, Jud. Decs. 1039 (1892).

[207] Sections 5 and 9 of this chapter.

[208] Matter of Appeal of McDonough *v.* Smith, Jud. Decs. 515 (1890). Acc.: Matter of Appeal from Action of Trustees, etc., 30 State Dept. Rept. 216 (1923).

[209] Matter of Appeal of McDonough *v.* Smith, *supra.*

should make a special effort in the instruction of such unfortunate ones they cannot be required to provide courses which might not reasonably be provided for in the public school.[210]

Probably a dispute over a child's demotion would not ordinarily reach the commissioner's ears but, where it practically amounted to a deprivation of school privileges bargained for, a different issue was presented. An appellant's children attended an academic school by virtue of a contract between their home district and the respondent board of education. Later these children were demoted to the elementary school of the latter's district. The appellant contends that having accepted his children for academic instruction the respondent board cannot give them another kind. In dismissing the appeal the commissioner addressed himself to an even larger audience than the litigants before him, when he said:

> The right of admission carries with it a responsibility to make use of the privileges granted. It would be entirely unreasonable to expect a community or the State to provide and maintain expensive school equipment and teachers for non-resident academic pupils who are either unwilling or unable to profit by the opportunities afforded. There is a feeling throughout the State that a not inconsiderable proportion of the high school students are failing to do the kind of work which justifies the expenditure which the State is making in their behalf. Both the State, which provides the funds, in part, for the instruction of non-resident academic pupils, and the local school authorities, who are responsible for the effective maintenance of the schools which such pupils attend, have the right and the power to insist upon a fair degree of accomplishment on the part of such pupils, and may provide for their classification or grading according to the work done by them.[211]

There are no modern cases involving the supervision of instruction in such a way as to be significant here. One early case, though an *ex parte* one, is worth quoting, however, to show the limitations which early state executives labored under, and at the same time to show how truly they were pointed in the right direction in the main. Local trustees applied to the superintendent of common schools for advice in a case where the inspectors of common schools had prescribed the number of hours children should spend on the different branches. The superintendent made reply that:

> The intention, however, so far as it can be gathered from the language of the law, was to give them (the inspectors of common schools) a general

[210] Matter of Appeal from Action of Trustees, etc., *supra*.

[211] Matter of Appeal of Van Tassell, 26 State Dept. Rept. 675 (1921).

supervision of the course of studies; and I think they should not, in ordinary cases, consider themselves called on to regulate mere details. Whether a child should read in one book or another, or write one line or six per day in his copy book, are matters which should be left to the teacher. The functions of the inspectors are of a higher order, and they should be content with exercising them according to the spirit of the law, from which their authority is derived. If the teacher is incompetent or unworthy of his place, they may annul his certificate; but they ought not to strip him of all authority by entering into the little arrangements of his school, and undertaking to determine the ability of each scholar to accomplish the particular task assigned to him. I do not wish to be understood, however, as intimating that the inspectors may not in case of any error on the part of the teacher in this respect point out and require him to correct it. The propriety of their interference must, as I have already observed, depend on the circumstances of the case.[212]

There is little to be said on the curriculum. Outside of health and physical training, it has been the subject of administrative regulation rather than statutory enactment. Much, anyway, is left to the discretion of the local community.[213] Where one of the by-products of a community's establishment of a domestic science course was the provision of free meals for the pupils, the commissioner sustained the local board's expenditure of money, not for free meals, but because foodstuffs had to be purchased to carry on the course.[214]

There was a time not so long ago when the extra-curricular activities of a school were well-nigh *extra* the school administrative authorities' control as well. In 1904 a case came before Commissioner Draper which necessitated the determination of the ultimate residence of control in the case of a student publication. While not altogether representative of the school, nevertheless, this particular publication purported to be so. When the student who was the leading spirit resisted the principal's effort to control the publication, he was suspended from school. An appeal from this action of the principal was taken. The decision handed down in the case is so characteristic of Commissioner Draper's sound educational statesmanship as well as his kindly manner that it is quoted somewhat at length:

[212] Trustees of School District No. —, Town of Warren, *ex parte,* Decs. Supt. Com. Sch., p. 180 (1834).

[213] Anonymous, Code of Pub. Instn. 1887, p. 605 (1887); Anonymous, Jud. Decs. 1294 (1880); Matter of Appeal of Niven *v.* School District, *Ibid.* 329 (1888); Matter of Board of Education, etc., 21 State Dept. Rept. 230 (1919).

[214] *Ibid.*

It seems to me that there can be no doubt about the legally constituted authorities of a school being wholly within their legal right in exercising control of the expressions and the business matters of a publication which is held out to represent the school. Not only are they legally warranted in doing it, but they are legally obligated to do it. Under the law they are charged with the duty of protecting the good name of the school; of keeping the organization free from whatever may discredit it, and of maintaining such a state of discipline among pupils as will insure harmony and effectiveness of procedure and accomplish the general ends for which the school is maintained.

The highest point of effectiveness is reached when this general principle is commonly assumed and the largest practicable freedom is accorded to the pupils; that is, when the pupils are capable of exercising the largest freedom without rebelling against the fact that in the last resort the legal and responsible governors of a school must govern.

There would be some pleasure in sustaining this energetic young manager, but he is in error. His error lies in the fact that he does not see, as he probably will when he is older, that a publication standing for the Monticello High School and appealing to the constituency of that school on that ground is not a private or personal affair. It becomes a public affair and so subject to public authority. The principal acted lawfully and moderately, firmly and wisely, and the board of education was correct in sustaining him.[215]

A somewhat different angle of the extra-curricular problem was presented several years later but it, too, received the same impress of the importance of keeping such matters well within the control of the school. Among other grievances of a teacher who had been dismissed from service was the fact that outside talent was brought in to aid the students in the preparation of a school entertainment instead of a demand being made on her services. Because she was regularly on the staff of the school she took this action as a distinct snub. Although Commissioner Draper sustained the board of education in its dismissal proceedings he threw out the caution that,

. . . it would be well to have all public school exercises of this character performed by those directly connected with the school. These exercises are given in the name of the school and stand for it and should be representative of its working forces, both pupils and teachers. If confined to these forces the authorities will avert such unpleasant and disagreeable community and school disturbances as occurred in this instance.[216]

The state department takes much the same attitude toward the choice of textbooks as it does toward the curriculum; it leaves it

[215] Matter of Appeal of Clark *v.* Board of Education, Jud. Decs. 94, 95 (1904).
[216] Matter of Application of Lamson, *Ibid.* 1091 (1906).

to local discretion.[217] In one instance it has passed on the question of what constitutes a textbook, holding a writing book to be such.[218] The state has had a law prohibiting frequent changes in textbooks which has been the subject of some litigation.[219] In one case the state superintendent pointed out that this law was neither aimed to benefit the publishers of books nor was it directed to prevent progress.[220] The commissioner will exercise a rigid scrutiny of textbook changes engineered by overzealous book agents.[221]

On the subject of school apparatus a citation that has only historical value can be cited. A very early case determined that "globes and apparatus" were not such necessary accessories as would legalize a tax therefor.[222] The regrets that the superintendent had in so advising this locality of course would be wholly unnecessary to-day.

In the early days of the commissioner's judicial power frequent demands were made on his advice with regard to the school district libraries.[223] Though one hardly ever finds the school library the subject of twentieth century appeals, it may be interesting to point out from one decision that the volumes of these early libraries were intended for the "intellectual improvement of the great body of the people, rather than to throw into school districts for the use of young persons works of a merely juvenile character."[224] This is quite a different idea from present school libraries, but then that was before the era of public libraries or other forms of adult education.

Only two precedents have resulted under the laws of the state providing for scholarships to higher institutions of learning. Both of these were formulated in the year 1890. In one case, Cornell University attempted to contend that mere failure of a scholarship holder to pass his university examinations did not constitute a

[217] Matter of Appeal of Chittendon *v.* Board of Education, Jud. Decs. 1227, 1231 (1887).

[218] Matter of Appeal of Ellsworth *v.* Board of Education, *Ibid.* 1232 (1888).

[219] Matter of Appeal of Chittendon *v.* Board of Education, *Ibid.* 1227 (1887); Matter of Appeal of Edson *v.* Board of Education, *Ibid.* 1222 (1887); Matter of Appeal of Curtiss, *Ibid.* 301 (1904).

[220] Matter of Appeal of Edson *v.* Board of Education, *Ibid.* 1222, 1225 (1887).

[221] Matter of Appeal of Curtiss, *Ibid.* 301 (1904).

[222] Trustees of School District No. —, Town of Arkport, *ex parte,* Decs Supt. Com. Schs., p. 280 (1834).

[223] See excerpts cited p. 328, Laws of N. Y., etc., and Digest of Decs.

[224] Commissioners of Common Schools, Town of Greene, *ex parte,* Decs. Supt. Com. Schs., p. 290 (1836).

permanent suspension from the privileges of the scholarship. The difficulty which the state superintendent found with this reasoning was that in as much as the suspension at best was indefinite, there might be a considerable interim when no ward of the state would be benefiting by the state's liberality. This he held against the public policy of the state which required that the scholarships always be filled. Consequently, he decided that any student who could not sustain himself beyond reasonable question would be obliged to give way to another who could.[225] In the second case, a first-year student of the City College of New York essayed the state scholarship examinations. His avenue to this bounty, however, was blocked when the superintendent held on appeal that candidates for these examinations were to be drawn only from the common schools and academies of the state, neither of which the City College of New York was.[226]

8. Religious Instruction in the Public Schools

The field of religious instruction, contrary to what one might expect, is one where the commissioner's judicial discretion is less hemmed in by legislative enactment than almost any other. For many years he had a clear field and it has only been since the end of the nineteenth century that the state constitution has given him such guidance as he has at the present time. That document now prohibits the devotion of public funds in aid of sectarian schools except for their examination and inspection.[227] But even before this provision was incorporated into the constitution, the superintendents of common schools and public instruction had taken precautions against an unsavory sectarianism in the schools. The first case, decided in 1839, has been sound enough to be controlling since. In an anonymous case of that date Superintendent Spencer laid down that religious services and instruction before the regular hour set for the opening of school were entirely proper providing that no one was compelled to attend. On the other hand, those refraining from attendance were enjoined to be careful not to interfere with those who wished the benefit from such projects.[228] Another anonymous decision in 1866 made more emphatic that regular school hours should not

[225] Matter of Appeal of McBarron *v.* Jasper, Jud. Decs. 984 (1890).
[226] Matter of Appeal of McBarron *v.* Jasper, *Ibid.* 984 (1890).
[227] Const., N. Y., art. 9, sec. 4.
[228] Jud. Decs. 526 (1839).

be used for religious instruction, especially when objected to, since the common schools were devoted to secular instruction and religious instruction was left to churches and Sunday schools.[229] Commissioner Graves has said comparatively recently that a teacher who persistently violates this fundamental state educational policy may subject himself to dismissal or even the revocation of his license.[230]

A very delicate variation of the facts already presented arose in the village of Suspension Bridge. There Catholic Sisters were teaching in one of the state aided schools. Although no religious services were conducted in the school nor any religious instruction given during school hours, nevertheless the sisters were at all times robed in the garb peculiar to their order and were addressed as "Sister." Objection was made to the superintendent of public instruction that this was as much a sectarian influence in the school as the holding of prayer or the reading of the scriptures. This point of view was sustained in one of the outstanding decisions of the department.[231] Superintendent Draper also took occasion in this case to condemn the preference which the board had shown for the class of teachers known as "Sisters" as an unfair discrimination against other eligibles. This he held to be a violation of the fundamental law of the state. A decade later Superintendent Skinner, in lending his unqualified approval to this earlier decision, made a further elaboration:

> To my mind, it is fundamental that teachers employed in the public schools of the State in fitting our children for useful citizens, should keep themselves in close touch with everything that will enhance their usefulness in this direction. To do this requires association with others engaged in like employment and familiarity with the every-day affairs of life with which the pupil in future years must battle for his own existence. They

[229] Jud. Decs. 527 (1866). Acc.: Anonymous, *Ibid.* 524 (1870); Matter of Appeal of Logue, *Ibid.* 527 (1909).

[230] Matter of Appeal from action of Board of Education, etc., 28 State Dept. Repts. 145 (1922).

[231] Matter of Appeal of Colt *v.* Board of Education, Jud. Decs. 533 (1887). Acc.: Matter of Appeal of Ferris *et al. v.* Sylvester, *Ibid.* 572 (1902); Matter of Appeal of Durant *et al. v.* Board of Education, *Ibid.* 538 (1896).

In Commissioners of Common Schools *v.* Windham, *ex parte,* Decs. Supt. Com. Schs. 231 (1835), the superintendent of common schools held against a minister of the gospel's becoming an inspector of schools.

In Proceedings for Removal of Members of Board of Education, 33 State Dept. Repts. 7 (1925), a physical education teacher, employed by the local board of education, taught several hours a week at a parochial school with the consent of his employers and during vacant periods. The commissioner refused to remove the board so long as the physical training work in the public school had not suffered.

should touch men and women in the multitudinous and intricate affairs of life which perplex and discipline us, and above all, the professional training which comes from association with educational representatives ought never to be barred from any teacher in the public schools. Transfers from one position to another, as the needs of a great city school system may require, ought always to be possible, and no teacher should be employed who owes such allegiance to any other institution, organization, or denomination as to make such transfers impossible.[232]

Public school buildings, themselves, because leased from a church whose own denominational buildings with their characteristic emblems and inscriptions were in close proximity, have also been held to convey a similar sectarian bias which will be sufficient to cause the superintendent of public instruction to hold against the lease.[233]

A widely different sort of religious case in the public schools arose during the World War. A Quakeress was charged with conduct unbecoming a teacher, because she considered it wrong to resist the invasion of this country by force, to urge her pupils to support the United States in the prosecution of the war, to abet the Red Cross in so far as it helped belligerency, and kindred concerns. She pleaded her religious scruples in defense of this conduct. None the less she was discharged. Her appeal from these proceedings was dismissed in masterful language cited from a war-time opinion in the Supreme Court:

> Where a person agrees with the state to perform a public duty she will not be excused from performance according to law merely because her religion forbids her doing so. While the petitioner may be entitled to the greatest respect for her adherence to her faith, she cannot be permitted because of it to act in a manner inconsistent with the peace and safety of the state.[234]

9. Discipline

The statutes composing the body of education law in the state have never spoken on the problem of school discipline. The penal code, however, lists the relation of teacher and pupil as one of the exceptions to the general prohibition against the exertion of force or violence toward the person of another, provided the force or violence be reasonable. Time was, though, when, as Superintendent Dix said, "The practice of inflicting corporal punishment upon scholars in any case whatever, has no sanction but usage.

[232] Matter of Appeal of Keyser *v.* Board of Education, Jud. Decs. 560, 562 (1898).
[233] Matter of Appeal of Durant *et al.* *v.* Board of Education, Jud. Decs. 538 (1896).
[234] Matter of Appeal of McDowell, 21 State Dept. Repts. 489, 491 (1919).

The teacher is responsible for maintaining good order, and he must be the judge of the degree and nature of the punishment required, where his authority is set at defiance; at the same time, he is liable to the party injured for any abuse of a prerogative which is wholly derived through custom." [235] This conception probably still holds. Consequent upon this state of affairs, rules and regulations governing matters of discipline are largely in the hands of local boards of education. Not only is it the duty of the teacher to conform to these, but it is charged upon the board to make none but such as are reasonable and will be sustained on appeal to the state department.[236]

This exposition leaves only the further question as to what is "reasonable" in either rules or in specific cases. A number of actual instances alone will illustrate this. To suspend a pupil from the privileges of school is, of course, among the most severe of disciplinary measures. All pupils are entitled to attend the common schools—are even compelled to do so since the compulsory attendance law—and therefore expulsion should only be resorted to in grave cases and where other means of correction have been tried and found unavailing.[237] Moral depravity,[238] violent insubordination threatening to disrupt the government of the whole school,[239] or grave contumacy,[240] will merit suspension. The same punishment might very well be imposed where a pupil damages school property, but to suspend him for refusing to pay a fine in the nature of damages for injury done goes too far.[241] Similarly a trustee was held to have abused his discretion in suspending a boy who refused to make an apology on his knees for an infraction of the school discipline.[242] Fully as unreasonable was a suspension of a girl just because her mother arranged her

[235] Trustees of School District No. 10, Town of Shawangunk, *ex parte,* Decs. Supt. Com. Schs., p. 101 (1833). Acc.: In the Matter of Petition of Fish, Jud. Decs. 492 (1894).

For appeals citing the penal code, see: Matter of Appeal of Mott *et al.* *v.* Board of Education, *Ibid.* 495 (1901); Matter of Stanbro, 30 State Dept. Rept. 633 (1924).

[236] In the matter of the petition of Fish, Jud. Decs. 492, 494 (1894).

[237] Anonymous, Decs. Supt. Com. Schs., p. 145 (1834); Matter of Appeal of Clark *v.* Board of Education, Jud. Decs. 1313 (1887); Matter of Appeal of Orth, 3 State Dept. Rept. (unofficial) 349 (1913).

[238] Anonymous, Code of Pub. Instn. 1856, p. 3 (1839).

[239] *Ibid;* Matter of Appeal of Clark *v.* Board of Education, Jud. Decs. 1313 (1887); Matter of Appeal of Brown *v.* Board of Education, *Ibid.* 517 (1888); Matter of Appeal of McAvoy, *Ibid.* 499 (1906).

[240] Matter of Appeal of Orth, 3 State Dept. Rept. (unofficial) 349 (1913).

[241] Anonymous, Jud. Decs. 514 (1873).

[242] Anonymous, *Ibid.* 515 (1872).

hair in a manner that did not suit the local trustee.[243] But if a child's breach of the school's rules is his parent's rather than his own fault, it will hardly be fair to punish the pupil with suspension.[244] An instance of a suspension that was sustained was a pupil's flat refusal to make his studying conform to the prescribed curriculum of the school.[245] If suspension is to be resorted to, it is probably well to consult the local administrative authorities first.[246] Corporal punishment is a very jealously guarded form of correction. The use of a small pine ruler or rubber tubing three-eighths of an inch in diameter on the approval of the board of education has been sustained.[247] It has been well decided, however, that the public has no right to call upon a teacher to match his physical powers against those of his pupils.[248] Merely to shove a pupil along the hall of the school has been held to constitute corporal punishment.[249] So mild a form of discipline, where the board had prohibited corporal punishment, as to require a pupil to attend one recitation rather than another would hardly be censured by the commissioner.[250] On the other hand, to order a pupil to sit next to a very hot stove as a punishment for whispering has been held an improper measure of correction for any offense.[251]

243 *Ibid.* 513 (1874).

244 Anonymous, Code of Pub. Instn. 1887, p. 603 (1875).

245 Anonymous, *Ibid.* 606 (1870).

246 Anonymous, Decs. Supt. Com. Schs., p. 145 (1834).

247 Matter of Petition of Fish, Jud. Decs. 492 (1894).

248 Matter of Appeal of Groom *v.* Hough, *Ibid.* 1188 (1888); Matter of Appeal of Brown *v.* Board of Education, *Ibid.* 517 (1888).

249 Matter of Appeal of Smith, 26 State Dept. Rept. 36 (1921).

250 Matter of Appeal of Lewis, 3 *Ibid.* (unofficial), 327 (1913).

251 Anonymous, Jud. Decs. 513 (1873). But examine the following decision where the petition was for the annulment of a teacher's license for "cruel and unusual" punishment.

"The severity of the punishment is conceded, but not to the extent nor in the manner charged. The facts appear to be that the pupil flatly refused to obey the teacher, by not taking the seat he was directed to take. The teacher came toward the boy, intending to compel him by force to take the seat assigned to him. The boy, with an oath, bade the teacher not to come near him, and, as the teacher approached, the boy struck at him several times. The teacher caught the boy, and with force put him in his seat, the boy meantime kicking, striking, yelling, and swearing. To stop this outrageous and unseemly noise the teacher took the most effectual means at his command; he intercepted the passage of air between the lungs and the vocal organs long enough to suppress the disturbance, but not long enough to injure the boy. But the boy was not subdued by any such gentle restraint, for no sooner was he left alone than he ran out of doors. The teacher pursued him, and brought him back to the schoolroom, not, it appears, without some considerable force, for the boy resisted with all his strength; and it would really not be strange if in the struggle he received some severe blows.

"And for this the Superintendent is asked to annul the certificate of the teacher.

While the school authorities have a complete disciplinary control over pupils in their charge during school hours, the same does not extend to out-of-school hours. Hence a suspension for leaving the school grounds during a noon recess was overruled on appeal.[252] Neither can pupils be censured for "attending parties" or "being absent from their rooms and studies at unusual and improper hours during school week." [253]

10. Social Class Lines

New York State has not been without its problems in social class conflict in its common school system. The influence of such stratifying forces as religion and politics has already been considered.[254] Color might be mentioned as another. On this point a very early case decided that, while the statute law made no prescription as to who might teach in the state-aided schools, nevertheless it was an unjustifiable exercise of authority for the trustee to select a colored teacher for a school of white children.[255] Whether the commissioner would feel himself bound by such a precedent at the present time in the light of constitutional amendments and the interpretations with which they have become overlaid, need not detain us here. Two appeals contemporary with the civil war period censured discrimination against colored children in the common schools.[256] A more recent decision than those already cited has approved a community's provision for different schools for the two races provided equal facilities are afforded each.[257]

The foreign-born have been another butt of discrimination which drew the following from the commissioner:

> It must be borne in mind . . . that in the public school, which is the most democratic of all institutions, the children of the foreign-born have equal rights and privileges with the children of native-born parents. It

"I decline to do anything of the kind. The teacher, in the matter of the boy, did no more than he was compelled to do; he might have done much more, and still be acquitted of inflicting cruel and unusual punishment. It was not cruel, and if it was unusual it was only so because the conduct of the boy was unusual." Anonymous, Laws of N. Y., etc., and Digest of Decs., p. 409 (1862).

[252] Matter of Appeal of Baldwin *v.* Streeter, Jud. Decs. 519 (1888).

[253] Anonymous, *Ibid.* 512 (1875).

[254] *Ante,* p. 118 ff.

[255] Anonymous, Jud. Decs. 1037 (1833).

[256] Anonymous. *Ibid.* 511 (1865); Anonymous, Laws of N. Y., etc., and Digest of Decs. p. 305 (1865).

[257] Matter of Appeal of Colored Residents, etc., 2 State Dept. Rept. (official) 613 (1914).

has always been held that no distinction shall be made in the character of instruction or treatment of any class of children attending the public schools. Questions of nationality may not enter into the determination of district boundaries as a controlling factor.[258]

The same principle applies in the case of discrimination against classes in our economic organization. Thus, the commissioner has refused to sanction creating a new district by dividing an old one where to do so would mean segregating the families of brick-yard workers from the rest of the community.[259] Finally, it is to be noted that the subventions from the state treasury are to go only in aid of public and not private schools. If a group wishes to maintain a school other than the one managed by the local public authorities, it must support it altogether by itself.[260]

11. School Sites

A very early *ex parte* opinion of the superintendent of common schools advised certain local trustees that if the owner of the site which they had selected for a school building would not sell it, they were without a remedy.[261] Of course the statute law has long since changed this situation, but the decision may be interesting as a reflection of a day when the school had not yet gained recognition as a public enterprise entitling the trustees to take advantage of the public's right of eminent domain.

> It has never been the policy of the Education Department to determine what site should be selected for a new building. This is a matter to be determined by the people themselves. On appeal cases . . . the general policy has been established by a long line of decisions that the . . . (department) . . . will not say what site must be selected; it will only determine what site shall not be selected.[262]

While the commissioner speaks judicially in this fashion, actually he will not hesitate to designate a site if asked to by the parties concerned.[263] The power to condemn a school site is not

[258] Matter of Appeal from Order of District Superintendent, 28 State Dept. Rept. 94, 97-98 (1922).

[259] Matter of Division of School District, etc., 2 *Ibid.* (official) 644 (1914).

[260] Inhabitants, etc. *v.* Trustees, Decs. Supt. Com. Schs., p. 55 (1829); Inhabitants of School District No. —, Town of Cairo, *ex parte,* Decs. Supt. Com. Schs., 119 (1833); Anonymous, Jud. Decs. 136 (1859).

[261] Trustees School District No. 4, Town of Hounsfield, Decs. Supt. Com. Schs., 26 (1828).

[262] Matter of Erecting a New School Building, 12 State Dept. Repts. 412, 421 (1917); Acc.: Anonymous, Laws of N. Y., etc., and Digest of Decs. 1866, p. 370 (1858); Anonymous, Code of Pub. Instn. 1887, p. 646 (1881); Matter of Appeal of Certain Residents, etc., Jud. Decs. 316, 317 (1905).

[263] Matter of Erecting a New School Building, 12 State Dept. Repts. 413 (1917).

included in a school commissioner's authority to condemn a school building; he may only advise.[264]

Since the selection of school sites is not the subject of administrative regulation as are school buildings, it may be well to mention here some of the attributes of a good site as they have been laid down in various decisions. Of course it should be centrally located so as to be easily accessible to as many children as possible.[265] The more grounds about it the better, especially if instruction in agricultural subjects is to be given.[266] If a community wishes to have its school building stand as an expression of its tastes, views, and judgment, and is going to spend enough money to make it such, the site certainly should be a "commanding and conspicuous" one.[267] Just as the statutes require that school buildings meet certain sanitary requirements, so should local authorities be guided by the same principles in the selection of school sites.[268] Where highways and tracks of public utilities must be crossed on the way to and from school, a decent regard must be had for the safety of the children exposed to these dangers.[269] In rural communities the fact that the site contains a good well will carry much weight.[270] And shade trees will always be a criterion of a desirable site.[271] Fencing the school property will generally follow the usual rules applied in court as to division fences.[272]

The most significant thing that the commissioner has said regarding a reasonable price to pay for a school site follows:

[264] Matter of Appeal of Ives, 2 State Dept. Repts. (official), 610 (1914); Anonymous, Code Pub. Instn. 1887, p. 655 (1879).

[265] Matter of Appeal from Order Dissolving School Districts, 6 State Dept. Repts. 521, 523 (1915); Matter of Erecting New School Buildings, 12 Ibid. 413 (1917).

[266] Matter of Appeal from Order Dissolving School Districts, 6 *Ibid.* 521, 523 (1915); 12 *Ibid.* 413, 420 (1917); Matter of Appeal of Certain Electors of School District, Jud. Decs. 918 (1907). In the sale of a portion of too extensive premises the department will scrutinize the proceedings to see that the community does not part with valuable rights. Cf. Matter of Appeal of Maidment, 3 State Dept. Repts. (official), 535 (1914); Matter of Appeal of Joralemon, 21 State Dept. Repts. 484 (1919); Anonymous, Code of Pub. Instn. 1887, p. 655 (1868).

[267] Matter of Erecting New School Buildings, 12 State Dept. Repts. 413, 420 (1917).

[268] Matter of Appeal of Van Sickle, Jud. Decs. 921 (1905).

[269] Matter of Appeal of Van Sickle, *Ibid.*

[270] Matter of Appeal of Van Sickle, Jud. Decs. 921, 922 (1905). A district may bargain away the well's surplus that would otherwise stand on the school grounds; Matter of Petition of Beach, Ann. Rept. State Ed. Dept. 1912, p. 477 (1911).

[271] Matter of Appeal of Van Sickle, Jud. Decs. 921 (1905); Matter of Appeal of Decker *et al.*, *Ibid.* 793 (1907).

[272] Anonymous, Code of Pub. Instn. 1887, p. 655 (1866); Matter of Appeal of Hodges *v.* Brown, Jud. Decs. 799 (1890).

. . . property is worth no more for manufacturing, hotel, or other business purposes than it is worth for school purposes. A school district may reasonably pay for a school site as much as an individual or a corporation may pay for such site or similar sites for business purposes.[273]

12. School Buildings

It is now settled policy in New York State that communities must own their school buildings except in the case of temporary exigency. Time was, however, when other counsels obtained. Before the public school gained the prestige it has in the popular mind at the present time, various arrangements for school facilities were contested before the department in its judicial capacity. One of the earliest, and one significant of the principle later to preponderate, arose in a community where the inhabitants had gone into partnership with a local academy for the erection of a schoolhouse. The state superintendent refused to confirm these proceedings because it prevented the district from having entire control of the building for the purposes of the local common school.[274] While this decision was probably the outgrowth of divided administrative control of education in the state,[275] and while it would hardly be possible to-day—unless the academy were a private one—it nevertheless lays down an important precedent, namely, that the local school authorities should aim at complete control of their school property.

Only a few years later Superintendent Spencer swerved from this rule by permitting district trustees to pay rent for the land on which they were about to build a schoolhouse by building a two-story house and permitting the lessor, the local Protestant church, to use the upper floor when the school was not in session.[276] It should be noted that while this case deviates from the earlier one it does not contradict it. The principle of control is maintained here, for the lease gave the district trustees uninterrupted enjoyment of the building during school hours and of the classroom downstairs, apparently, at all times. In 1874 Superintendent Gilmore seems to have taken an opposite view of such an arrangement, but, as the report of his decision is so scant as not to show the terms of the agreement, it is difficult to appraise

[273] Matter of Appeal of Hall *et al., Ibid.* 911 (1905).
[274] Bank of Orleans *v.* Trustees, etc., Jud. Decs. 803 (1835).
[275] *Ante,* p. 4 f.
[276] Anonymous, Code of Pub. Instn. 1856, p. 3 (1839).

it.[277] Up to almost the close of the century, the statutes of the state were not very articulate on this problem although they did clearly recognize the right of the community to lease its school facilities.[278] As far as the conditions of the lease were concerned the annotations of the school code published in 1887 show the departmental policy to have been a composite of these early decisions. Thus, it did favor a community's owning its own building to insure complete control. But if its means were too scant, no objection was interposed to an arrangement like the one that Superintendent Spencer passed upon, namely: a lease covenanting for control of the entire building during school hours, unqualified possession at all times of the schoolroom, etc.[279]

The Appeal of Durant v. Board of Education,[280] decided by Superintendent Skinner in 1896, is the next source of light on the evolution of departmental policy. There the lease of a building used for public school purposes was under fire because it ran from one of the local church denominations and because the appellants did not think that the school so maintained was entirely free from sectarian influences. When the respondent board cited its statutory right to lease buildings, Superintendent Skinner made the qualification that:

> . . . such provisions have never been held to authorize school authorities to lease rooms except temporarily to supply the lack of schoolhouses and rooms in buildings the property of the district, or during a time when the district does not own sufficient school accommodations, and pending action on the part of the school authorities or the inhabitants of the district to supply such deficiency.[281]

This opinion sounded the death knell of the custom of long and continued leasing of property for school purposes. While leases may have been drawn to give the public school authorities an appropriate control of the school premises, yet the decision of this appeal brings strongly to the foreground for the first time that covenants for control will not compare in the long run with possession of the fee. Leasing was, therefore, relegated to a temporary expediency. Judging from earlier precedents it is diffi-

[277] Anonymous, Code of Pub. Instn. 1887, p. 583 (1874).

[278] E.g., Laws of N. Y. 1864, as amended to 1889, ch. 555, title 7, sec. 15.

[279] Code of Pub. Instn. 1887, pp. 258-60. See also: Matter of Appeal of Girvan, Jud. Decs. 954 (1889).

[280] Jud. Decs. 538 (1896). Cf. Matter of Appeal of Colt *v.* Board of Education, Jud. Decs. 533 (1887).

[281] *Ibid.* p. 546.

cult to agree with Superintendent Skinner that this always had been the departmental policy, unless to say so is but another way of asserting that the department had always encouraged ownership of school buildings. After determining that no temporary emergency existed in West Troy, the superintendent decided against the lease on the further grounds that insufficient control of the buildings was reserved in it and that the building was not entirely free from sectarian influences. Two years later, another case involving these same issues arose again. After finding that the community could and should afford school buildings of its own, Superintendent Skinner once more asserted the necessity of undisputed ownership of school buildings by local school authorities. This time, however, he rested the requirement, not on uncontradicted precedent as he had before, but on an intent which he had gleaned from the revision of the education laws in 1894.[282] Just what provisions he had in mind and why he did not cite them in the earlier decision in 1896 he does not set out. The similarity of the statute before and after 1894 makes one wonder the more. The judicial policy of these last two decisions, nevertheless, remains the present one, and is incorporated in no indefinite language in the present statute.[283] There seems little doubt but that this is a sound working principle.

To allow some one to live in part of the school building as a dwelling is open to the same objections already mentioned.[284] Yet, on the other hand, where a school building in a secluded position had suffered from the invasions of marauders at night, the state superintendent was only too glad to allow the janitor the privilege of living there to protect it.[285]

Another aspect of school buildings that has afforded not a little litigation before the commissioner is the provision of the school laws permitting the school commissioner to condemn school buildings when they have become wholly inadequate for the purposes for which they were originally intended. In the first place, this power has been rightly held a very summary one and only to be exercised where a district is unwilling to provide a proper and

[282] Matter of Appeal of Kennedy *et al. v.* Board of Ed., Jud. Decs. 554 (1897).

[283] Laws of N. Y., 1910, amended to 1925, ch. 140, secs. 275 and 310. See also: Matter of Appeal of Roche, 26 State Dept. Repts. 217 (1921); Matter of Appeal of Rawley, 22 State Dept. Repts. 392 (1920).

[284] Tyler *et al., ex parte,* Decs. Supt. Com. Schs., 51 (1829).

[285] Matter of Appeal of Greene *et al. v.* School District No. 8, Jud. Decs. 845 (1887).

suitable school building.[286] It has been said that "a schoolhouse is not 'worth repairing' within the meaning of the statute, when it is so dilapidated or inadequate that it cannot be repaired to meet the requirements of the law and the regulations of this department, within the sum which must be expended for the erection of a new building sufficient for the needs of the district." [287] But to condemn a building merely because it is "wholly inadequate to accommodate the pupils attending" is obviously short of the statute because it gives no indication whether "repairing" might not make it quite adequate.[288] Again, condemnation proceedings should be referred to the conditions existing at the date of condemnation and not to some contemplated future conditions, for example, an anticipated consolidation.[289] While the commissioner has realized that he cannot criticize a trustee for not submitting a contract for repairs to bids, yet, where the amount of money involved is great, he has recommended that this be done.[290] It was early settled that the mere fact that the school building might be out of repair was no excuse for not opening any school at all.[291]

The size, design, orientation, and like matters of school building construction have long been subject by statute to the regulations of the state department. They are not, however, the matter of frequent appeal. A few items, nevertheless, are significant. The department has definitely decided that in anticipation of future growth a community is justified in erecting a larger school building than present needs require.[292] In Matter of Erecting a New School Building, etc., an objection was raised to the way the plans adopted in a district meeting had been so altered, when submitted to the state department for approval, that they no longer could be considered the plans that had been submitted to the district.[293] The overruling of this objection will show again how far the center of gravity has shifted from localities to the state in educational matters.

[286] Matter of Appeal of Scott *et al.*, 4 State Dept. Repts. (unofficial) 588 (1914); Anonymous, Code of Pub. Instn. 1887, p. 629 (1869); Matter of Appeal of Mathewson *v.* Thompson, Jud. Decs. 852 (1894).

[287] Matter of Appeal of Arnold *et al.*, 1 State Dept. Repts. (official) 537, 538 (1914); Acc.: Appeal of Ives, 2 *Ibid.* (official) 610 (1914).

[288] Matter of Appeal of Barney *v.* Burdick, Jud. Decs. 850 (1902).

[289] Matter of Appeal of Scott *et al.*, 4 State Dept. Repts. (official) 588 (1914).

[290] Matter of Appeal of Gonyo, 22 State Dept. Repts. 573 (1920).

[291] Anonymous, Laws of N. Y., etc., and a Digest of Decs. 1866, p. 359 (1858).

[292] Matter of Appeal of Reese *et al.* *v.* School District No. 15, Jud. Decs. 832 (1887); Cf. Matter of Appeal of Austin *et al.* *v.* Humphrey, *Ibid.* 1291 (1891).

[293] 12 State Dept. Repts. 413 (1917).

As is commonly known, school bonds are issued to pay for the school site and the school building, but a separate appropriation must be made for school equipment. The validation of school bonds was contested in one instance because the resolution voting the bonds included "fixtures" as well. On this the commissioner said:

> . . . it has been held that ordinary school furniture does not constitute a part of the building; but that furniture that is built into the walls or that is otherwise so related to the building that it must be treated as a permanent fixture properly falls within the purposes for which a school district's bonds may be issued and sold.[294]

There are a number of decisions where a school commissioner's order that a district install new and modern equipment has been contested.[295] The school commissioner's order in this case is a summary one, like his order condemning school buildings as beyond repair, and usually not exercised unless he has a clear-cut case. Consequently, the state commissioner of education will generally be found to support him. While fifty years ago the superintendent of public instruction could find no authority in the school law whereby a district might purchase an organ for its school, it is quite probable that he could find such authority to-day.[296]

Only one decision was found concerning the insurance of school buildings against fire.[297] The appeal there was from a vote of the district to apply the proceeds of a policy toward general expenses. The commissioner was of the mind that this sum of money should only be so used where the replacement of the school building and school property had first been cared for.

13. Use of the School Plant for Other Than School Purposes

For many years the school laws dealt only inferentially with the problem of using the school building for other than strictly school purposes. The statute put the building in the custody of the local authorities and the implication was that their custody

[294] Application of Board of Education, 20 State Dept. Repts. 199, 202 (1919).

[295] Matter of Appeal of Folts *et al.* *v.* Knapp, Jud. Decs. 792 (1838); Matter of Appeal of Pond *v.* Conlon, *Ibid.* 788 (1893); Petition of Ryther, *Ibid.* 786 (1898); Matter of Appeal of Moss, etc., 2 State Dept. Repts. (unofficial) 393 (1913).

[296] Anonymous, Code of Pub. Instn. 1887, p. 583 (1872).

[297] Matter of Appeal from Action of District Meeting, etc., 26 State Dept. Rept. 434 (1921).

was for the purposes enumerated in the school laws. As other than educational matters were not mentioned there, a strict construction of the laws practically made it incumbent upon the commissioner and his predecessors to hold against the many demands that were made on local authorities for the use of the school plant out of school hours. Such a rigid interpretation, however, never gained favor. Almost from the very start permission was given to use the schoolhouse for other activities, especially religious activities.[298] As stated in a later day, though, when the state was still largely agricultural:

> Frequently in the rural districts, the schoolhouse is the only suitable place in the district for holding a meeting of any character and such policy has greatly promoted the convenience as well as the intellectual and moral activity of the district.[299]

Yet the permission has been hedged about with some restrictions. In an *ex parte* opinion tendered in the year 1833, Superintendent Dix founded a rule of policy which in the main has been followed as precedent to the present time. After recognizing the results of a strict reading of the statute, Superintendent Dix goes on to say,

> I do not consider the voice of a majority of the inhabitants of a district as a proper criterion for determining the propriety of applying a schoolhouse to other uses than those for which it was designed. The law has determined this question. It can not with strict propriety be applied to other than common school purposes. It may be otherwise used by the general consent of the parties interested. But if such use were likely to distract the district, by breeding dissensions, and a respectable minority should apply to me for an order to confine the schoolhouse to its legitimate purposes, I should not consider myself at liberty to deny the application.[300]

Even after the legislature had directed that those wishing to use the school plant for other than school purposes must first gain the consent of all the trustees and then use the school only for the purpose of "giving and receiving instruction in any branch of education or learning or in the science or practice of music," the state department still maintained the policy laid down by Superintendent Dix, of deviating from the statute and recognizing other uses if not objected to.[301] The statute was not a dead letter, how-

[298] E.g., Trustees School District No. 3, Town of Massena, *ex parte,* Decs. Supt. Com. Schs., 91 (1832).

[299] Code of Pub. Instn. etc., and Digest of Decs. p. 641 (1887).

[300] Trustees of School District No. 4, Town of Champion, *ex parte,* Decs. Supt. Com. Schs., 99 (1833); also reported in Jud. Decs. 877.

[301] In the Matter of Appeal of Baker *v.* Hull, Jud. Decs. 878 (1887).

ever, for when it was attempted on appeal to justify a Sunday school in the schoolhouse on the ground that it taught the history and geography of the ancient world, the superintendent of public instruction refused to be misled as to the true character of the instruction.[302] If an organization is successful in gaining the use of the schoolhouse, it will be responsible, and not the public, for the lighting and heating of the building during use and also for sweeping and cleaning afterwards.[303] If any damage is done to the school premises as a result of the occupation, the trustee will be liable,[304] for not only is he responsible for granting permission for their use, but he is their custodian as well. At first it was thought that no one, not even on appeal to the superintendent of public instruction, could compel local authorities to give permission for extraordinary use of the school premises, because, in spite of the precedents of the state department, the statute did not require them to.[305] More recent legislation, however, has specifically made this discretion appealable to the commissioner.[306] Although this same legislation has also increased the number of enumerated uses to which the school plant may be put out of school hours, the basic criterion still remains the same. Its latest enunciation by Commissioner Graves, where the American Civil Liberties Union sought permission from the board of education to use a school building to discuss "old-fashioned free speech" and was refused, is worth quoting:

> While I recognize the importance of both religion and politics, as well as many other activities, yet, no matter how worthy the object or how just the cause for which the use of the school buildings is sought, the use should not be granted if there is any probability that it will be resented by a considerable number of the people of the district, village, or city. It would be better to err on the side of exclusion than on that of inclusion.
>
> The question before us in this matter is not the sanctity of free speech. We all believe in free speech within the limits of the Constitution and the law. Nor is it so much a question of the definition of free speech. Its limitations have been settled by the highest court in the land.

[302] *Ibid.*

[303] Matter of Appeal of Smith *v.* Conklin, Jud. Decs. 882 (1896); Trustees School District No. 9, Town of Paris, *ex parte,* Decs. Supt. Com. Schs., 289 (1836).

[304] Matter of Appeal of Kennedy, 2 State Dept. Repts. (official) 625 (1914).

[305] Anonymous, Jud. Decs. 525 (1860); Anonymous, *Ibid.* 525 (1862).

[306] For at least two cases where local authorities were overruled by the commissioner, see: Matter of Appeal of Vernon High School Alumni Association, 15 State Dept. Repts. 476 (1918); Matter of Appeal from Action of Trustees, etc., 33 *Ibid.* 118 (1925).

The real question, then, is whether the use by the American Civil Liberties Union of the Stuyvesant High School in the City of New York for a meeting to discuss "old-fashioned free speech" is such a use as will promote the welfare of the schools in that city, or whether it is such an activity as, like religion and politics, should be debarred from the public schools and left to be sponsored by other institutions.[307]

14. Formation, Alteration, and Dissolution of School Districts

In the early days of the New York State common school system, appeals arising out of disputes concerning the formation and alteration of school districts were among the most numerous that the state superintendents were called upon to adjudicate. Indeed, they remained so as long as unoccupied parts of the state were being settled by an ever-expanding population. Of course the factor which gave prominence to so apparently unimportant a professional matter was the fact that the district unit had a large office in the apportionment of the state common school fund. Some of the general principles on which superintendents and commissioners have operated in the disposition of these cases are to be noted here, but it should be borne in mind that the element of fact, rather than law, is so large in this type of case that a number of cases should be read to gain a firm grasp of the application of the principles.

By 1841 the rather obvious though none the less important dictum had been made that, "The formation and alteration of school districts must be guided by a sound judgment upon various facts

[307] *New York Times,* Dec. 6, 1926. *Illustrating the above principles further: Religion:* Anonymous, Jud. Decs. 525 (1862); Matter of Appeal of Cogan *et al. v.* Coolidge, *Ibid.* 880 (1888); Matter of Appeal of Shettler *v.* Angel, *Ibid.* 880 (1898); Anonymous, Code of Pub. Instn. etc., and Decs. Relating to Com. Schs. 1887, p. 608 (1870); Anonymous, Code Pub. Instn. 1856, p. 70 (1855); Matter of Appeal of Kennedy, 2 State Dept. Rept. (official) 625 (1914). *Politics:* Matter of Appeal of Smith *v.* Conklin, *Ibid* 882 (1896); Matter of Appeal of Griggs *et al.,* 3 State Dept. Repts. (unofficial) 337 (1913). *For private tuition students:* Matter of Appeal of Baker *v.* Board of Education, Jud. Decs. 1330 (1889). *Temperance societies:* LeFever *v.* Milgate, Jud. Decs. 890 (1887); Matter of Appeal of Mayer *v.* Barnes, *Ibid.* 887 (1896); Trustees School District No. 14, Town of Catlin, *ex parte,* Decs. Supt. Com. Schs., 156 (1834). *Music and entertainment:* Matter of Appeal of Twiss *et al. v.* McCutcheon *et al.,* Jud. Decs. 899 (1901); Matter of Appeal of Freer *v.* Van Aken, *Ibid.* 903 (1891); Matter of Appeal from the Action of Trustees, 31 State Dept. Rept. 447 (1924). *Woman's club:* Matter of Appeal of Women's Civic Club, etc., 31 State Dept. Rept. 396 (1924). *Mother's Club:* Matter of Appeal from the Action of Trustees, 33 *Ibid.* 118 (1925). *School alumni association:* Matter of Appeal of Vernon High School Alumni Association, 15 State Dept. Rept. 476 (1918). *Fraternal Organizations:* Anonymous, Code of Pub. Instn. etc., and Decs. Relating to Com. Schs. 1887, p. 630 (1869); Matter of Appeal of Johnson *v.* Winston, Jud. Decs. 894 (1895).

and circumstances, such as the number of children, the amount of taxable property, the extent of territory, and the convenience of the inhabitants." [308] Superintendent Benton spoke more definitely a few years later, when he declared it a "uniform rule" not to permit the formation of new districts having less than thirty-five to forty children between five and sixteen years of age and not to sanction any alteration that would reduce the number of pupils below what had been found sufficient to give full employment to a competent teacher.[309] The support that might be expected for the teacher's salary from the "rate bill" probably influenced this working principle.[310] But at a later day Superintendent Ruggles had to warn a litigant that there was no departmental precedent defining the number of taxpayers that would be requisite to authorize the setting up of a new district.[311] Superintendent Benton's "uniform rule" was repudiated by Superintendent Crooker for he claimed that there was nothing in the statutes or departmental rules that defined any prerequisite number of children for either the formation or maintenance of a district school.[312] Although perhaps not well informed in departmental precedents on this point, Superintendent Crooker seems to have stated the better working hypothesis. As was pointed out in the preceding chapter,[313] it is indispensable for the individualized application of the educational laws that the department avoid circumscribing its discretion in advance on matters that vary so much from case to case. But not always does the creation of a new district depend upon a minimum school population. Sometimes it may hinge on a community's independence and isolation from already existing school facilities.[314] To urge the creation of a new district by cutting an old one in two, just because one part has urban interests and the other rural, was frowned on recently because the commissioner held the diversity of occupations an advantage rather than a disadvantage to the community.[315] Apart from such reasons he has opposed bisecting a single village into two school districts. Running a division line

[308] Anonymous, Jud. Decs. 7, 8 (1841).

[309] Anonymous, Code of Pub. Instn. 1856, p. 57 (1847).

[310] Anonymous, Code of Pub. Instn. 1856, p. 5 (1839).

[311] Anonymous, Code of Pub. Instn. 1887, p. 560 (1884).

[312] Matter of Appeal of Kane *v.* Pollard, Jud. Decs. 757 (1895).

[313] *Ante,* p. 38 ff; 43 f.

[314] Matter of Long Beach, etc., 1 State Dept. Rept. (unofficial) 425 (1912).

[315] Matter of Appeal from Refusal of District Superintendent, etc., 28 State Dept. Rept. 449 (1922).

arbitrarily through the center of a community serves no good end.[316] Similarly, it has been found undesirable to have a district lie in more than one county.[317]

Even after districts had been formed in the early days, disputes were not infrequent as to such a formal existence of them as would entitle them to share in state school funds. Sometimes the written records of districts became lost; sometimes the legal formalities of forming a new district never had been perfected. Yet such conditions might well be expected in a frontier state. The state superintendent early created a precedent making allowances in this direction by recognizing the validity of a district if for a number of years it had been commonly so treated.[318] If the very existence of districts was hazy, it can well be imagined that their boundaries were no less so. On this point the department has been more strict. In describing territory which is to form a new district or be annexed to another district, it is prescribed that the description "should be so complete and definite that a surveyor, at any future day, may run its boundaries without reference to any other document than the order forming, altering, or describing the territory." [319] Natural and permanent monuments and distances by rod and chain should be given rather than perishable and transitory marks as ownership of the soil, etc.

Throughout the history of the district system in New York State there has been a constant pressure exerted on district boundaries to shape them now this way and now that. It was early established as precedent, however, that any alteration of boundaries is to be referred to the resulting educational conditions of the districts concerned and not the personal or temporary preference of some one of the residents.[320] The point of reference may also be the future educational needs of the community as well

[316] Matter of Appeal of Keller *et al.* *v.* Whitcomb, Jud. Decs. 638 (1887).

[317] Matter of Appeal of Thomson *et al.* *v.* Harris, Jud. Decs. 605, 606 (1889).

[318] Inhabitants of Joint School District No. 13, Towns of Rome and Lee *v.* Commissioners of Common Schools, Jud. Decs. 746 (1834); Trustees of School District No. 13, Town of Edmeston *v.* Commissioners of Common Schools, Decs. Supt. Com. Schs., p. 79 (1831).

[319] Matter of Appeal of Rickmyer *et al.* *v.* Davis, Jud. Decs. 627, 628 (1897); Matter of Appeal of Cole *v.* Davis, *Ibid.* 1359 (1902).

[320] Trustees of School District No. 20, Town of New Paltz *v.* Commissioners of Common Schools, Decs. Supt. Com. Schs., p. 255 (1835); Anonymous, Laws of N. Y. etc., and Digest of Decs., p. 320 (1857); Anonymous, Code of Pub. Instn. 1887, p. 532 (1879); Anonymous, *Ibid.* (1883); Anonymous, *Ibid.* (1885); Matter of Appeal of Greenan *v.* Pollard, Jud. Decs. 616 (1895); Matter of Appeal of Van Deusen *et al.*, Jud. Decs. 648 (1907).

as the immediate ones.[321] The alteration of boundaries is not to be resorted to as an expediency for ridding a district of a troublesome resident, for such a policy would permit one under guise of a quarrel to gain his mere personal ends in being set off to an adjoining district.[322] Of course it goes without saying that a trustee will not be permitted to assent to such an alteration of his district as will settle him in another district, thus vacating his office.[323] Probably the most conspicuous and underlying consideration in the alteration of district boundaries is the financial one. The problem of strong and weak districts runs through most of the cases cited above with usually inferior schools in the weak districts and relatively lighter tax burdens in the strong districts. Since New York State is committed to the district system, and since the policy of consolidation has only been energetically pushed in the last decade or so, it early became precedent to prevent alterations of district boundaries which would weaken already weak districts, when it was not clearly shown that by so doing the persons occupying the transferred territory would enjoy greater convenience.[324] Peculiarly, though perhaps rightly enough, the department refused to sanction alterations which had as their sole motive the equalization of tax burdens.[325] The superintendent of public instruction feared that if he were to adopt any other policy there would be such a constant struggle for the annexation of property that the people of the state would be involved in endless controversy. Certainly, in this respect, equalization of tax burdens is more satisfactorily brought about by consolidation rather than alteration of districts, for then there is not the bitter competition.

In an important decision of Superintendent Ruggles in 1883, it was determined that no alteration of a district's boundaries would be equitable where that district had an outstanding bond

[321] Matter of Appeal of Trustees, etc., 6 State Dept. Rept. 557 (1915).

[322] Anonymous, Laws of N. Y. etc., and Digest of Decs., p. 321 (1859).

[323] Anonymous, Code of Pub. Instn. 1887, p. 545 (1885); Matter of Appeal of Ward *et al.* *v.* Wells, Jud. Decs. 600 (1890); Matter of Appeal of Sawyer *et al.* *v.* Chick, *Ibid.* 601 (1900).

[324] Matter of Appeal of Saunders *v.* Benedict, Jud. Decs. 599 (1700); Matter of Appeal of Parks *et al.* *v.* Wardner, *Ibid.* 603 (1888); Matter of Appeal of Parsons *v.* Barr, *Ibid.* 619 (1890); Matter of Appeal of De Clercq *et al.*, *Ibid.* 1353 (1896); Matter of Appeal of Rickmyer *et al* *v.* Davis, *Ibid.* 627 (1897); cf. Matter of Alteration of Districts, etc., 1 State Dept. Rept. (unofficial) 408 (1912).

[325] Van Dyne *v.* Smith, Jud. Decs. 662 (1886); Matter of Appeal of Wilson, *Ibid.* 630 (1896); Matter of Appeal of De Clercq *et al.*, *Ibid.* 1353 (1896).

issue.[326] But wherein lies the absence of equity? Almost inescapably one surmises that Superintendent Ruggles had in mind the possibility of an increased tax rate in so much of the old district as would have been left unaltered. Superintendent Draper seemed to think it lay in a different direction. He thought it consisted in permitting the set-off section to escape a just burden of taxation. Whichever view is taken becomes important in the disposition of the hypothetical case he states in the Appeal of Sagendorph *et al.,* v. Drumm.[327] While in that case Superintendent Draper affirmed and applied Superintendent Ruggles' decision, yet he hinted that if the set-off area would have to bear a bonded indebtedness in its new situation, there would be no case for the application of the anonymous precedent of 1883. But next, what of the section of a district which presumably had no outstanding indebtedness when it was transferred to one that had such indebtedness? Could it object to being required to aid in paying off the indebtedness incurred for the erection of a new school building? This proposition has been decided in the affirmative; perhaps the newcomers did not have a vote in incurring the burden, but they will participate in its benefit and therefore should share the former as well as the latter.[328] If the school building has already been paid for by the time a territorial addition is acquired, there is at least *ex parte* authority for saying that that liquidated obligation will not be reopened to require the new inhabitants to assume a part.[329] Finally, what are the rights of the set-off area to school property in the old district which they had helped to pay for before separation? Apparently none, not even where a contract exists for the division of school property.[330] If, however, a district is divided up and annexed to others so that a complete dissolution of the old district occurs, the latter's former school property will be sold, debts deducted, and a pro rata partition of the proceeds among tax-payers take place. But this is a statutory remedy.[331] In these latter circumstances, one who moves into the district

[326] Anonymous, Code of Pub. Instn. 1887, p. 559 (1883).

[327] Jud. Decs. 655, 656 (1891).

[328] Appeal of Pendleton, *Ibid.* 707 (1907); Matter of Appeal from Action of Board of Education, etc., 34 State Dept. Repts. 591 (1926).

[329] Cooper *et al., ex parte,* Decs. Supt. Com. Schs., 32 (1829).

[330] Commissioners of Common Schools, etc., *v.* Commissioners, etc., Decs. Supt. Com. Schs., p. 55 (1829); Matter of Appeal of Riley *et al.,* Jud. Decs. 666 (1890). But see a dictum in Anonymous, Laws of N. Y. etc. and Digest of Decs., p. 328 (1865).

[331] Laws of N. Y. 1847, ch. 480, sec. 50; continued in modified form in Laws of 1910, ch. 140, sec. 138, as amended to 1925.

after the construction and payment of the building, but prior to partition and dissolution, will be entitled to share if he is a taxpayer.[332]

A problem of some historical interest arose in those districts which before the modern era of school financing had built up school funds of their own, the income from which was used to defray the expenses of the local support of education. One such district subsequently was formed into a joint district and then the issue arose whether it would have to share its frugality with its sister district. The state superintendent held in the negative.[333] One cannot help but wonder how many, if any, of these independent funds still exist to-day.

If a school district is too weak to maintain an efficient school, its annulment will be sustained on appeal.[334] A want of interest on the part of the inhabitants in maintaining a school will result in the same fate for the district.[335] Such a condition will not be held to exist, however, just because a majority of the inhabitants of the district are in favor of dissolving the district or discontinuing the school. If a respectable minority wish a school near home and the district is financially able to support it, an appeal by this group will be sustained.[336] Of course to dissolve a district in order that its school may become the practice department of a state normal school is quite proper.[337]

15. Consolidation of Districts

As every one knows, the large versus the small unit of administration for local schools has been an issue in our educational system ever since the American educational renaissance of the early nineteenth century. While New York State still had a frontier, and before the era of the automobile and macadamized highways, it is quite natural that the tendency in the state should have been toward division and multiplication of districts rather

[332] Commissioners of Common Schools, Town of Henderson, *ex parte,* Decs. Supt. Com. Schs., p. 246 (1835).

[333] Commissioners of Common Schools, Town of Edmeston, *ex parte, Ibid.* 124 (1833).

[334] Anonymous, Laws of N. Y. etc., and Digest of Decs., p. 324 (1859); Anonymous, Code of Pub. Instn. 1887, p. 551 (1880).

[335] Matter of Contracts for Instruction of Pupils, 1 State Dept. Rept. (official) 540 (1914); Matter of Appeal from Order Dissolving District, 23 *Ibid.* 40 (1920).

[336] Anonymous, Code of Pub. Instn. 1887, p. 532 (1884); Anonymous, *Ibid.* 617 (1881).

[337] Matter of Appeal of Hasbrouck *v.* School District, etc., Jud. Decs. 418 (1891).

than consolidation and contraction in number. Yet the decisions of so outstanding a superintendent of common schools as John A. Dix clearly show that he was well aware that much of the weakness in the quality of education offered in the schools of the state was due to the limited means of small territorial units.[338] It is not surprising, then, that it early became settled precedent to sanction the consolidation of districts so weak that their continuance necessitated an undue sacrifice of public money of the state.[339] But if a district was strong enough financially and numerically to maintain a home school of its own and the majority of the local inhabitants were eager to do so, their resistance to consolidation in an appeal to the state department had every chance of being sustained, at least down to about 1913 or 1914.[340] In some instances the threat of future consolidation was held over a district's head in order to make it exert itself in raising its educational standards.[341] From the general policy one must not think that the commissioner has been unmindful of the advantages of consolidation—the larger school, better grading, up-to-date equipment, and more competent teachers[342]—especially in union free school districts.[343] But even though he has conceded these benefits, yet, down to the end of the first decade of the twentieth century he still adhered fundamentally to the precedents evolved during nineteenth century rural New York. In one of the last decisions, before a change in policy occurred, it was remarked,

"Our present law recognizes the existence and maintenance of small rural schools. . . . The advantages of a small school in an agricultural community must be recognized. A school with a single competent teacher whose work is supervised by an experienced superintendent, will afford effective instruction to the young pupils in the neighborhood. Such a school serves the immediate locality; it is accessible to children who could not

[338] Inhabitants of School District No. 14, Town of Richland *v.* Commissioners of Common Schools, Decs. Supt. Com. Schs. 136 (1833); Inhabitants School District No. 2, Town of Stamford *v.* Commissioners of Common Schools, *Ibid.* 220 (1835).

[339] Anonymous, Laws of N. Y., etc., and Digest of Decs., p. 324 (1859); Matter of Appeal of Fogarty *et al.* *v.* Jones, Ann. Rept. Dept. Pub. Instn. 1892, pp. 66, 67 (1890).

[340] Anonymous, Code of Pub. Instn. 1856, p. 57 (1843); Matter of Appeal of Kneale *v.* Smith, Jud. Decs. 1347 (1893); Matter of Appeal of Knight, *Ibid.* 715 (1907); Matter of Appeal of Done *v.* Griffin, *Ibid.* 742 (1899); Matter of Appeal of Gulick *v.* O'Neill, *Ibid.* 740 (1891); Matter of Dissolution of School District No. 2, *Ibid.* 717 (1908); Matter of Appeal of Fogarty *et al.* *v.* Jones, Ann. Rept. Dept. Pub. Instn. 1892, p. 66 (1890); *Contra:* Matter of Appeal of Larmon *v.* Barbur, Jud. Decs. 703 (1889).

[341] Matter of Appeal of Donel *et al.* *v.* Knapp, Jud. Decs. 706 (1890).

[342] Matter of Appeal of Milks, *Ibid.* 646 (1907).

[343] Matter of Appeal of King, *Ibid.* 1333 (1905).

attend, without great inconvenience, the more distant graded school; it has beneficial local influence, and should not be abandoned so long as there are pupils to be accommodated and a majority of the patrons desire its maintenance.[344]

Just as alteration of district boundaries had been resisted when for the sole purpose of equalizing tax burdens, so, too, and for the same reasons, did the commissioner frown on consolidation for that limited purpose.[345] In 1912, however, he weakened on this principle so far as to declare an exception to the rule.[346]

After 1913 the decisions of the commissioner on appeal cases arising out of disputes over the consolidation of districts take a distinct turn in favor of consolidation. As has already been pointed out,[347] this was not a change primarily in the commissioner's judicial policies. Rather did the commissioner's decisions reflect a redirection of policy in the legislature.[348] New legislative enactments not only paved the way to consolidation by vote of qualified electors, but they also considerably increased the quotas from the state treasury to consolidating districts. With the legislature thus inclined to consolidation, it is natural to expect a corresponding bending of the commissioner's precedents.[349] From this time forward, the issues receiving most discussion in his decisions concern, not the majority sentiment of the individual districts, but rather the advantages of a central school with its broader curriculum, its possibilities of grading with consequent better instruction, its equipment, the location of highways, transportation facilities, community spirit, and the like.[350] Of course all these advantages require a larger unit than the old common school district for purposes of administration and taxation, and, if consolidation does increase taxation, the commissioner is optimistic in thinking that it will be outweighed by the advantages enumerated. In some cases he even holds out hope for more

[344] Matter of Appeal of Birdseye, 1 State Dept. Rept. (unofficial) 395 (1912); Acc.: Matter of Appeal of Garling *et al.*, Ann. Rept. State Ed. Dept. 1912, p. 454 (1911); Matter of Appeal of Duell, Jud. Decs. 720 (1906).

[345] Matter of Appeal of Jones *et al.*, *Ibid.* 709 (1905).

[346] Matter of Appeal of Mehaffy *et al.*, Ann. Rept. State Ed. Dept. p. 464 (1911).

[347] *Ante*, p. 56 f.

[348] Laws of N. Y. 1913, ch. 129 and 1914 ch. 101.

[349] Matter of Bonner, 9 State Dept. Rept. 611, 613 (1916).

[350] Matter of Dissolution of School Districts, 4 State Dept. Rept. (official) 614 (1915); Matter of Appeal of School Districts, etc., 6 *Ibid.* 525 (1915); Matter of Consolidation of School Districts, *Ibid.* 615 (1915); Matter of Dissolution of School Districts, 5 *Ibid.* 625 (1915).

economical operation under consolidation.[351] This change in precedent in the disposition of appeal cases on consolidation was not without its storm of protest. This was answered in a lengthy review of the whole question both in New York and in other states in the Matter of Dissolution of School Districts.[352] Even though some of the commissioner's judicial language has been so strong as to assert that the advantages of consolidation "must be conceded without discussion,"[353] nevertheless one must not fall into the error of thinking that every appeal was decided in favor of consolidation.[354] Concomitantly with the change in policy just noted came a new attitude toward consolidation for the purposes of equalizing tax burdens. Although still adhering to his former precedent on this point, where only the alteration of district boundaries was concerned, the commissioner launched out now to justify such proceedings where effected through consolidation.[355] In 1917 a still further step in the direction of consolidation and larger local administrative units was taken in the Township Law.[356] The law, however, was so short-lived, that it did not get a thorough treatment at the hands of the commissioner's judicial tribunal.

In the new line of precedents from 1913 on, there is nowhere the express reflection of changed social and economic conditions which have given birth to it. The former policy was admittedly adjusted to a rural New York. Just as definitely, if not so expressly, the new one mirrors a different New York. The increasing keenness in economic competition has necessitated more adequate preparation both in industrial and agricultural pursuits. To meet this, curricula have been expanded. But this expansion has required money, and more money than common school districts could muster. The great popularity of secondary education has extended to rural communities. But, again, a more powerful taxing unit was necessary before its advantages could become very widespread. Finally, neither of these advantages could have been utilized—perhaps even popularized to their present degree—except

[351] Matter of Order Dissolving School Districts, 6 *Ibid.* 521 (1915).

[352] 4 *Ibid.* (official) 614 (1915).

[353] Matter of Order Dissolving School Districts, 6 *Ibid.* 521, 523 (1915).

[354] E.g., Matter of Dividing School District, 9 *Ibid.* 616 (1916).

[355] Matter of Appeal of Ockers, 9 *Ibid.* 606 (1916); Matter of Appeal from Order Dissolving School District, 21 *Ibid.* 479 (1919); Matter of Appeal of Ploss, 4 *Ibid.* (official) 647 (1915); Matter of Appeal of School District, etc., 6 *Ibid.* 548 (1915); Matter of Altering Boundary Line, 22 *Ibid.* 677 (1920).

[356] Laws of N. Y. 1917, ch. 328.

for the tremendous growth in the automotive industry. The great economies effected there and the wide uses for which automobiles have become available revolutionized the social and economic life of the state. Except for this and the transformation of the highways of the state from dirt roads to hard-surface roads, this new judicial policy might never have come into being, not even with the legislation commencing with 1913. Hardly any decision now, affecting consolidation, is complete without some consideration of transportation facilities. This topic, therefore, is properly the next one to be examined.

16. Branch Schools—Transportation of Pupils

As already indicated, the success of the state's tendency toward a single large central school instead of numerous small ones serving the same area is quite dependent on adequate transportation facilities. Excessive distances to and from school, however, were a problem long before the era of consolidation. The difficulty was then more likely to be met by the establishment of a new district or of a branch school within the same district. An early anonymous decision states that, "Whenever in any remote locality of the district a number of scholars sufficient to make a respectable school are debarred, from the fact of such remoteness, from attending school, the establishment of a branch school will be directed." [357] Decisions on this point have been crystallized into statutory form at present.[358] Inclement weather and impassable roads at certain periods of the year have been added as reasons for justifying the establishment of branch schools.[359] The number of children from whom a branch school will be formed is indefinite.[360] Three children have been held as too few, especially when all came from the same family,[361] but less than ten have been interpreted as a "considerable number" within the meaning of the statute.[362] The commissioner states his general policy very well in the Matter of Appeal of Sherman:

> Unless a considerable number of children are to be accommodated by the school, it should not be established notwithstanding the remoteness of

[357] Anonymous, Laws of N. Y., etc., and Digest of Decs. p. 356 (1857).

[358] Laws of N. Y. 1910, ch. 140, sec. 275, subdiv. 19, as amended to 1925.

[359] Matter of Appeal of Yousey, 28 State Dept. Rept. 298 (1922).

[360] Matter of Appeal of Sherman, Jud. Decs. 143 (1909); Matter of Appeal of Yousey, 28 State Dept. Rept. 298 (1922).

[361] Matter of Appeal of Sherman, Jud. Decs. 143 (1909).

[362] Matter of Appeal of Yousey, 28 State Dept. Rept. 298 (1922).

the children and the hardships to be endured by them in reaching the main schoolhouse. The children of the petitioner are entitled to the benefits of the school in the district, but the trustee may not be compelled to take the school to their door. There is also a parental obligation resting upon the petitioner to give his children educational advantages. He should not be permitted to shift this burden upon his neighbors. If his business takes him into a remote district and his family goes with him his children must either suffer the hardship of attending a school located a long distance from their home, or must be given equivalent instruction at home. . . . It is not necessary for a determination of this appeal to decide what would be a "considerable number" within the meaning of the statute.[363]

Much the same attitude was taken to a later appeal in 1914, but it is significant there that the commissioner hinted *obiter* that transportation was probably the proper alternative to the branch school.[364]

From the dates of its first authorization to the present, the statute on transportation has been permissive rather than mandatory. It is to be invoked where children live so remotely that they are deprived of school privileges during any portion of the year.[365] Even though transportation found a place in the law as early as 1896, its early judicial significance was not chiefly in connection with consolidation. The beginnings of the contract system [366] called it as much to the foreground of attention as anything else. The leading early case, In the Matter of the Petition of Nulty,[367] defines what is probably the basic position of the department at the present time on transportation. This was an instance where one district was contracting with another for the education of its children and subsidizing each family of the home district at the rate of ten dollars a child for transportation. Since most of the families concerned were put to no extra effort or trouble whatever, the subsidy was clear gain. Such a practice was very severely condemned. Not only did Commissioner Draper point out that this practice came dangerously close to an improper influence on the resident to vote for the contract system in preference to a home school when the district could afford one, but he also asserted that public aid in transportation commences only

[363] Jud. Decs. 143, 144 (1909). Acc.: Matter of Appeal of Flanders, 8 State Dept. Rept. 623 (1916).

[364] Matter of Appeal of Valentine *et al.*, 3 State Dept. Rept. (official) 531 (1914).

[365] Laws of N. Y. 1896, ch. 264, sec. 5; continued in subdiv. 18, sec. 206, of ch. 140 of Laws of 1910 as amended to 1925.

[366] Laws of N. Y. 1903, ch. 265.

[367] Jud. Decs. 151 (1905).

at the point where private families could not provide it. Citing the Nulty case in another appeal arising the same year, he said of the statute relating to transportation:

> It cannot be successfully contended that this provision of the law was enacted for the purpose of relieving parents from any of the obligations which they owe their children in the matter of providing for their education. A parent in providing for the education of his children as well as in providing for their other necessities must first discharge his parental duties and obligations before he can ask the community to help him. It is just as much the duty of the appellant to educate his children as it is to feed, shelter, or clothe them or to otherwise provide for their health and comfort. In appeal no. 5219, decided by me October 31, 1905, I held as follows: "The moral and legal obligation rests upon every parent to give his child the advantage of the school facilities afforded by our system of public education. He should do this even at great inconvenience and expense if necessary. He should not expect remuneration, nor should it be given, for such trouble as may reasonably be expected of a parent to enable his children to attend school.[368]

While the statute leaves the provision of transportation up to a vote of the district, on appeal the commissioner may, and he frequently does, direct a community to provide transportation.[369] For the commissioner's decision to make mandatory what the statute leaves permissive would seem justified in the light of the fact that the legislature has favored transportation by allowing quotas from the school moneys therefor.[370] In the Appeal Relating to the Transportation of Certain Children,[371] however, the commissioner's power to do this was questioned. As has already been pointed out,[372] the case was carried beyond the commissioner and up to the Court of Appeals where the commissioner was sustained.

Granting that a pupil's parents cannot afford him transportation, how far from school must he live to be able to command the aid of the district? One early appellant tried to fix this distance at two miles, but the commissioner refused to accept any such arbitrary figure either as a departmental rule or as a judicial precedent.[373] Neither will the commissioner lay it down that a

[368] Matter of Appeal of Turner, *Ibid.* 1234, 1236 (1905). Acc.: Matter of Application of Loomis, *Ibid.* 1233 (1908). Matter of Appeal of Chapman *et al.*, 1 State Dept. Rept. (official) 524 (1913).

[369] E.g., Matter of Appeal of Fisher, 32 State Dept. Rept. 371 (1925).

[370] *Ibid.* See also Laws of N. Y., 1923, ch. 716 and of 1924, ch. 192.

[371] 31 State Dept. Rept. 85 (1924).

[372] *Ante*, p. 46 ff.

[373] Matter of Appeal of Sackett, Jud. Decs. 915 (1906).

pupil entitled to transportation may demand it from his doorstep.[374] In order to meet the convenience of all, it may be necessary for him to walk to meet the lorry. But a family that moves into a part of a district difficult of access to school, after, and with full knowledge of prior consolidation proceedings which abandoned a nearby school building, will have difficulty in making out any case at all for the transportation of its children.[375] On the other hand, where a district contracts with a union free school district for the instruction of its children, it may not make a separate contract with a common school district nearer to one family in order to avoid the expense of transportation of that family to the union free school.[376] Once transportation is directed, the district has no further control over the trustee in his arrangements.[377] In making these arrangements, the trustee can not be required to let a contract for conveyance to the lowest bidder "unless the bidder is a suitable person to drive the conveyance and the means afforded are adequate." [378] But in any event, the contract for conveyance must be either "with a proper person who is to furnish a comfortable and safe means of conveyance, or, if the children are conveniently accessible to a trolley line or railroad, the trustee should provide for the payment of their fares during the time that they are in attendance." [379]

17. The Contract System

As noted already, prior to 1912 the commissioner's judicial power was exercised in the direction of favoring a home school rather than consolidation if there were sentiment, numbers, and financial ability to maintain it.[380] The same preference is to be noted for the corresponding period where contracts for neighboring districts have been the subject of appeal.[381] A district that provides for its educational responsibilities by the contract system is not to be let out of them easily. Thus, the commissioner

[374] Matter of Appeal of Chase, 26 State Dept. Rept. 86 (1921).

[375] Matter of Appeal Relative to the Transportation of Certain Children, 27 *Ibid.* 247 (1922).

[376] Matter of Transportation of Children, 4 *Ibid.* (unofficial) 591 (1915).

[377] Matter of Appeal of Rombach, 27 *Ibid.* (1922); Matter of Appeal Relating to the Transportation of Children, 31 *Ibid.* 721 (1924).

[378] Matter of Appeal of Rice *et al.*, 2 *Ibid.* (unofficial) 397, 399 (1913).

[379] Matter of Contract for Instruction of Children, 19 *Ibid.* 271, 272-73 (1919).

[380] *Ante,* p. 139.

[381] Matter of Appeal of Abrams *et al.*, Jud. Decs. 156 (1909). See, too, Matter of Appeal of Maher, 25 State Dept. Rept. 542 (1921).

will require that the contract engage the best possible opportunities and, if more than one contract is necessary for this with more than one district, then he will direct that that course be pursued.[382] Or, again, he may only approve a contract if satisfactory conveyance is supplied.[383] The commissioner has even held that:

> A district is not relieved from the duty of maintaining its school building in good condition by contracting with another district for the instruction of its pupils. A school building in a contracting district must be kept in such a state of repair that it may be again used for such purposes without the expenditure of an unreasonable amount of money should the district desire to abandon the contract system of instruction and provide for its children in its own school.[384]

Finally, while a resident may not as a matter of strict legal right compel his district to contract with some particular district for the instruction of his children, yet, his wishes are entitled to consideration and, other things being equal, his preferences should be recognized.[385]

It is mandatory upon a district to provide education of the elementary level either by maintaining a home school or by contract. To do the same on the academic or secondary level, however, was optional until the Appeal of Fraser was determined.[386] After that case an appellant could expect success in forcing his district against the wish of the majority of voters to contract for his child's secondary education. The theory of this case was that the pupils, whose interests were litigated in this appeal, were still within the compulsory age limits after they had completed the elementary school course and, if no advanced work were provided for them, they would have to mark time by repeating in the district school till they grew beyond the legal age limit. Two decisions not long after this case made secondary education available even for those beyond the compulsory school age.[387] But yet a third decision was necessary to round out this truly notable

[382] Matter of Appeal of Hildreth *v.* Ryant, *Ibid.* 172 (1908).

[383] Matter of the Contract for the Instruction of Children, 1 State Dept. Rept. (official) 531 (1914); Matter of Contract for the Instruction of Children, 19 *Ibid.* 271 (1919); Matter of Appeal Relative to the Transportation of Children, 26 *Ibid.* 695 (1921).

[384] Matter of School District No. 18, *Ibid.* (unofficial) 441 (1912).

[385] Matter of Appeal of Casey, 1 *Ibid.* (unofficial) 438 (1912). Cf. Matter of Appeal of Blacket, 15 State Dept. Rept. 509 (1918).

[386] 20 State Dept. Rept. 170 (1919).

[387] Matter of Academic Tuition, 20 *Ibid.* 186 (1919) and Petition of Goettel, 27 *Ibid.* 285 (1922). By the time the latter case was decided the statute law had been liberalized in accordance with Fraser's Appeal: Laws of N. Y. 1921, ch. 383.

extension of secondary educational opportunities through the commissioner's judicial power. Matter of Appeal from the Action of Trustee, etc.,[388] was a case where the district recognized its duty to contract for secondary education. The appellant's case, however, was unique. Although he had acquired enough Regents credits in three years, at the academic school to which his district had been sending him, to entitle him to the school's diploma, yet, on trying to enter college, he found his credits insufficient in number to gain him admittance. He then returned for a post-graduate course to earn the remaining necessary regents credits. The district contested its obligation to pay for this fourth year of instruction. The commissioner was deaf to the claim. On the other hand, he held that the appellant had not "completed his high school course within the fair meaning of that term. . . . A full high school course is recognized in this state as consisting of four years of academic work, and it has been generally understood that a pupil is entitled to instruction in high school for at least four years." [389]

One step farther the commissioner might have gone but that he refused to do, or, better, perhaps he could not expect a district to afford. In the Matter of Appeal of Flint,[390] a district that already maintained a high school was made a respondent by a parent who wished the district to contract for his daughter's secondary education outside the district because the local school did not offer courses in stenography and typewriting. In as much as the local school was giving instruction in all the subjects required by the state, the commissioner refused to order the district to provide for special classes or courses to accommodate individual pupils.[391] The opportunities for academic education through the contract system are not to be open to those who have not completed the elementary school.[392] Neither can one claim these

[388] 32 State Dept. Rept. 321 (1925). [389] *Ibid.* p. 322.

[390] 23 State Dept. Rept. 441 (1920).

[391] A similar result was reached even where the home district maintained no high school but, in choosing between several possible academic institutions, picked one without a commercial course. Matter of Appeal from Action of Annual District Meeting, 31 *Ibid.* 455 (1924).

Mere sentimental reasons are not enough on which to base a preference either. Matter of Appeal from Action of Annual School Meeting, 34 *Ibid.* 11 (1925).

On the other hand, if a child moves into a district in the middle of the year, he will be entitled to complete the term at his present school even though that is not the designated school of his new home. Matter of Appeal from Designation of School, 31 *Ibid.* 240 (1924).

[392] Matter of Appeal of Smith, 20 *Ibid.* 185 (1919).

advantages without first making an application to the trustees or board of education.[393] But the cost of transportation to, or maintenance at an academic school under the contract system will not be made a charge on the home district.[394]

The statute makes no specifications as to the terms on which districts shall contract with each other. These terms are, nevertheless, reviewable by the commissioner.[395] He has held that the district offering secondary education facilities cannot lay down terms impossible or impractical for outlying districts to comply with. It may not, for instance, require the payment of tuition at the beginning of the term, since at that time district trustees do not always know how many pupils will be in attendance, and, even if they did know, they could not levy and collect a tax soon enough.[396] In another case the commissioner pared fifteen dollars off the rate charged per pupil.[397]

Although not strictly a subject under the heading of the contract system, yet, since a consideration of this topic has carried the discussion over into the field of secondary education, it may be well to point out that the Appeal of Fraser was anticipated in Matter of Academic Instruction of Children.[398] In this case the local board of education had refused to act on a petition of the residents to provide secondary school facilities. After pointing out that "There is no provision of the Education Law or of the Constitution which limits the obligation of a district to the furnishing of instruction for the children therein in so-called elementary or common school branches," the commissioner passed on to note that it had for some time been departmental policy to look upon secondary education as a necessity. In as much as he had supervisory control over this district's provision for its educational need, and, in as much as the district had the financial resources for maintaining it, the commissioner directed the establishment of high school facilities. The state policy of furnishing equalization quotas for academic departments has more recently fortified this policy.[399]

[393] 20 *Ibid.* 180 (1919).

[394] Matter of Appeal of Millar, 20 *Ibid.* 178 (1919).

[395] Laws of N. Y., 1910, ch. 140, sec. 493, subdiv. 6 as amended to 1925.

[396] Matter of Appeal from Action of Board of Education, 34 *Ibid.* 237 (1926).

[397] Matter of Appeal of Board of Education, etc., 28 *Ibid.* 710 (1923).

[398] 10 *Ibid.* 449 (1916).

[399] Matter of Appeal of White *et al.*, 33 State Dept. Rept. 229 (1925); Laws of N. Y. 1925, ch. 675.

18. School Term, Attendance, and Like Matters

While a minimum school term is prescribed by the state law, no appeal will lie because a community wishes to exceed bare requirements.[400] Of course it is desirable for a pupil to enter school at the beginning of the term and inconvenient for the school if he enters later, but a board of education cannot on that account have a rule against admitting pupils except at the beginning of the term.[401] To hold otherwise would often deprive children of a year's schooling, which would surely be against the policy of the school laws which make the public school available to all without limit to the time of entrance, except as to the pupil's age. Looking at the problem from this point of view shows less advantage is to be gained from observance of such a rule than from overruling it.

What time of day the school should open and close is left a matter of local discretion, as it should be. The "daylight saving" law, nevertheless, has caused enough excitement to generate several appeals to the commissioner.[402] But they have not been treated as exceptions to the rule. The number of hours that will constitute a school day has depended on local custom from almost the beginning of the system.[403] At first the designation of school holidays had only local custom to conform to.[404] While this freedom probably still remains, it is hedged in by the statute which, on the one hand, prescribes certain holidays, and, on the other, requires that school be taught a minimum number of days if a community expects to share in the public moneys.[405] Though the statute now omits Saturdays from the count of days the school must officially be in session, time was when the superintendent of common schools was asked about the propriety of a Saturday whole or half holiday.[406]

Compared with the length of the educational history of the state, compulsory attendance is a recent development. Never-

[400] Matter of Appeal of Woodward *v.* Hill, Jud. Decs. 1151 (1894).

[401] Matter of Appeal of Nichols *v.* Board of Education, *Ibid.* 1315 (1891).

[402] Matter of Appeal from Action of Board of Education, etc., 29 State Dept. Rept. 663 (1923); Matter of Appeal from Decision of Trustees as to Time, 33 *Ibid.* 226 (1925).

[403] Elkins, *ex parte,* Decs. Supt. Com. Schs., p. 88 (1832).

[404] Anonymous, *Ibid.* 139 (1833).

[405] Laws of N. Y., 1910, ch. 140, sec. 492, subdivs. 2, 3, as amended to 1925.

[406] Anonymous, Decs. Supt. Com. Schs., p. 121 (1833); Anonymous, Code of Pub. Instn. 1856, p. 37 (1848).

theless, while the early parent could not be compelled to send his child to the district school, especially if he preferred a private one,[407] the local board was justified in requiring regular and prompt attendance of those who did patronize the public school.[408] Relatively few formally contested appeals have arisen under the compulsory attendance law. In one case the commissioner held that he has no authority to excuse a child from the operation of the law even though the circumstances seem so distressing that an exception ought to be made.[409] Of course physical inability of a child to attend school will be a good excuse for non-attendance, but the mere say-so of the parent as to his child's physical disability need not be accepted as final. If school authorities had to labor under such a restriction the compulsory attendance law would soon become a dead letter.[410]

19. District Meetings

The district meeting has long been heralded as American democracy in education in its simplest terms. This democracy, however, operates within an area pretty well delimited by statute, at least in the important details. Far from being the source of all educational authority in the district, the district meeting has some definite boundaries to its power. Perhaps outstanding here is the fact that it cannot control the district trustee in his selection of a teacher. The time span of the cases cited will show how long it has taken to become accustomed to that curb on a purer democracy.[411] Their only compensation is that decisions have recommended that trustees follow the wishes of the community so far as possible.[412] On the other hand, certain functions delegated to the district meeting by statute cannot be vested by them in a committee of their number, as, for instance, the selection of a school site.[413] If such a committee is appointed, its

[407] Anonymous, Decs. Supt. Com. Schs., p. 169 (1834).

[408] Anonymous, Code of Pub. Instn. 1887, p. 770 (1866).

[409] Matter of Rau, 1 State Dept. Rept. (unofficial) 420 (1912).

[410] Matter of Application to Remove Roe, Jud. Decs. 443 (1906).

[411] Trustees School District No. ——, Town of Colesville, *ex parte*, Decs. Supt. Com. Schs., p. 62 (1830); Matter of Appeal of Nieman *et al.*, Jud. Decs. 1252 (1906); Matter of Appeal of Ingersoll, 5 State Dept. Rept. 601 (1915).

[412] Matter of Appeal of Nieman *et al.*, Jud. Decs. 1252 (1906).

[413] Anonymous, Code of Pub. Instn. 1856, p. 6 (1839); Matter of Appeal of Rood, Jud. Decs. 955 (1886); Matter of Appeal of Tait *et al.*, *Ibid.* 933 (1888). See also: Matter of Appeal of Baker *et al.*, *v.* Board of Education, *Ibid.* 1244 (1887).

function will be wholly advisory.[414] So entirely dependent on statute is the school district meeting for its authority to act that there is one case on record where the superintendent of common schools could find no way to authorize a district's purchase of "globe and apparatus" other than by private subscription.[415] Neither could a school bell be purchased as a "necessary appendage," [416] although a fence about the school property,[417] or a stove and pipe could be so purchased.[418] At a later day a district was allowed to authorize the digging of a well on the school property for drinking water.[419] Any one of the preceding activities seems properly within the province of modern local legislation, but, the question of erecting a monument to the members of a district who served in the World War seems too remote from education and its incidents.[420]

When the district meets to debate the purchase of a heating apparatus or textbooks, it must be free from the undue influence of the agents of any particular appliance or company. An agent may present his wares, but, if he engineers the meeting that adopts them,[421] the state department will be strongly inclined to vacate the proceedings on account of undue influence. Little quarrel can be found with this result.

In appeals to set aside the proceedings of district meetings on account of alleged irregularities, the state department has made a policy of inquiring into "the bona fides thereof. Were the things done such as it was proper to do? Has any one been misled, imposed upon, or wronged? If mistakes and irregularities have occurred, will the greater hardship be imposed upon individuals by setting aside or sustaining such acts?" [422] Certainly there is too much danger of prejudicing a majority's interest where a meeting is convened without a reasonable allowance of time for

[414] Matter of Appeal from Action of Board of Education, etc., 29 State Dept. Rept. 624 (1923).

[415] Trustees School District No. —, Town of Arkport, *ex parte,* Decs. Supt. Com. Schs., p. 280 (1835).

[416] Trustees School District No. 2, Town of Brighton, *ex parte, Ibid.* p. 28 (1828).

[417] Trustees School District, No. 12, Town of Glen, *ex parte, Ibid.* 235 (1835).

[418] Anonymous, Code of Pub. Instn. 1856, p. 61 (1847).

[419] Matter of Appeal of Waldron, Jud. Decs. 1252 (1900).

[420] Matter of Appeal of Valk, 21 State Dept. Repts., 692 (1919).

[421] Matter of Appeal of Curtiss, Jud. Decs. 301 (1904); Matter of Appeal of Stevens *et al.,* 2 State Dept. Rept. (official) 605 (1914).

[422] Matter of Appeal of Britton, Jud. Decs. 324, 327 (1895). Acc.: Matter of Appeal of Bagg *et al. v.* Union Free School, *Ibid.* 343 (1891); Alfred *et al. v.* The Trustees, etc., *Ibid.* 386 (1886).

the main body of inhabitants to arrive and participate therein.[423] A willful failure to observe a local custom of ringing the school bell to warn of the time of the school meeting must receive the same criticism.[424] The state superintendent, on the other hand, has had less patience with a local custom of not calling the meeting to order till the lapse of an hour after the stated time.[425] In no case, however, will proceedings be set aside because a majority of the inhabitants did not turn out when they easily might have, had they been so minded.[426] Again, if the meeting is satisfactorily convened, but its proceedings are so disorderly and tumultuous as to assure no guarantee that the final decision of the group was in truth the sober and sane judgment of the community, sufficient cause will exist for setting the proceedings aside on appeal.[427] Instances of this last case have been all too frequent.

"So far as the binding obligation of common parliamentary rules is concerned, it must ever be held subordinate to the will of any organized meeting, every such assemblage being free to establish its own rules." [428] Yet, while presumably each district meeting may determine the order of its own business, the commissioner has suggested that the usual custom among districts is to have reports of officers presented, then the budget for the ensuing year, and, finally, the election of officers.[429]

The rule in the calling of special meetings is a simple one—the trustee must call these meetings if a respectable number of the qualified voters desire it and if the object is one that warrants the assembling of the community.[430] Such a condition does not exist, however, where the district has already had an opportunity to express itself on the matter proposed for special meeting.[431]

[423] Ross *v.* Inhabitants, etc., Decs. Supt. Com. Schs., p. 131 (1833); Tilden *v.* Inhabitants, etc., *Ibid.* 219 (1835); Matter of Appeal of Middlemist, Jud. Decs. 350 (1895).

[424] Matter of Appeal of Huntley *et al.* *v.* School District, *Ibid.* 341 (1891).

[425] Anonymous, Laws of N. Y. etc., and Digest of Decs., p. 339 (1859).

[426] Anonymous, *Ibid.* 340 (1858); Matter of Appeal of Murphy *v.* School District, Jud. Decs. 978 (1889).

[427] Anonymous, Code of Pub. Instn. 1887, p. 575 (1872); Matter of Appeal of Childs *v.* the Action of a Joint Meeting of Residents of District, Jud. Decs. 328 (1888); Matter of Appeal of Petregal, 1 State Dept. Rept. (unofficial), 387 (1912).

[428] Anonymous, Laws of N. Y. etc., and Digest of Decs., p. 338 (1860). Acc.: Anonymous, Code of Pub. Instn. 1856, p. 90 (1855).

[429] Matter of Appeal from Action of Annual District Meeting, 33 State Dept. Rept. 61 (1925).

[430] Matter of Appeal of Griffin *v.* Lounsbury *et al.*, Jud. Decs. 376 (1896).

[431] Matter of Refusal of Trustees to Call a Special Meeting, 24 State Dept. Rept. 196 (1920).

20. School District Voting

Disputes over the results of voting and the right to vote have always been a prolific source of litigation before the state department. It always reaches high tide right after the period of the annual district meetings. Since legislative enactments have always pretty fully covered suffrage qualifications, there is little that a discussion of appeal cases can add. What constitutes owning land within the meaning of the statute has sometimes not been altogether clear. The possession of a dower interest [432] or that of a reversioner [433] have both been held insufficient to meet the statute. In the case of a leasehold interest, which will enable one to vote, the difficult question of fact arises whether the alleged lease is in fact a lease or an agreement describing the relation of master and servant.[434] In any case, to try to circumvent the letter of the law by conveying an interest in land for the day of the voting will be too open a violation of the spirit of the statute to escape judicial censure.[435]

Colored people never seem to have been under a disability to vote in school district meetings in New York if possessed of other necessary qualifications.[436] On the other hand, a similar liberality shown toward aliens at first [437] has since been revoked by statute which sets down United States citizenship as an indispensable prerequisite to the right of suffrage.[438] It is a significant milestone in the growing importance of the judicial power of the state department that when the state admitted women to suffrage rights in school district matters, the state superintendent was held in high enough esteem to pass authoritatively on the question of the constitutionality of the statute.[439]

Parents of children who are attending the school of a neigh-

[432] Matter of Appeal of Wilcox *v.* School District, Jud. Decs. 1426 (1888).

[433] Matter of Appeal of Preston *et al., Ibid.* 1420 (1908).

[434] Matter of Appeal of Russell *et al., Ibid.* 1428 (1898); Matter of Appeal of Allen, *Ibid.* 1432 (1907).

[435] Matter of Appeal of Preston *et al., Ibid.* 1420 (1908).

[436] Inhabitants School District No. 10, Town of Schodack, *ex parte,* Jud. Decs. 1419 (1836).

[437] Anonymous, Decs. Supt. Com. Schs., p. 76 (1831). Potter *et al. v.* Commissioners, etc., *Ibid.* p. 147 (1834), holding that an alien could not be an office holder, was apparently overruled by Anonymous, Code of Pub. Instn. 1856, p. 17 (1842). In the latter case the view was taken that if the alien could vote he could also hold office.

[438] Matter of Appeal of Cudney *v.* McDermott, Jud. Decs. 1435 (1896); Matter of Election of Trustee etc., 6 State Dept. Rept. 597 (1915).

[439] Anonymous, Jud. Decs. 1450 (1883).

boring district under the contract system are entitled to vote at the annual meeting of the home district by virtue of their parenthood in spite of the fact that the law declares parenthood is only a qualification where the parent sends his child to the school of the district where the meeting is to be held.[440] This result is reached by holding that the school of the district contracted with, in essence, is the school of the home district. Formerly where a child was domiciled with a family other than his own, only the man or wife was thereby entitled to vote under the statute,[441] but a change in the present wording of the statute would probably lead to a different result were the case to arise again.

Where the appellant conceives himself aggrieved by illegal voting at the district meeting and therefore seeks to have the proceedings set aside on appeal, he will only succeed when he can show that the illegal voting materially affected the result.[442] Bribery is always a bad taint to voting,[443] but probable bidders on a contract, the subject of a district meeting's vote, will not be disfranchised from voting thereon because they are financially interested.[444]

21. The District School Trustee

Not much remains to be said about the office of district school trustee as a separate topic. Much has already been described indirectly in a consideration of other headings into which he enters, as selection and dismissal of teachers, alteration of district boundaries, the contract system, and many similar concerns. Not infrequently a trustee's election to office is defective but, nevertheless, he poses as trustee for the district. It has been held for a long time that such trustees are at least *de facto* officers and that since they hold office under color of title thereto that their acts will be binding upon the district at least as regards third

[440] Matter of Appeal from Order Consolidating Districts, 32 State Dept. Rept. 527 (1925).

[441] Matter of Appeal of Wentworth *et al.*, Jud. Decs. 411 (1895).

[442] Brewer *v.* Inhabitants, etc., Decs. Supt. Com. Schs., p. 84 (1831); Trustees School District No. 2, Town of Italy *v.* Inhabitants, *Ibid.* p. 176 (1834); Anonymous, Code of Pub. Instn. 1856, p. 99 (1856); Anonymous, Code of Pub. Instn. 1887, p. 523 (1884); Matter of election of a member of the Board of Education, Jud. Decs. 175 (1905). For other cases see Jud. Decs., pp. 175-285. Matter of Appeal of Merritt, 2 State Dept. Repts. (unofficial) 408 (1913).

[443] Trustees School District No. —, Town of Solon, *ex parte,* Decs. Supt. Com. Schs., p. 247 (1835); Matter of Appeal of Case *et al.*, Ann. Rept. State Ed. Dept. 1912, p. 437 (1910).

[444] Matter of Appeal from Action of Special District Meeting, 29 *Ibid.* 403 (1923).

parties.[445] A number of the older cases show numerous attempts of the school trustee to hold other district offices, as clerk,[446] librarian,[447] and even teacher,[448] but in every case the two positions were held incompatible and the trustee compelled to vacate one or the other office. This is sound because in each case the second capacity is one that owes responsibility to the trustee and it would be contrary to public policy in such cases to allow one to be responsible to himself. A trustee whose residence is set off to another district in proceedings for the alteration of boundaries will automatically vacate his office.[449] If the trustee moves out of the district so that he cannot perform his duties, he will not later be able to return and try to resume them by claiming that he never had changed his domicile.[450] There have been enough occasions necessitating the removal of trustees from office for neglect of duty or willful disobedience but the number who have been removed for sheer incompetence is very small.[451]

Of course the trustee is expected to act in the interests of the district and not his own. To insure this end the statute was passed requiring ratification by the district meeting of any teacher contract of his with a blood relation. The same question of fiduciary relationship is raised where the trustee awards a janitorship [452] or a contract for transportation [453] to his minor son. The fact that the child is a minor raises too strong an inference that the parent is financially interested, and therefore may be tempted to ignore the best interests of the district. The case is even more clear where trustees award themselves district contracts for materials and labor.[454]

While the statute law allows a trustee his expenses in suits where he has officially represented the district, such can hardly

[445] Anonymous, Code of Pub. Instn. 1856, p. 11 (1841); Anonymous, Code of Pub. Instn. 1887, p. 709 (1884); Matter of Appeal of Welch *et al.*, Jud. Decs. 221 (1894).

[446] Trustees School District No. 7, Town of Lexington, *ex parte*, Decs. Supt. Com. Schs., p. 142 (1833).

[447] Anonymous, Code of Pub. Instn. 1856, p. 7 (1839); Anonymous, Code of Pub. Instn. 1887, p. 520 (1875).

[448] Anonymous, *Ibid.* p. 765 (1871).

[449] Anonymous, Code of Pub. Instn. 1856, p. 5 (1839).

[450] Anonymous, Code of Pub. Instn. 1887, p. 787 (1874).

[451] Matter of Application for Removal of Lewis, Jud. Decs. 1272 (1888); Matter of Appeal of Lynch *et al.* *v.* Gibney, *Ibid.* 1248 (1891). See also: Anonymous, *Ibid.* 470 (1859).

[452] Matter of Appeal of Mudge *et al.*, *Ibid.* 296 (1904).

[453] Matter of Appeal from Action of Trustee, etc., 32 State Dept. Rept. 578 (1925).

[454] Matter of Removal of Oakley *et al.*, Jud. Decs. 448 (1905).

be the case where he is sued for misconduct in office.[455] It is not even the case where he sues the district for a counsel fee incurred because he had to sue the district for a claim it owed him.[456] It hardly needs mention that any judgment gained against a trustee in his official capacity cannot be collected by a levy and sale of the schoolhouse.[457]

22. Boards of Education—The City Superintendent

The preceding section and the present one undoubtedly shade into each other and many principles apply equally to both. For instance, just as school trustees are not allowed to hold other district offices which might be incompatible with that of trustee, so board members are similarly limited.[458] Again, neither a district nor a board meeting may so vote at one session as unalterably to bind any future one.[459] Other principles applying equally to both are more often found in connection with board organization. Thus, to act effectively the board must meet and act as a board; no valid action can be taken where conclusions are reached by individual members in places separated from each other or at different times even though they will come to the same decision.[460]

On some points there is a distinct difference. A trustee may reengage a blood relation of his as teacher without putting such a contract up for the approval of the district as the law requires in the first term of employment.[461] A board of education, however, must give a statutory majority every year such a relative of a member of a board is retained.[462] Again, while the statute

[455] Matter of Appeal of Miller, 9 State Dept. Rept. 580 (1916).

[456] Anonymous, Code of Pub. Instn. 1887, p. 745 (1879).

[457] Trustees of School District No. 3, Town of Chenango, *ex parte,* Decs. Supt. Com. Schs., p. 127 (1833).

[458] Anonymous, Code of Pub. Instn. 1887, p. 771 (1873); Matter of Appeal of Mansfield *v.* Board of Education, Jud. Decs. 1417 (1901); Matter of Board of Education, etc., 10 State Dept. Rept. 444 (1916).

[459] Anonymous, Code of Pub. Instn. 1887, p. 773 (1886); Matter of Appeal of Chittenden *v.* Board of Education, Jud. Decs. 1227 (1887).

[460] Anonymous, Code of Pub. Instn. 1856, p. 28 (1848); Anonymous, Laws of N. Y., etc., and Digest of Decs., p. 397 (1860); Anonymous, Code of Pub. Instn. 1887, p. 543 (1870); Matter of Appeal of Barnard *v.* Board of Education, Jud. Decs. 1201 (1894); Matter of Appeal of Wolcott *et al. v.* Gale, *Ibid.* 649 (1895); Matter of Proceedings and Acts of Trustees, etc., 7 State Dept. Rep. 570 (1915). Also note the same principle in connection with district meetings, Matter of Appeal of Cruikshank, Jud. Decs. 1103 (1904).

[461] Matter of Appeal of Witbeck *et al. v.* Trustees, etc., Jud. Decs. 1138 (1897).

[462] Matter of Appeal of Browne, 12 State Dept. Rept. 459 (1917).

only mentions defraying the costs of litigation against the community, whichever its educational administrative organization is, it has been judicially held that a board of education may levy taxes to pay for litigation which it instigates itself.

> It has been repeatedly held by the courts that such board of education not only possesses the specific powers that are conferred by statute but, in addition thereto, the functions and authority conferred by other statutes and such as corporations enjoy by the rules of common law. . . . When a corporation is duly created, all other incidents are tacitly annexed to it. These are numerous and important, and include all which are needful to the life and well-doing of such creatures of law. . . .[463]

Most distinctive of board organization as compared with the simpler common school district form are the broader powers generally conferred upon it; especially is this the case in city charters [464] and the city education law of 1917.[465]

The department has not been enthusiastic about bipartisan boards of education. Although not having this feature of administrative organization under its immediate control, it has denounced it in no uncertain terms:

> Whatever may have been the operation elsewhere of this modern legistion to keep politics out of the school by this method of bipartisan boards, the direct result in this city has been to inject politics into the school to the extent that every other consideration has been lost sight of—even the school itself.[466]

The board should be discreet in its choice of a place to meet. Proceedings carried on in a barber shop while the proprietor plied his trade were vacated on just that account in an anonymous opinion in 1875.[467] Neither will a country tavern with all the accessories of a saloon do.[468] In both the appeals cited, the department recommended the schoolhouse as the desirable and appropriate place for the board of education to meet. On convening, the same rules governing a quorum will obtain that control other similar bodies.[469] All meetings of the board are generally open to the public except when it goes into executive session.

[463] Matter of Appeal from Action of Board of Education, etc., 31 *Ibid.* 238 (1924).
[464] Matter of Appeal of Lichterman, 7 *Ibid.* 593 (1916).
[465] Matter of Appeal of Hughes, etc., 13 *Ibid.* 416 (1917).
[466] Matter of Appeal of Flewwellin *et al.* *v.* McLeese *et al.*, Jud. Decs. 121 (1897).
[467] Code of Pub. Instn. 1887, p. 568.
[468] Matter of Depan *et al.*, Ann. Rept. State Ed. Dept. 1913, p. 428 (1911).
[469] Anonymous, Code of Pub. Instn., 1887, p. 766 (1884); Matter of Appeal of Bausch *et al.*, Jud. Decs. 108 (1895).

The board is permitted to exercise reasonable discretion in determining what business shall be done in executive session. But the board may not declare all its meetings to be executive and exclude the public therefrom. Meetings at which the ordinary and regular business of the district is to be transacted are to be public. If a meeting has before it business of a special nature which, in the judgment of the board, may not properly be discussed in public, the board may move to take up the matter in executive session and thereupon proceed with the business in executive session. If the board acts fairly in the matter, and resolves itself into executive session in good faith and with a legitimate end in view, a qualified elector or taxpayer is not aggrieved thereby, and will not be heard to complain on appeal.[470]

The old colonial conception of the town visiting committee, where on visiting days the minister and patriarchs of the community might interrupt the teacher in the conduct of her class or even take it out of her hands, has passed. Where the visiting committee of one board harked back to these methods the state superintendent was constrained to say:

A visiting committee of a board, visiting a school, has no authority to interfere with the methods of instruction pursued by the teachers, nor to give orders to the teacher, nor to interfere in the recitations or assume to conduct such recitations, nor to conduct examinations on their own account, without advising with the teachers, nor to interfere with the seating of the pupils. Such committee should visit the school at such times as it shall deem necessary and proper, and watch carefully the methods pursued by the teacher, the government and discipline of the school, whether or not the teacher maintains good order and discipline, etc., etc., and report the facts relative to such matters to the board. If, in the opinion of the board, the condition of the school is such that, in its judgment, it is not for the best educational interests of the school, then it should call the attention of the teachers thereto. No members of a visiting committee or the board should criticize or reprimand a teacher in the presence of the school or any pupil attending the same, as such a course will be in the highest degree detrimental to the best educational interests of the same.[471]

There is quite clearly evident in the judicial mind of the state superintendent just revealed, a distinction between the lay and professional aspects of educational administration. As the city school superintendency has forged to the fore this distinction has greatly increased in importance. The evolution of this office continued naturally and spontaneously till 1917, when educational

[470] Matter of Appeal of Hughes, Ann. Rept. State Ed. Dept. 1913, pp. 423, 424 (1911); Acc.: Matter of Meetings of Board of Education, etc., 6 State Dept. Rept. 517 (1915).

[471] Matter of Appeal of Barnard *v.* Board of Education, Jud. Decs. 1201, 1207 (1894). Cf. quotation p. 187.

theory and practice was crystallized into statute form in the law of 1917.[472] It can hardly be the purpose of these pages to set forth the provisions of this progressive statute; its spirit, however, can be shown here by the citation of one of the leading cases under it, the Appeal of Hughes, etc.[473] In that instance, Superintendent Hughes of Syracuse had made recommendation to his board of education for the appointment of certain teachers to certain positions. The board ignored them and filled these vacancies on its own initiative. From this action the superintendent appealed and was sustained. The controlling view was that the power to initiate recommendations to the teaching force belonged to the superintendent and that the board possessed only the right of rejection. The theory of the legislation of 1917 was stated to be that.

> . . . the Legislature intended to make the superintendent of schools the chief professional officer of the school system. If the proper functions of a superintendent of schools are not to pass judgment upon the professional affairs in the school system before action is taken by the board of education, it is difficult to conceive what his function should be. The superintendent is required to possess training and experience which qualify him to determine such questions and he is a paid officer in the school system for rendering such service. The board of education is composed of business men who are not competent to pass judgment upon the technical professional questions involved in the administration of a school system. The board employs a superintendent to do that very work.
>
> The conferring upon a superintendent of schools of the proper professional functions which that officer should perform does not impair in any way the prestige or dignity of a board of education. The board of education under the law is the supreme controlling body of the school system. It determines the broad general policy under which the schools shall be managed. . . . In short it may meet any social or intellectual need of a city that may be reached through a public school system. . . .
>
> In the enactment of this law the Legislature undoubtedly took into consideration that members of a board of education are generally business men and have limited time which may be devoted to the important matters relating to the management of a school system. It recognized the necessity of providing for a paid staff which should be responsible for the details of administration. Ample check for the proper performance of the duties of members of such staff is placed in the hands of the board of education.[474]

The last remark was inserted because counsel for the board evidently thought that the superintendent's professional eminence

[472] Laws of N. Y. 1917, ch. 786.
[473] 13 State Dept. Repts. 416 (1917)
[474] *Ibid.* pp. 421-42.

was rapidly approaching the status of an autocrat. If the board could only select through the power of rejection, what would happen if the board and superintendent could never agree? What would happen if there was a temporary vacancy in the superintendency? Or what would be the remedy if the case should arise of a superintendent who persistently recommended inferior teachers in order to embarrass the board? These difficulties of counsel were all met by the commissioner. The simple remedy for the last, and one that should be used without hesitation, is removal from office. In case of a vacancy, a temporary appointment to the superintendency would carry on. Inability to agree apparently did not strike the commissioner as much of a possibility. It should readily be seen by this time that the Appeal of Hughes is a notable landmark in the development of professional influence in education.[475]

Probably the position of city superintendent of schools is not protected by the state tenure law. The statute assures tenure to "clerks, draftsmen, inspectors, chemists, tabulating machine operators, auditors, secretaries, etc. . . . and all other administrative employees of a board of education."[476] The position of "business superintendent"—and doubtless the same would be said of the post of superintendent as well—was held not to be an "other administrative employee" of the board of education.

> The resolution of the board of education which created this office in the beginning and the resolution which was later adopted defining and amplifying its powers and duties, together with the minutes of the board of education, clearly show that this position was one with broad and sweeping powers that were not merely clerical, that the performance of the duties of this position required skill, judgment, trust and confidence. It is an executive position and not that of a subordinate employee. I am unable to convince myself that this position is *ejusdem generis* with the positions specifically enumerated in the statute.[477]

[475] The same distinction between lay and professional functions in city educational administration is carried out in the arrangement of hours for recitation and study periods: Proceedings for the Removal of Members of Board, 33 State Dept. Rept. 7 (1925). So, too, where a board undertakes a survey of the school system without the superintendent's coöperation: 23 *Ibid.* 32 (1920). The board of examiners in New York City and its relation to the superintendent and board of education is a special case but tends to illustrate the same principles: Matter of Jurisdiction of Board of Examiners, 25 *Ibid.* 275 (1921); Matter of Appeal from Action of Board of Education, etc., 29 *Ibid.* 505 (1923); Matter of Appeal of Certain Members of the Board of Examiners, 34 *Ibid.* 183 (1926).

[476] Laws of N. Y. 1910, ch. 140, sec. 872, subdiv. 2-a, as amended to 1925.

[477] Matter of Appeal of Sweeney, 35 *Ibid.* 573 (1926).

Perhaps one further specialization of educational administration is to be noted here, that of health. In admitting children to school who have been exposed to contagious disease the board should rely on the judgment of the board of health rather than call in independent medical talent.[478] But in any event, the board is quite within its rights in insisting on the advice of a licensed practitioner of medicine rather than that of agents of other therapeutic cults.[479]

[478] Matter of Appeal of Crowell, Jud. Decs. 506 (1907).

[479] Matter of Appeal of Gilmore, 24 State Dept. Repts. 716 (1921).

CHAPTER IV

CRITICAL REVIEW

Having now observed the circumstances, legal and educational, which the judicial power of New York State's Commissioner of Education was designed to accommodate, and having described at some length its actual operation, an appraisal of the total situation, aims, accomplishments, and probable tendencies will now be taken up. Let the point of departure be made in the statement of one of America's foremost legal scholars, Dean Roscoe Pound of the Harvard Law School:

> About twenty-five years ago we began to take subjects of controversy away from courts and confide them to administrative boards and commissions. But some of these in effect have become courts. The justice they administer is going the way of judicial justice. Others have made little progress in developing a technic of individualized application of law, so that their offhand executive justice has proved as unsatisfactory in one direction as slow-moving judicial justice in the other direction. At present there is a reaction against further extension of the former without any clear program for improvement of the latter.[1]

How does the commissioner's judicial power measure on this yardstick?

At the very outset it seems almost impossible to accuse the commissioner's justice of being "off-hand." It is difficult to think that any state would tolerate a hundred years of that kind of administration of justice, and not only that, but constantly magnify the tribunal dispensing it. But there are even more positive guarantees to litigants before the commissioner that their grievances will not be disposed of arbitrarily. Foremost is the fact that the legislature affords the commissioner a rather complete manual of directions in the statute law. His discretion, therefore, is not one that knows no limits.[2] In the second place he has built up a body of precedents in his interpretation of the legislative will which enables individuals to predict the legal con-

[1] Pound, Roscoe, The Crisis in American Law, Harper's Magazine, Jan. 1926.
[2] *Ante*, p. 37 f.

sequences of their acts. It is maturing these principles which distinguishes "justice according to law" from oriental or "off-hand" justice. Thirdly, these precedents have been reinforced in their validity by the commissioner's practice of drawing liberally from the courts for precepts that have stood the test of criticism at the bar.[3] Another assurance to parties before the commissioner that their rights will receive adequate protection is the fact that the commissioner's judicial conscience is in the trained and expert keeping of the members of the state bar who compose the law division of the education department. In fact, some state superintendents of public instruction, as Ruggles and Draper, for instance, were themselves legally trained. Although a point of doubtful value in some political philosophies, it is worth pointing out that the commissioner of education, and consequently his appointees in the law division, too, hold office during good behavior, the ideal tenure of any judiciary. Finally, security for a fair and impartial administration of justice lies in the fact that some types of cases may be carried beyond the commissioner to the courts of the state.[4]

But are not the forces just enumerated as injecting stability into the judicial career of the state department of education also the very ones which are slowly making this administrative tribunal over into a judicial one pure and simple? Will they not even-

[3] In his annual report for 1886 Superintendent Ruggles called attention to the fact that:

"The questions of law involved in these appeals, although arising primarily out of matters within, or supposed to be within the scope of some provision of the school statutes, are, nevertheless, very wide in their range, branching out into almost every department of common and statutory law . . . constitution and statutory construction; taxation—including regularity of appropriations, assessments, tax warrants, property liable or exempt, liability, of tax collections and trustees for erroneous proceedings, and many questions incidental to the system of local taxation for school purposes.

"Real estate, particularly titles to school sites, adverse possession, prescriptions, dower, rights of way, easements of various kinds and liens.

"Contracts, particularly for teaching, building, repairing, bonds of school districts, supervisors, collectors and sureties.

"Boundary lines, division fences and fixtures.

"Statutes of limitations.

"Titles to offices and contested elections, involving questions of citizenship, residence, qualifications of voters, rights of husband and wife, parent and child, guardian and ward, and master and servant. . . .

"Principles of the law of evidence.

"Construction of wills.

"Municipal corporations.

"Parliamentary law, and numerous other subsidiary and incidental questions often necessarily involved in the examination and decision of the principal questions in issue on appeal." Ann. Rept. Dept. Pub. Instn., 1886, pp. 11-12.

[4] *Ante*, p. 57 ff.

tually snuff out the initial advantages of administrative justice and revert to the slow and less flexible methods of the courts? It is very difficult to foretell. The advantages of expedition and economy sought in the act of 1822 seem still to adhere to the functioning of the office. While the instances of individualized application of the law—that departure from abstract and generalized rules in favor of specific, concrete cases—have varied from time to time with the incumbent of the state superintendency and the later state commissionership, there seems no reason yet to think that these advantages do not still attach to the administration of justice in this department. Dean Pound is of the mind that this free rein accorded executive officers, as compared with strictly judicial ones, is probably a passing phase of the law.[5] It is the way the law gives evidence of growing pains. When the law catches up with the tremendous changes which have occurred in our social fabric, there will be no need for such a flexible tribunal. Both Roman and English equity, as distinct from law, commenced with administrative officers. Both later submitted to standardization. The present growth of administrative law is thus, perhaps, a glimpse at history repeating itself.

But even should this be the case, there apparently is one advantage in the growth of the commissioner's judicial power which will be permanent, namely, the administration of the educational laws by a tribunal technically expert in the field of education. To the great extension of public welfare legislation and to the increasingly minute specialization in human pursuits, there seems no other answer but a degree of judicial specialization. The English authority, Mr. Dicey, in reviewing the part which two cases arising in the British educational system had played in the development of administrative law there, remarked, that the management of such a public undertaking is not like a law trial; "The two things must in many respects be governed by totally different rules." [6]

Doubtless the concentration of executive, legislative, and judicial powers in a single man such as the commissioner of education is a violation of the American principle of the separation of powers. Yet, viewing the size and complexity of the state's

[5] Pound, Roscoe, Justice According to Law, Columbia Law Review, vol. xiii, pp. 696-713; and vol. xiv, pp. 1-26, 103-21.

[6] Dicey, A. V., Development of Administrative Law in England, 31 Law Quarterly Review, 148, 150.

educational enterprise, it seems excellently adapted to the effective administration of education. With the growth toward centralization of administration in New York State[7] has come a measure of necessary and desirable uniformity which may sometimes disregard local differences and submerge individual interests. Too much friction and heat will be generated in this process unless localities and individuals have some means of airing their complaints with a real assurance of having them weighed in a judicial manner. Investing the commissioner of education with appellate jurisdiction makes a fine adjustment and accommodation to this danger point in state educational administration.

Of course it is of the utmost importance that these grievances may be disposed of almost as quickly as they arise and with little or no expense to the parties concerned. On the other hand, it is thought by some that the very cheapness and expedition with which appeals may be made to the commissioner are in themselves a cause of much litigation which otherwise might never reach judicial ears. Perhaps this is so, but every superintendent and commissioner who has made public utterances on it has felt that the benefit to the smooth working of the system far outweighed any possible disadvantages.

Finally, not only does the commissioner's judicial power clarify and afford a guide to trails already blazed by the legislature, but it is also a blazer of trails itself. Not only is it an ancillary to the efficient working of the whole education system, but it is its directive force as well. To the extent that it is a policy-forming instrumentality, an alarm may at once be sounded that the traditional separation of powers is again in danger, that the commissioner has confused legislative and judicial functions. That fear may as well be dismissed. Administrative justice cannot be cast in the traditional mold. Unmistakably charting new courses without precedent of the department or enactment of the legislature to guide the way have been the decisions of such appeals as those involving the right of teachers to wear distinctive religious garb,[8] the compatibility of professional duties with those of maternity,[9] and the requirement of school districts to provide by contract for opportunities of instruction on the secondary or academic grade.[10] Any residuum of anxiety on this point should be put at rest by

[7] See Introduction; also, Fairlie, J. A., Growth of Centralization of Administration in New York State.

[8] *Ante*, p. 119 f. [9] *Ante*, p. 102 ff. [10] *Ante*, p. 146 ff.

recalling those excellent words of Andrew S. Draper on the interrelationship of his administrative and judicial duties.

There is a different relation between the Commissioner of Education and a proceeding before him from that which obtains between a court and a proceeding before it. A court is disinterested in all questions except the facts and the law. The Commissioner of Education is the administrative or supervisory officer of the whole educational system of the State. He is bound to have an interest in the equity, right, and justice of all questions having a bearing upon the administration of the educational system. He must determine judicial questions with a view to the general effect upon the school system as well as to the technical requirement of the law.[11]

[11] *Ante*, p. 41. Election of Member of Board of Education, etc., Jud. Decs. 175, 183 (1905).

ABBREVIATIONS

Acc.—Decision is in accord with previous one.

Affd.—Affirmed.

Ann. Rept. Dept. Pub. Instn.—Annual Report of the State Department of Public Instruction.

Ann. Rept. State Ed. Dept.—Annual Report of the State Education Department.

Ann. Rept. Supt. Com. Schs.—Annual Report of the State Superintendent of Common Schools.

App. Div.—Court Reporter of the Appellate Division of the Supreme Court.

Assem. J.—Assembly Journal of the State Legislature.

Barb.—Barbour's Reports of the Supreme Court.

Code of Pub. Instn. 1856—Code of Public Instruction 1826.

Code of Pub. Instn. 1887—Code of Public Instruction of the State of New York Containing the Laws and Decisions Relating to Common Schools with Comments and Instructions.

Decs. Supt. Com. Schs.—Decisions of the Superintendent of Common Schools.

Denio—Denio's reports of cases in the Supreme Court and Court for the Correction of Errors.

Hun—Hun's Reports of the Supreme Court.

Jud. Decs.—Judicial Decisions of the State Superintendent of Common Schools, State Superintendent of Public Instruction, and the State Commissioner of Education.

Laws of N. Y., etc., and Digest of Decs.—Laws of New York Relating to Common Schools with Comments and Instructions and Digest of Decisions.

Misc.—Miscellaneous Reports (Supreme Court Reporter).

N. Y.—New York State Court of Appeals Reporter.

State Dept. Repts.—State Department Reports.

Wend.—Wendell's reports of cases in Supreme Court of Judicature and in the Court for Trial of Impeachments and the Correction of Errors.

BIBLIOGRAPHY

STATUTES

Statutes of the State. 1822-1926.

COURT REPORTS

Reports of the Courts of Record in New York State.

DEPARTMENTAL DECISIONS

Decisions of the Superintendent of Common Schools. Croswell, Van Benthuysen & Burt, Albany, N. Y., 1837. 479 pp.

Code of Public Instruction. Weed, Parsons & Co., Albany, N. Y., 1856. 492 pp.

Laws of New York Relating to Common Schools with Comments and Instructions and Digest of Decisions. Weed, Parsons & Co., Albany, N. Y., 1868. 720 pp.

Code of Public Instruction of the State of New York Containing the Laws and Decisions relating to Common Schools with Comments and Instructions. Weed, Parsons & Co., Albany, N. Y., 1887. 1070 pp.

Judicial Decisions of the State Superintendent of Common Schools, State Superintendent of Public Instruction, State Commissioner of Education. University of the State of New York, Albany, N. Y., 1914. 1508 pp.

Annual Reports of the State Department of Public Instruction. 1887-1904.

Annual Reports of the State Education Department. 1905-1913.

State Department Reports. Vols. 1-35.

ANNUAL REPORTS TO THE LEGISLATURE

Annual Reports of the Superintendent of Common Schools. 1812-1853.

Annual Reports of the Department of Public Instruction. 1854-1904.

Annual Report of the State Education Department. 1905-1925.

PERIODICALS

Albertsworth, E. F. Judicial Review of Administrative Action. Harvard Law Review, 35:127-53, Dec. 1921.

Dicey, A. V. Development of Administrative Law in England. Law Quarterly Review, 31:148-153, Apr. 1915.

Pillsbury, W. Administrative Tribunals. Harvard Law Review, 36: 405-25, 583-92, Feb. and March, 1923.

Pound, Roscoe. Justice According to Law. Columbia Law Review, 13: 696-713, Dec. 1913; 14:1-26, 103-21, Jan. and Feb. 1914.

Pound, Roscoe. Administrative Application of Legal Standards. Reports of the American Bar Association, 1919, pp. 445-65.

Pound, Roscoe. The Crisis in American Law. Harper's Magazine, Jan. 1926.

Wigmore, J. H. Administrative Boards and Evidence Rules. Illinois Law Review, 17:263-282, Dec. 1922.

MISCELLANEOUS

Cubberley, E. P. Public School Administration in the United States. Houghton Mifflin Company, Boston, 1922, 479 pp.

Fairlie, J. A. Growth of Centralization of Administration in New York State. Columbia University Press, New York City, 1898, 210 pp.

Freund, E. Growth of American Administrative Law. Thoms Law Book Company, St. Louis, Mo., 1923, 190 pp.

Hedden, Stuart. Historical Outline of Policy: New York School Legislation, 1922. Carnegie Corporation of New York.

Gambrell, E. Smythe. Judicial Decisions Relating to Education in New York State from 1815 to 1921, 1922. Carnegie Corporation of New York.

Randall, S. S. History of the Common School System of the State of New York. Ivison, Blakeman, Taylor & Co., New York & Chicago, 1871, 477 pp.

INDEX